Education Reform and Education Policy in East Asia

I0125130

This book assesses the impact of globalization on the education systems of key East Asian countries, examining how the increasingly interdependent economic system has driven policy change and education reform.

It discusses how policymakers have responded to changes required in educational outcomes in order to equip their societies for new global conditions; it explores the impact of new approaches and ideologies related to globalization, such as marketization, privatization, governance changes, managerialism, economic rationalism, and neoliberalism; and it makes comparisons across the region. The countries covered are China, including Hong Kong, Japan, and the "tiger economies" of South Korea, Taiwan, and Singapore.

Based upon indepth research, fieldwork, literature analysis, policy document analysis, and the personal reflections of academics serving in the education sector, this volume recounts heated debates about the pros and cons of education restructuring in East Asia. The discussions of national responses and coping strategies in this volume offer highly relevant insights into how globalization has resulted in restructuring and draw lessons from comparative public policy analysis and comparative education studies.

Ka Ho Mok is a chair professor in East Asian Studies and director of the Centre for East Asian Studies, University of Bristol. He was previously associate dean and convener of the Comparative Education Policy Research Unit at the City University of Hong Kong. His recent books include *Centralization and Decentralization: Educational Reforms and Changing Governance in Chinese Societies* (Kluwer, 2003) and *Globalization and Marketization: A Comparative Analysis of Hong Kong and Singapore* (Edward Elgar, 2004).

Routledge Advances in Asia-Pacific Studies

Education Reform and Education Policy in East Asia

Ka Ho Mok

Routledge
Taylor & Francis Group
LONDON AND NEW YORK

First published 2006
by Routledge
2 Park Square, Milton Park, Abingdon, Oxon OX14 4RN

Simultaneously published in the USA and Canada
by Routledge
711 Third Ave, New York, NY 10017

Routledge is an imprint of the Taylor & Francis Group

First issued in paperback 2013

© 2006 Ka Ho Mok

Typeset in Times New Roman by
Newgen Imaging Systems (P) Ltd, Chennai, India

British Library Cataloguing in Publication Data
A catalogue record for this book is available from the British Library

Library of Congress Cataloging in Publication Data
A catalog record for this book has been requested

ISBN 978–0–415–36814–8 (hbk)
ISBN 978 0–415–64740–3 (pbk)

To God, in whom I faithfully trust, who is the origin of wisdom and knowledge

Also to Jasmine, Esther and Lucinda, my beloved wife and daughters

Ka Ho Mok

Contents

Figures

Tables

Preface

This book represents the fruit of my strong research interest in comparative education policy and the culmination of several years of research into the impact of globalization, privatization, and marketization on education in selected societies/countries in East Asia. I started my academic career in the early 1990s after returning from my PhD studies at the London School of Economics and Political Science, University of London. During my studies in London, I got the chance to learn from one of the most eminent professors of sociology of development, Leslie Sklair, who is my ex-supervisor and also the author of *Sociology of the Global System*. I was greatly impressed by the work of Leslie, despite the fact that I did not engage in a PhD project related to globalization in the early 1990s. Nonetheless, I was exposed to the debates of globalization during my years of studying in London. Such a discourse has inevitably shaped my intellectual journey.

When I started my academic career at the Department of Public and Social Administration of City University of Hong Kong in 1993, I was assigned to teach a course on comparative policy in the mid-1990s; at the time this subject area was entirely new to me. Nonetheless, the shift to teaching comparative policy has taken me to a new research field, driving me to make attempts to research topics related to development studies and comparative public policy. In the past ten years, I have been researching on comparative education policy in East Asia, with particular reference to how globalization has affected education policy change, education reforms and education developments, and changing governance in Hong Kong, Singapore, Taiwan, South Korea, Japan, and mainland China. By conducting research projects related to comparative education policy and changing governance, I have also been exposed to literature on educational changes and reforms in Western societies like the United Kingdom, the United States of America, and Australia and New Zealand in the Pacific region. Undoubtedly, the exposure to comparative public policy has provoked my profound interest in comparing and contrasting education policy change and developments in the Asia Pacific region.

This book is a collection of papers based upon the research findings generated from fieldwork, literature analysis, policy and document analysis, as well as the personal reflections of academics serving in the education sector. Some of the chapters are revised papers based upon some of my international journal articles/book chapters or internationally refereed conference papers; others are newly written for this volume. The completion and publication of this book could be seen as a landmark of my academic endeavor, especially when I have taken up a new academic appointment as chair professor in East Asian Studies and concurrently as founding director of the Centre for East Asian Studies at the University of Bristol from January 2005.

I recognize that the pace of education reform is breathtaking in all the selected places and that some of what appears in the book will already be out of date by the time it appears in print. Nevertheless, I feel that it is worth documenting what has taken place over the past two decades, if only to serve as signposts through which later policy developments might be better understood. The publication of this book hopefully contributes to the existing heated debates with regard to education reforms not only in Hong Kong but also in other Asian societies. What makes the book most timely is that its publication comes at a time when the selected Asian societies are undergoing different forms of education reforms and restructuring. Heated debates about the pros and cons of the education restructuring experiences in the selected Asian societies are documented and analyzed in this book. The discussion on national responses and coping strategies in Part II of this book hopes to offer some comparative insights for readers to reflect upon how globalization has resulted in education restructuring in East Asia and what lessons we can draw from the comparative studies for Hong Kong.

Acknowledgments

Throughout the process of researching on issues related to globalization and education policy change and reform in East Asia, a great many people and institutions deserve special thanks for their help and assistance in enabling the author to conduct field visits and fieldwork during the past ten years. I want to express my gratitude to the following institutions, which have offered me a great deal of assistance to complete the project.

The Research Grants Committee of City University of Hong Kong and the Government of the Hong Kong Special Administrative Region, as well as the Sumitomo Foundation, granted me research funds to go for fieldwork and field interviews, whereas the following institutions made arrangements enabling me to conduct fieldwork and field interviews: National Institute of Education, Nanyang Technological University, Singapore; Ministry of Education at Singapore, Taiwan, South Korea, and mainland China; Education Department and Education and Manpower Bureau of the HKSAR Government; Korean Educational Development Institute; Higher Education Research Institute, East China Normal University, Shanghai and Tsinghua University, Beijing; Research Institute of Higher Education, Hiroshima University; and National Institute of Academic Degrees and University Evaluation in Japan.

In the past few years, many of my good friends and research collaborators have offered help and assistance to me one way or another; I cannot list out all the names here to show my gratitude. Even when I am aware of intellectual debts, I may have missed out some of them; in particular, many indirect influences have not been mentioned here. I will try my best to repay these scholarly debts in the most appropriate coin by continuing my research to promote better understanding of education policy change and development from a comparative perspective.

The completion and publication of this book have very much depended upon the kind support of the following publishers for granting permission for the author to reprint chapters or articles already published. As some of the chapters in this volume have been revised based upon previous work, I must acknowledge the original sources of papers.

Chapter 1 of the volume is a revised paper based upon a keynote speech presented at the Annual Conference of the Comparative Education Society of Hong Kong in December 2002. Chapter 3 is a revised version of a book chapter originally published in I. Holliday and P. Wilding (eds.) *Welfare Capitalism in East Asia: Social Policy in the Tiger Economies* (Basingstoke: Palgrave Macmillan, 2003), pp. 37–69. Chapter 4 is a revised chapter based upon an article published in *Globalization, Societies & Education* Vol.1, No.2, pp. 201–21. Chapter 6 is based upon another keynote speech that I presented at an international symposium organized by the Civil Service College, Singapore government in October 2003, while Chapter 7 is based upon a revised version of various journal articles and book chapters I have published in recent years. Chapter 8 in this volume is based upon a revised version of a paper originally published in *Journal of Education Policy* Vol.15, No.6, pp. 637–60, and Chapter 9 is a revised version of my journal article published in *Public Administration & Policy* Vol.10, No.2, 149–74.

I must thank Prof. Leslie Sklair, Prof. Philip Altbach, Prof. Andy Green, Prof. Roger Dale, Prof. Susan Robertson, Prof. Mark Bray, Prof. Paul Wilding, Prof. Anthony Cheung, Prof. Jon Pierre, Prof. Anthony Welch, Prof. Philip Jones, Prof. Jan Currie, Prof. Ian Holliday, Prof. Julia Kwong, Prof. Mark Bray, Prof. Po Chen, Prof. Alvin So, Prof. Ruth Hayhoe, Prof. Jun Oba, and Prof. Yonezawa and others for stimulating and encouraging me to join the field of comparative education policy and comparative public policy studies, through which I have learned a lot and enjoyed the academic journey. I must thank Kennis Cheng, my research assistant, for assisting me to prepare the manuscript for publication. Last but not least, I must thank my beloved wife, Jasmine, for giving me her full support, love, and encouragement in venturing in an entirely new academic environment after coming over to the United Kingdom to take up the directorship and chair in East Asian studies at the University of Bristol. Jasmine has made tremendous sacrifices for my new venture; hence she should be given special credit. Without the very enjoyable and meaningful family life offered by Jasmine and my two lovely daughters, I would not have been able to complete this book project.

I dedicate this book to those who are interested in comparative education and comparative public policy. As I have just left the City University of Hong Kong for my new academic position at Bristol, special thanks must be expressed to my colleagues and students, who have offered me encouragement and support, stimulating me to think and reflect deeply about education issues throughout the past decade while teaching and researching at City University of Hong Kong. This book is also dedicated to God, in whom I faithfully trust, who gives me wisdom, knowledge, energy, and strength in pursuing an academic career.

Ka Ho Mok
Bristol, UK
March 2005

Introduction

The rise of the knowledge economy has developed new global infrastructures in which information technology has played an increasingly important role. The popularity and prominence of information technology has changed the nature of knowledge, and is currently restructuring higher education, research, and learning. The changes in the socioeconomic context as a result of the globalized economy have inevitably led to changes not only in the university sector but also in the school sector.

The principal goal of this introductory chapter is to set out the wider socio-economic context for the discussion to be followed in the book. This chapter examines the common challenges in East Asia, followed by how education developments and formulation of education policies have been affected by the growing impact of globalization. In addition, I will briefly outline whether there are any common trends in education developments in East Asia. Before I draw a close to the introduction, I will briefly discuss how the chapters in this book are organized and what are the central arguments of the following chapters.

Common challenges in East Asia

A better understanding of education change and education development in East Asia can be obtained only when we contextually analyze the education policy changes and transformations in education governance in the light of the changing socioeconomic and sociopolitical environments of different Asian societies. As we are living in an increasingly globalizing economy, modern states are confronted with challenges of a similar nature. This is particularly true when technology, information, and telecommunications have become so advanced that things happening anywhere in the world will be widely reported across different parts of the globe. Modern states have tried very hard to identify good policy practices and management initiatives elsewhere to improve local public policy delivery and public management (Common 1998).

Economic, social, and political developments in East Asian societies, as in other parts of the globe, have been increasingly influenced by the growing impact of globalization (Mok and Welch 2003). In order to enhance their competence in the global marketplace, governments in Hong Kong, Singapore, Taiwan, South

Korea, Japan, and mainland China have started to review their education systems, and different reform measures have been introduced to improve the overall quality of education in order to enhance their competitiveness in the globalizing economy (Mok 2003c,e). According to Townsend and Cheng, there are a few major challenges common to all East Asian societies, including:

- ever-increasing rate for human progress;
- the rise of the knowledge economy and the changing university;
- the growing significance of information and technology in education delivery;
- massification of higher education and the need for quality control;
- the East Asian financial crisis and the post-crisis adjustments;
- the social and political changes and the need to change higher education.

(2000)

As we head into an age of communication and information, there is a strong need to rethink the nature of knowledge and the way education is operated and run. According to Townsend (1998), we have successfully "conquered the challenge of moving from a quality education system for a *few* people to having a quality education system for *most* people" in the past few decades (248, original italics). But what we are now confronting is the move from having a quality education system for *most* people to developing a quality education system for *all*. In order to promote lifelong learning/continual education and to make any society a learning society, the way that education is managed should undergo a fundamental change. In addition to the challenges generated by the newly emerging knowledge economy, education policy and development in different parts of the globe have been increasingly affected by globalization.

Another major contextual variable that we should take into consideration in analyzing education policy change and transformation in education governance in selected Asian societies (namely, Hong Kong, Singapore, Taiwan, South Korea, and mainland China) is the impact of the Asian financial crisis in 1997 and its subsequent impacts on these societies, especially how the economic downturn in the post-crisis era has led to changes in economic, social, and political arenas. Such post-crisis transformations and changes have shaped the way in which education policy is formulated and the strategies that these Asian governments have adopted in coping with the challenges of globalization (Holliday and Wilding 2003; Tan 2003).

Globalization challenges to education

When reflecting upon the impact of globalization on education, it is believed that the corollary effects of globalization on education may lead to delegitimizing public education, treating education as a business, emphasizing performance indicators, embracing privatization and decentralization, and noneducational groups generating curricula. As Cowen has suggested, global forces can have an impact on formal schooling in at least three interlinked ways, including "the generation of a globally tiered education system; the enlargement of the private sector; and the reform of the curriculum" (1996, p. 105). Martin Carnoy argues in the same vein that "globalization enters the education sector on an ideological horse, and its effects in education are largely a product of that financially driven, free-market ideology, not a clear conception for improving education" (Carnoy 2000, p. 50). Despite the fact that different scholars put forward diverse interpretations of the impacts of globalization on education, no one can deny the fact that education policy change and education development have been increasingly shaped by a finance-driven reform and that strategies along the lines of decentralization, marketization, privatization, and corporatization have become increasingly popular (Currie and Newson 1998a; Mok and Welch 2003).

Education in the marketplace

The growing concern for "efficiency and quality," "value for money," and "public accountability" has altered people's value expectations. All providers of education today inhabit a more competitive world, where resources are becoming scarcer, but at the same time, providers have to accommodate increasing demands from the local community as well as the changing expectations of parents and employers (Currie and Newson 1998a; Curlson 1999). In an increasingly market-driven society, scholars have been discussing the relationship between education and the market. Issues and problems relating to the application of market principles in educational provision have been explored and debated (Pring 1987; Bridges and McLaughlin 1994; Apple 2000). By bringing market elements into education, people believe that they will have more choices and eventually better-quality education. The British scholar Stephen Ball, through his studies of education reforms in the United Kingdom and elsewhere, has identified five major elements in the educational marketplace in general, namely, choice, diversity, funding, competition, and organizational style (Ball 1990).

It is within such a policy context that notions such as diversity of schools, parental choice, school autonomy, and school accountability have become increasingly significant forces shaping educational development not only in Western societies like the United States and the United Kingdom but also in the Asia Pacific region, including the four Asian Tiger economies, Japan, and mainland China (Harmer 1994; Harkim *et al.* 1994; Lai 2002; Mok 2003c; Richard and Mok 2003). In order to make education systems more responsive to the social and economic changes outlined earlier, ideas and practices along the lines of marketization, privatization, and decentralization are being adopted to transform the way educational institutions are managed and governed. This is particularly true when common concerns over widened access, funding, accountability, quality, and managerial efficiency have been perceived as prominent global trends related to education (Tsang 2002; Mok and Tan 2004).

Similar trends in education developments in East Asia

Although it is difficult to make generalizations about the patterns, trends, and models in higher education developments in these four East Asian Tigers since each country/society may have its own stage and own speed of development, different comparative studies of a similar kind have reported some interesting patterns and trends common to the development of education in the Asia Pacific region. Some of the typical ones are as follows:

*   the reestablishing of new aims and a national vision for education;
*   the expansion and restructuring of education;
*   the assurance of education standards and a quality education;
*   the use of market forces and the balance between education equality and encouraging of competition to promote excellence;
*   the privatization and diversifying of education;
*   the shift to decentralization and school-based management;
*   the emphasis on the use of development planning and strategic management;
*   parental and community involvement in school education;
*   the use of information technology in learning and teaching;
*   the development of new curricula and methods of learning and teaching;
*   the changes in examination and evaluation practices;
*   the search to enhance teacher quality; and
*   the need for continuous professional development for teachers and principals.

(adapted from Cheng and Townsend 2000, p. 319)

Similarly, Mok and Welch compare and contrast educational developments in the Asia Pacific region, with particular attention given to examining the relationship between the growth of globalization and educational restructuring. After completing a series of comparative studies, they find that educational developments in the region, including Hong Kong, Taiwan, Singapore, South Korea, mainland China, Japan, the Philippines, Cambodia, New Zealand, and Australia, have been affected by the trends of marketization and corporatization (Mok and Welch 2003). Governments in these societies are increasingly concerned about the role of education in improving the competitiveness of their countries, and their place in regional and global markets. Therefore, they are very keen to promote the idea of "life-long learning" and "quality education" in preparing their citizens for the knowledge-based economy (Mok *et al.* 2000; Weng 2000b; Tse 2002).

Privatization of either whole or parts of educational institutions, or indeed sectors of education (and other areas of social activity), is often now an instrument of economic and social (including education) policy, as is a more user-pays philosophy in education (World Bank 1995b,c; Mok 1999). In many societies, even socialist states such as Vietnam and China, this has been part of a wider set of changes whereby foreign direct investment has been encouraged, and public sector activity has been pruned, often substantially, and public sector wages have been held down, while private economic activities have been encouraged within the climate of increasing deregulation and the economy has been reshaped toward more export growth-oriented industries, and away from state responsibility for areas of social policy such as health, transport, communications, and education (Mok and Welch 2003). In turn, state ministries and other public authorities are increasingly subjected to efficiency principles and made to compete as though they were private industries (Welch 1996, 1998).

It is within this wider policy context that an increasing number of institutions of higher learning are being established with new missions and innovative configurations of training, to serve populations that previously had little access to higher education. Nonetheless, the rapid expansion of higher education in the past few decades in many countries has also raised social concern over quality assurance. To address the issues related to the massification of higher education, higher education institutions are required to set up systems to maintain high academic standards. Meanwhile, higher education institutions are required to improve their administrative efficiency and accountability in response to the demands of different stakeholders such as government, business, industry, and labor organizations, students and parents as well (Currie and Newson 1998a; Mok and Welch 2003). In short, globalization accelerates higher education restructuring along the lines of "marketization," "corporatization," and "privatization."

Similarly, school education and school governance have undergone changes under the same policy environment. In order to respond to the rapid socioeconomic changes, schools are called upon to engage in the diversification process by changing their school governance models and curriculum design to accommodate the changing needs of the knowledge economy. In the past decade or so, different school reform measures have been introduced in different Asian societies. In Hong Kong, school-based management has been adopted to allow more flexibility and autonomy to schools in making the school system more responsive to changes. In addition, a direct subsidy scheme was introduced with the intention to make the school system more diversified. A similar practice has been adopted in Singapore, where independent and autonomous schools are allowed to have more flexibility and autonomy in curriculum design and school management. In Taiwan and South Korea, diversification and decentralization processes have also taken place in the school systems to make their students more creative, innovative, and responsive to external and internal changes. Even in mainland China, school and university systems have been diversified, especially when nonstate sectors and actors have started to play an increasingly significant role in financing and providing education services. In Japan, national universities are going through the process of corporatization; the Japanese government is very keen to inject market ideas and strategies to reform its national university system by making it more flexible and responsive to the changing global environment.

Mok and Welch's recent edited volume has clearly illustrated the macro and micro impacts of globalization on the educational and other public policies of governments in the Asia Pacific region (1993). Despite the similarities in terms of reform agendas and strategies in education, Mok and Welch have pointed out how important it is to note the differences between countries, their motivations, actions, and solutions. When reflecting upon globalization and education changes, many aspects are the same worldwide, while a closer scrutiny may lead to different conclusions since each country has individual and unique challenges to face and overcome. Therefore, we should go beyond the reform rhetoric to the reform realities, carefully teasing out the complexities and interactions between the structures and agents and contextually analyzing recent education governance changes and reforms.

About the book

Like other contemporary societies, the East Asian societies selected for study in this volume—Hong Kong, Singapore, South Korea, Taiwan, mainland China, and Japan—have been talking about the challenges of globalization since the mid-1990s. Realizing that their future depends very much upon how they can maintain competitiveness in the global marketplace, these East Asian economies have begun to review their education systems. Associating quality education with further socioeconomic development, and believing that the global competence of their societies very much relies upon quality people, all the selected Asian governments have started education reforms in the past decade in order to produce high-quality graduates.

The choice of the case studies

The selection of these six Asian societies is based upon their comparability in terms of their similar sociohistorical backgrounds and socioeconomic develop-ment experiences, given that they have been classified as newly industrializing economies in East Asia except Japan. The central focus of this book is to examine how these Asian societies have responded to the growing impact of globalization, to explore how these governments have attempted to reform their education sys-tems, and to reflect upon the changes in education governance in the wider context of globalization. I hope that this book will arouse interest in comparing and con-trasting the education policy changes and education reforms in the selected Asian societies, with particular reference to issues relating to changing governance in education. Three major areas, namely, education financing, provision, and regula-tion, are prominent, especially as modern states struggle to boost higher education enrollment rates in times of economic uncertainty. More specifically, in the second part of the book I have chosen to focus on how individual states or societies have responded to the pressures and challenges resulting from globalization.

Major research questions

A few major research questions that the present volume attempts to address include

- What are the historical and socioeconomic backgrounds for education reforms in these Asian societies?
- In what way have the selected Asian societies attempted to reform their education systems?
- How and to what extent are the reform strategies similar and different?

- Why are the governments in the selected societies different in their reform strategies? How are the reform strategies adopted by these societies similar? So what?
- Are there any fundamental changes taking place in education provision, financing, and regulation? How and why?
- Are there any significant changes observed in education governance models in these Asian societies?
- Are there any common trends in education policy/education reform strategies in these Asian societies?

Structure of the book

This book has two main parts. After this introduction to the policy context, Part I focuses on education systems, policy changes, and education reforms in the selected Asian societies, with particular reference to issues related to education provision, financing, and regulation issues. There are four chapters in this part. The first chapter is the theoretical framework of this book, trying to set out the theoretical/conceptual issues for the ensuing discussion in this book. This chapter also identifies, examines, and discusses issues related to globalization challenges and educational restructuring, especially analyzing education governance from the policy instrument approach. In addition, a few key issues related to the changing state and education relationships and new regulatory arrangements when education service providers and funding providers are increasingly diverse will be discussed in this chapter.

Chapter 2 provides an overview of the education systems of these Asian societies, outlining the recent policy changes and education reforms in these Asian economies; while Chapter 3 focuses on examining the education regulation, provision, and funding issues in four Tiger economies, namely, Hong Kong, Singapore, Taiwan, and South Korea. Chapter 4 of Part I discusses whether and how similar education development patterns have evolved in the selected Asian societies, with particular attention given to examining how marketization and decentralization have affected higher education governance in the Tiger economies and whether common trends and challenges have emerged in the education sector in East Asia.

Part II adopts a theme of "globalization and national responses" by examining how different Asian societies have responded to the impacts of globalization by changing the way that education is managed and governed. In particular, the six chapters in Part II mainly focus on how different higher education systems in the selected Asian societies have responded to globalization challenges by changing their governance models, closely examining the specific reform strategies that the selected Asian governments have adopted in strengthening their higher education systems. The major objectives of Chapter 5 are to examine how the Chinese government has attempted to adopt strategies of diversification and decentralization to create more higher education opportunities and raise the overall education standards of the Chinese citizens. Despite the fact that a policy of decentralization has been adopted in reforming the higher education system and changing the governance of higher education in mainland China, people working in the higher education sector generally feel that the central government has still maintained tight control over the development of higher education. The chapter critically examines the dilemmas that the Chinese regime is now facing because of the policy of decentralization introduced in the mid-1980s, revealing the politics of education decentralization in post-Mao China.

Chapter 6 discusses how the government of the Hong Kong Special Administrative Region (HKSAR) has tried to strengthen the relations between the university sector, industry, and the business sector by developing the triple-helix network system to encourage universities in Hong Kong to venture into entrepreneurial activities. The case study on Hong Kong vividly shows how a less interventionist East Asian state has attempted to set out new policy frameworks in promoting further collaborations between universities, business, and industry. The quest for entrepreneurship has significantly changed the relationships between the HKSAR and universities, business, and industry. Such governance changes have clearly shown that the universities in Hong Kong are becoming more market driven and that they must become more entrepreneurial in nature.

Chapter 7 focuses on Singapore's strategies to make its university system more competitive in the global marketplace by implementing fundamental reforms in higher education. Openly recognizing the lack of a spirit of inventiveness and risk thinking, and, at the same time, worrying about the lessening of its competitiveness in the globalizing economy, the Singapore government has begun to launch projects in promoting entrepreneurship. Having been too paternalistic, the Singapore government has put the promotion of entrepreneurship to the top of its political agenda in recent years. In particular, the Singapore government has deliberately changed its governance model in higher education. The injection of market competition, the introduction of the first private university, Singapore Management University, and the stress on performance and international benchmarking, etc. are intended to make the Singapore university sector more dynamic and responsive to the changing demands in the global marketplace.

Chapter 8 examines how the Taiwan government has changed the governance model in higher education to make its university system more internationalized. Chapter 9 will investigate South Korea's responses to globalization by looking into the specific reform strategies adopted by the Korean government to make its higher education more diversified and specialized in coping with globalization challenges. Common to Taiwan, South Korea, and Japan, the recent higher education restructuring taking place in these Asian societies has been closely related to liberalizing the overly and stubbornly sustained "centralized" governance model in higher education through the adoption of decentralization, marketization, diversification, and corporatization ideas and strategies to lessen the unnecessary state control in order to make their systems more responsive and flexible in coping with changes generated both domestically and globally.

Chapter 10 focuses on the recent higher education restructuring and governance changes in Japan. In order to cope with the ever-changing environment, the

Japanese government has introduced a new policy of corporatization in the national university sector. By 2005, all national universities have been incorporated and they are now subject to far more quality assurance and evaluation measures. Since the present Japanese government strongly believes in the ideas of neo-liberalism, the higher education sector, like other public sector areas, has been experiencing significant restructuring along the lines of marketization and corporatization. This chapter will provide an overall view of the most recent reforms and governance changes in Japanese national universities, reflecting upon the policy implications and dilemmas that the university sector is now facing in Japan. The book concludes with an extensive discussion and analysis of the observations/major findings in the previous chapters in the light of the theoretical framework set out at the beginning of the book.

A note for readers

This book is written for general readers who are interested in education policy change and education reform in East Asia and for those students who enroll in comparative education, policy studies, Asian studies, and comparative policy courses. Readers may find some repetition between chapters, but this is deliberate. All chapters in this book have been written to stand on their own and I believe that students and readers may therefore profitably read individual chapters or parts—though obviously they need to do more than that. For this reason, it is unavoidable that readers may find some repetitions in historical and contextual discussion or statistical data from chapter to chapter in analyzing the most recent changes in education policy and reform in the selected Asian societies.

Part I

Education systems, policy change, and education reforms

1   Globalization and new governance

Changing policy instruments and regulatory arrangements in education

Introduction

Over the past decade, people have begun to talk about the impact of globalization on economic, social, political, and cultural fronts. Seeing globalization as very complicated processes of economic transactions and worldwide telecommunications, sociologists generally believe that the impact of globalization is profound as it is restructuring the ways in which we live and creating a new hybridity of cultural styles and mixes. Albeit no country is immune from the impact of globalization, there are heated debates about positive and negative consequences of globalization. No matter how we assess the impact of globalization, it is undeniable that contemporary societies are not entirely immune from the prominent global forces. Within the same context of globalization, some scholars in the field of education studies also believe education policy and development is not immune from globalization pressures, while many others argue we should avoid an overly deterministic view of globalization's impact on education policy. This chapter attempts to identify, examine, and discuss issues related to globalization challenges and educational restructuring, especially analyzing education governance from the policy instrument approach. The present chapter will focus on a few key issues related to changing state and education relationships and new regulatory arrangements when education service providers and funding providers are increasingly diversified.

Globalization challenges to contemporary development

Globalization is a central concept in this book but it is important to note that "globalization" is a highly contested term. To different people, globalization has different meanings. Some scholars believe one can obtain a better understanding of contemporary society only when we analyze the impact of globalization processes, while others reject such a thesis by criticizing the overstatement of global impacts on social, economic, cultural, and political developments (Sklair 1995; Sassen 1998; Hirst and Thompson 1999; Mittelman 2000). Despite the disagreements over and diverse interpretations of the impacts of globalization on contemporary society, no one can deny that there has been a growing literature in globalization discourse and that many have examined how globalization processes have affected public policy formulation and modern governance (see, for example, Massy 1997; Pierre and Peters 2000; Yeates 2001).

There are three major theories of globalization, namely, strong globalists, skeptics, and transformationalists; they have different interpretations of the impacts of globalization on modern states (Held *et al.* 1999). At the crudest level, "strong" globalization theory argues the global economy is dominated by uncontrollable global forces in which nation-states are structurally dependent on global capital that is primarily determined by transnational corporations (TNCs) (Yeates 2001). The emerging complexity of the global economy has inevitably led to changes in state structures. It is believed globalization processes create great uncertainty in the global economy that, in turn, requires nation-states to act in ways that will promote stability in the domestic economic order. In addition, the growing complexity also constrains the capacity of nation-states to coordinate political bargaining and compensate interest groups (Woods 2000; Jayasuriya 2001). To strong globalists, globalization means a drastic shift in structural power and authority away from nation-states toward non-state agencies and from national political systems to global economic systems and they also believe the world will a converge in the context of globalization (Strange 1996; Held 2000).

In contrast, scholars who oppose the convergence thesis criticize the strong globalists for overstating and overgeneralizing the convergence tenets of globalization. Instead, they point out the importance of nation-states and heterogenization in terms of national, regional, and local responses to global processes or imperatives (Hirst and Thompson 1999; Held 2000; Waters 2001). The skeptics, in contrast, maintain that contemporary levels of economic interdependence are not historically unprecedented. Criticizing strong globalists for being fundamentally flawed and politically naive since they underestimate the enduring power of national governments to regulate international economic activity, the skeptics point out the important role that regional organizations perform in the world economy. They also assert that in comparison with the age of world empires the international economy has become considerably less global in its geographical embrace (Held *et al.* 1999; Smith *et al.* 1999).

The transformationalists, like the strong globalists, perceive globalization as an unprecedented driving force for rapid political, economic, and social changes in modern societies. Nonetheless, they reject the thesis of global convergence. Instead, they believe the existence of a single global system is not evidence of global convergence or of the arrival of a single world society. Instead, the transformationalists consider globalization would result in "global-stratification" since some states, societies, and communities are enmeshed in the global order at the expense of other countries, thus marginalizing some so-called less competitive economies in the process of globalization. Such new patterns require reformulation of vocabulary from North/South and first/third world, acknowledging that new hierarchies cut across and penetrate all societies and regions of the world (Held *et al.* 1999; Waters 2001).

In my view, globalization processes are complex and often contradictory and therefore we need to avoid an overly deterministic view of globalization. On the one hand, we cannot deny that globalization is real, not a virtual phenomenon, and its effects are enhanced and even transformed by the revolution in communications and the continuing advancement of technology-driven innovation. On the economic front, globalization is a process for removing restrictions, hence leading to increased trade and economic growth and the benefits of having a more liberal trade environment. On the other hand, we should not underestimate the social and political costs of globalization. We can easily see growing inequalities in some countries, environmental degradation, commodification of culture and education, rises in unemployment, greater uncertainty and risk, and reduction of power in states as unacceptable consequences (Hsieh and Tseng 2002; Stiglitz 2002). The extreme form of globalization may have led to the consequent acceleration in economic integration which privileges market capitalism. These processes place economic power in the hands of TNCs, for many of them have been dominated by Western developed economies primarily based in the United States and Europe. Similar processes have also resulted in "international stratification of national powers," making the developed economies far more powerful and dominant in international affairs, while marginalizing those developing economies and threatening their social, economic, political, and cultural developments. Therefore, we should be cautious about the growing impact of globalization instead of overstating the benefits that globalization processes have brought to us.

Globalization challenges to modern governance

The growing impact of globalization has caused a number of modern states to rethink their governance strategies to cope with rapid social and economic changes. When examining the capacity of modern states in the context of globalization, both the skeptics and transformationalists believe nation-states still retain the ultimate claim of legal legitimacy within their territories even though they have to respond to external pressures generated by international laws and authorities (Pempel 1998; Jayasurya 2001). Contrary to strong globalists' arguments, the institutionalized state-society linkages (i.e., the mobilization of nonstate sources and actors to engage in social/public policy provision and financing) may not necessarily diminish the state's capacity. Instead, globalization could be conducive to the reconfiguration of modern states, creating forces to drive modern states to restructure their governance models and reform the ways they manage the public sector (Pierre 2000). These changes could also be seen as productive forces for modern states to shift from "positive coordination"[1] to "negative coordination," whereby the state can choose to perform the role of regulator, enabler, and facilitator instead of being heavily engaged in the role of provider and funder (Scharpf 1994; Jayasurya 2001). The debate just outlined here clearly indicates that scholars in public policy and governance have begun to reflect upon how far globalization pressures have really weakened state capacity in shaping local public policies and directing public sector management.

A close scrutiny of the impacts of globalization on public policy/public sector management has led some scholars to conclude that even though there may be similar trends and patterns in the public policy and public management domain along the lines of privatization, marketization, commodification, and corporatization, different governments may use similar strategies to serve their own political purposes. Modern states may tactically make use of the globalization discourse to justify their own political agendas or legitimize their inaction (Mok 2003c). Other studies report that public sector reform and reengineering of the government in Asian societies have become "tools" or "instruments" adopted by governments in Asia to build state capacity (Cheung and Scott 2003). Similarly, the revitalization of nonstate sectors (including the market or private actors) in public policy provision and social service delivery may not necessarily weaken state capacity (Knill and Lehmkuhl 2002) but instead may drive modern states to reconstitute and restructure their systems to become activist and proactive in shaping policy agendas and policy directions. In short, such restructuring processes could strengthen the capacity rather than weakening the role of modern states (Salomon 2002; Yang 2003).

Seen in this light, processes of globalization have prompted individual states to change their roles and reform their institutions in order to accommodate, and not just adapt to, the demands and pressures generated from the external environments (Giddens 1999; Waters 2001; Mok and Currie 2002). Marginson and Rhodes (2002) clearly describe the challenges posed by globalization to modern states, stating that the role and functioning of the state in the context of globalization is skewed toward the competitive state (see also Cerny 1996), which prioritizes the economic dimensions of its activities above all others. Therefore, maximizing welfare to promote enterprise, innovation, and profitability in the private and public spheres is becoming popular. It is in such a context that Dale argues that the world is in the process of becoming wholly commodified, both through the recommodification of those elements of public provision that the welfare state decommodified and much more by the extension of the commodity form into all those areas of the world that were previously concealed from it (Dale 2000, p. 95).

Emerging new forms of governance

Despite the disagreements over and diverse interpretations of the impacts of globalization on state capacity in governance, new forms of governance and new governance philosophies have emerged in recent years in order to maintain the competitiveness of modern states. Fundamental transformations have taken place in public policy instruments and public management (Faulks 2000; Lane and Ersson 2002). Theories of "new governance" propose that modern governments are adapting to radical changes in their environments by turning to new forms of governance that are "more society-centred" and focus on "co-ordination and self-governance" (Pierre 2000, pp. 2–6). Peters (1995) highlights four governance models as alternatives to the traditional system, namely, the market model, the participatory state model, the flexible government model, and the deregulated government model. Central to these governane models is the involvement of sectors other than the state such as the market, society, and other nonstate sectors in governing the public domain. Instead of relying solely upon government bureaucracy in terms of delivery of goods or services, there has been a massive proliferation of tools and policy instruments such as dizzying array of loans, loan guarantees, grants, contracts, insurance, and vouchers to address public problems. Diversified policy tools and instruments may render the conventional governance model inappropriate. This is particularly true when many of these tools are highly indirect. They rely heavily on a wide assortment of "third parties" such as commercial banks, private hospitals, industrial corporations, universities, social service agencies, and other social organizations (Salomon 2002). Therefore, networks and partnerships supplant hierarchical command and control (Rhodes 1997, 2000); in the delivery of services, public authority is shared between governments and with nongovernment actors—what Salomon (2002, p. 2) calls "third party government"; services are decentralized and in some cases privatized, and the role of governments in managing the economy is more sharply delineated and circumscribed by new arm's length (from government) market-supporting instruments, in some cases relying on self-regulation (Gamble 2000, pp. 130–31; Jayasurya 2001). Many possible causes have been highlighted: ideological changes such as the discrediting of "statist" models, fiscal and bureaucratic "overload" problems, the growth in supranational bodies that undermine a government's control, and economic globalization eroding state "steering capacities."

Central to the changing governance is the emerging trend of "zations" or coexisting "processes" that have transformed the way public sector is managed and public policy is formulated. One of these trends is privatization. Privatization has been a common theme in evolving patterns of government-business relations in some countries (e.g., Malaysia and South Korea) (Gouri *et al.* 1991; World Bank 1995). Pressures for broad governance changes have been strong, coming to a head in the financial crisis of 1997. A feature of these pressures is the presence of influential international agencies such as the IMF and World Bank. Their preferred models of governance reflect many of the same tendencies noted earlier:

> a less interventionist and arbitrary state; a strengthening of "juridical" forms of regulation (often associated with fundamental legal reform); more disaggregated and decentralised forms of government, including partnerships and a stronger "co-production" role for civil society groups; and a preference for market-like mechanisms over bureaucratic methods of service delivery
> (World Bank 1995)

Hence, it is not surprising that strategies, measures, and policy instruments along the line of marketization, corporatization, commodification, and managerialization are becoming popular practices in public policy and public management (Minogue 1998; Lane and Ersson 2002; Mok and Welch 2003).

Globalization and educational restructuring

Our earlier discussion has suggested globalization is not the only driving force for the recent changes and transformation taking place in governance and public sector management. If we put the most recent reforms in public sector management and transformations in public policy domain into historical perspective, strategies along the lines of marketization, privatization, and decentralization have long been adopted by modern states to resolve the problems generated from competing and growing social demands. The continual growth in "welfare" has already drawn many modern states to transform the way social services and public policy are managed. This is particularly true when modern states encounter a fiscal crisis. In the late 1970s and the early 1980s, the British government under Margaret Thatcher and the US government under Ronald Reagan used similar measures to improve public policy delivery and the efficiency of public administration. Hence, globalization may be understood as forces *accelerating* current changes and transformations in public administration or public sector management. More important, we must also pay particular attention to the unique social, political, economic, and cultural contexts in which policy and governance changes are introduced, trying to examine how local forces interact with regional and global variables in formulating public policy, implementing governance change, and launching reform in the public sector (Cheung and Scott 2003).

Nonetheless, some policy analysts argue that education policy and development, just like other public policy domains, are not immune from the impact of these globalization processes (Burbules and Torres 2000; Pierre and Peters 2000). Some scholars in the field of education even believe it is becoming increasingly difficult to understand education without reference to such processes (Currie and Newson 1998a; Jones 1998; Crossley 2000; Welch 2000, 2001; Mok 2001c; Currie 2002; Mok and Chan 2002; Mok and Lo 2002). A close scrutiny of comparative education literature has well documented that there seems to have been a convergence of curricula on a global scale. International organizations such as UNESCO, the World Bank, the OECD, and research institutes such as the IEA, by virtue of their recommendations, funding power, and cross-national comparisons have inevitably influenced the way curricula are designed and changed the mindsets of education ministries in different parts of the globe. It is remarkable that reform rhetoric is becoming increasingly similar across different education jurisdictions; all education reform proposals talk about the importance of competition, global competence, diversity, and choice, etc. (Mok and Welch 2003; Gopinathan 2005). In spite of Green's assertion of the essentially national nature of education systems, he also asks whether there is an emergent "common world education culture?" (Green 1997).

In order to make individual nation-states more competitive, schools and universities across the globe have been under tremendous pressures from government and the general public to restructure/reinvent education systems in order to adapt to the ever-changing socioeconomic and sociopolitical environments. As Martin Carnoy has pointed out, "globalization enters the education sector on an ideological horse, and its effects in education are largely a product of that financially driven, free-market ideology, not a clear conception for improving education" (Carnoy 2000, p. 50). According to Carnoy, education reforms within the context of globalization could be characterized by a finance-driven reform emphasizing decentralization, privatization, and better performance (2000).

Likewise, numerous major publications by the World Bank in the 1990s, for example, propounded a view of how education should be reshaped, in particular so as to more precisely serve the assumed demands of national and international economic growth and competitiveness. This set of reforms was to be accomplished with increased financial inputs from families and individuals and decreased inputs from the state (World Bank 1991, 1994b, 1995a), and it was to be paralleled by increasing privatization and the reform of the public sector, including substantial devolution to the local level, and the reform of public authorities in education on more businesslike principles (Watson 1996; Welch 1998, 2000). This subjection of education to the confines of the language and logic of neo-liberal economics is arguably part of a larger process of commodification, which Dale (2000), citing Cox, terms an "ontological shift."

With heavy weight being attached to the principle of "efficiency and quality" in education, schools, universities, and other learning institutions now encounter far more challenges and are being subjected to an unprecedented level of external scrutiny. The growing concern for "value for money" and "public accountability" has also altered people's value expectations. All providers of education today inhabit a more competitive world, where resources are becoming scarcer, but at the same time, providers have to accommodate increasing demands from the local community as well as the changing expectations of parents and employers. Governments across different parts of the globe have to expand higher education but they are facing increasing financial constraints in meeting people's pressing demands for higher education. In order to create more higher education opportunities, modern universities have started to change their paradigm in governance by adopting the doctrine of monetarism, which is characterized by freedom and markets, to replace Keynesianism (known as static options) (Apple 2000). In order to generate additional revenue, an increasing number of universities have turned into "wealth creation" machines (Slaughter 1998). In this way, the "third responsibility," other than teaching and research, namely, revenue generation, has become an increasingly important mission of contemporary universities. Therefore, a process of "academic capitalization" is becoming increasingly popular in shaping the higher education sector across the globe (Slaughter and Leslie 1997; Clark 2002; Mok 2001c).

In addition, similar developments and experiences of marketization can be easily found in the school sector. Stressing the importance of "choice" for students and parents, school governance and management has become increasingly important. According to Schneider *et al.*:

> In the past, most educational reform movements focused on curriculum and teaching methods. Today's reform, however, centres more on issue of governance...Education cannot be improved unless actors are brought into the decision arena, changing the way which educational policy decisions are made, shifting power toward parents, and exposing overly bureaucratic school systems to some form of market discipline.
>
> (2000, p. 21)

More and more school activities, including teaching and learning, have been oriented toward market-driven ideas and practices. The ranking of schools or the introduction of "league tables," coupled with calls for strengthening the parents-school relationship by making parents and community a more prominent part of the governance processes in school, has clearly indicated that modern schools are under intensified market pressures within a competitive environment (Bridges and McLaughlin 1994; Good and Barden 2000; Leung 2003). Obviously, schools and universities are now much governed by market ideologies and the corporate discourse of efficiency and effectiveness, which also suggests that the lifestyle of teachers and academics has been affected as well (Mok 2001c; Mok and Chan 2002).

State, market, and civil society in education and changing governance

With heightened expectations for better education, how do modern states/governments finance and provide education sufficient to meet the pressing demands of their citizens, particularly when an increasing number of modern states are confronted with economic downturn and financial constraints? A number of scholars in the field of education have emphasized the importance of changing governance in education, paying heed to transformations and changes taking place in educational financing, provision, and regulation in education.

One exemplary work related to changing governance in education is Dale's framework (1997). According to Dale, in relation to the changing role of the state in education, we should closely examine the roles that the three major coordination institutions, namely the state, the market, and the community, play in terms of governance activities including funding, regulation, and provision/delivery. Core research questions are related to how education is funded, how it is provided (or delivered), and how it is regulated (or controlled) (Dale 1997). Against a changing socioeconomic and sociopolitical environment, especially in the context of globalization, Dale believes "it is not necessary for the state to carry out all of these activities [i.e., the three main governance activities in education], while remaining in overall control of education" (1997, p. 275). In view of the intensified financial constraints that modern states are now facing, it is anticipated that nonstate actors or sectors, including the market, the community, and the third sector, or civil society at large, will assume increasingly important roles in education financing/funding and education provision/delivery, while the state will restructure its roles in education by actively getting involved in performing the roles of enabler, regulator, quality controller, facilitator, and coordinator of services.

Such changes are accelerated when more governments are exploring additional resources from the civil society or the third sector. One seminal work shows an increasing number of countries have started to revitalize the nonstate sectors, including the market, the community, the third sector, and civil society, to engage in education (Meyer and Boyd 2001). Scholars who support the diversification of education services point out the problems with state action in education.

Reconsidering the society-based tradition of education as represented by writers such as Humboldt, Jefferson, de Tocqueville, and Mill seems timely and appropriate under the conditions of cultural pluralism (Meyer 2001). The myriad social ties that connect actors in a community—in the case of education: students, parents, teachers, and neighbors—could generate rich social resources as "social capital" that modern education systems could tap into or use (Coleman 1990). In short, the diversification of education service providers and funding providers, coupled with the revitalization of the third sector or civil society involvement in education, opens new venues and arenas for modern states to reconsider the way education governance activities are to be managed.

With diversified actors/coordinators in education provision and financing, there is a need to redefine the relationship between state and nonstate education (Rhodes 1997; Peters 2000; Pierre 2000; Salomon 2002). Such trends are consistent with other public policy domains where notions such as "co-production," "bringing society back in," and "coordinative relations" among state, society, and other nonstate sectors are stressed. Not surprisingly, the nonstate sectors now share more power of control and influence in governing education policy and educational development. "Co-arrangement," "coproduction," and "co-management" relationships between the state and the nonstate sectors (including the market, the community, the family, individuals, and other social forces) are experiencing changes; hence there is an urgent need to evolve new coordination efforts and governance modes. As Salomon has rightly suggested, the proliferation of policy tools and instruments requires "an elaborate system of *third-party government* in which crucial elements of public authority are shared with a host of nongovernmental or other-governmental actors, frequently in complex collaborative systems that sometimes defy comprehension" (2002, p. 2). Therefore, public-private partnerships in running the public sector or in delivering social services have started to take shape in different countries (Broadbent and Gray 2003; Klijn and Teisman 2003; Reeves 2003). During such a restructuring process, the role of the government has shown signs of fundamental change from "provider of welfare benefits" to "builder of markets", whereby the state actively builds markets, shapes them in different ways, and regulates them (Sbragia 2000).

Changing mix of policy instruments

As discussed earlier, globalization processes have accelerated changes to the public sector, driving more modern governments to engage in public sector reforms in search of alternative "policy tools" or "policy instruments" to solve public problems. Hence, new governance models are evolving and different kinds of management reform measures are developing to improve public sector performance. Theories of new governance are contested and in some respects appear contradictory (Peters 2000). They grapple with a broad set of "mega-trends" across a wide range of institutions and relationships that are not easily or precisely operationalized in testable propositions. To try to overcome this, the approach adopted here is to focus on one important dimension of new governance: changes

Table 1.1 Illustrative tools of education

Illustrative tools	Vehicle	Delivery system
Direct government	Direct provision	Public agency
Grant	Grant award/cash payment	Lower level of government, nonprofit
Direct loan	Loan	Public agency
Loan guarantee	Loan	Commercial bank
Tax expenditure	Tax	Tax system
Fees, charges	Tax	Tax system
Government corporations	Direct provision/loan	Quasi-public agency
Vouchers	Consumer subsidy	Public agency/consumer

Table 1.2 Changing governance paradigm

Traditional public administration	New governance
Program/agency	Tool
Hierarchical relation	Network and synthesis
Public vs. private	Public + private
Command and control	Negotiation and persuasion
Management skills	Enablement skills

Source: Adapted from Salomon 2002, p. 9.

to the mix of policy instruments. Instruments can be distinguished in a number of ways. One can draw up more or less exhaustive lists (direct government provision, social and economic regulation, grants, information collection and dissemination, and so on) (Salomon 2002, p. 21). For instance, Table 1.1 illustrates some major tools that modern states could adopt in education delivery and financing. Tools range from direct government delivery to loan guarantee delivered by commercial banks.

The proliferation of policy actors in general and diversification of policy instruments in particular have suggested that the relationship between the state and other nonstate actors in education delivery and financing has changed from a "hierarchical" to a "network" relationship; thereby the conventional governance mode of "command and control" has shifted to a "negotiation and persuasion" model (see Table 1.2). Such a critical and reflective analysis could throw more light on changing roles and relationships between the state and other nonstate sectors/actors in education governance activities. Such fundamental changes have therefore led us to call for new governance approaches and a new regulatory framework in education.

Following Salomon (2002), there are four dimensions along which policy instruments can be distinguished:

Coerciveness—the extent to which an instrument constrains behavior rather than encouraging or discouraging it.

Directness—the extent to which the government body that authorizes and finances a public policy is directly involved in implementing it.

Visibility—the extent to which the instrument's costs and impacts are conspicuous.

Automacity—the extent to which the instrument makes use of existing social and economic mechanisms rather than having to use government authority to create alternative ones.

Many new governance theorists make claims that most of the changes involve a shift in a similar direction along each of these "scales" (from more to less coercion, from more to less direction, and so on). Salomon (2002, p. 9) makes this link in distinguishing classical public administration from new governance as a field of study (the latter being concerned with the particular issues raised by an increasingly significant range of new governance "tools" or instruments). The "instruments approach" seeks not only to make clear distinctions between types of instruments but also to explain their adoption. In this regard, the search for a clear logic of design and adoption has had mixed results. In order to achieve a better conceptualization and clearer understanding of the changing roles of the state in education and the roles that other nonstate actors perform in the education sector, we can closely examine the mix of policy instruments and assess how the four dimensions that Salomon highlighted along which policy instruments can be distinguished (namely, coerciveness, directness, visibility, and automacity) have affected the adoption of policy instruments. In addition, a few major criteria (namely, effectiveness, efficiency, equity, manageability, legitimacy, and political feasibility) are adopted to assess which "policy instrument" or "policy tool" should be chosen in education delivery. With diversified "policy tools" or "policy instruments" in education, it is intellectually stimulating to examine the changing relationships between the state, the market, and the other nonstate actors, especially exploring the different roles they are now playing in education. In addition, when planning and designing the way that education services are financed and by whom they are run, education researchers should examine how different coordination institutions (i.e., state or local governments, market, family, community, the third sector, and other social forces in civil society) differ in the four dimensions of policy instruments, and individual tools of education might perform differently in terms of the five assessment criteria. More specifically, tool choices are highly political processes rather than purely technical choices because they involve value judgment. Tool choices involve issues related to the capacity of governance and manageability, legitimacy, and the political feasibility of the society introducing different policy options. Therefore, we should examine the impact of different interests and perspectives on tool choices (Peters 2002).

Changing public-private mix and new regulatory arrangements

Our earlier discussion has pointed to a very important development: the revitalization of nonstate actors and the proliferation of actors in education provision and financing imply potential governance contributions from private or nonstate sectors that might compensate for the decreasing capacities of nation-states to provide education services. Despite the fact that we do not suppose a hollowing-out of the state, the increase in nonstate and private contributions to education will certainly challenge the conventional regulatory arrangements in the education sector. The major shift in national politics from maximizing welfare to promoting entrepreneurial culture, innovation, and profitability in both the private and public sectors has led modern states to adopt the techniques of steering from a distance. Through adopting the means of regulation, incentive, and sanctions to make autonomous individuals and quasi-governmental and nongovernmental institutions such as universities behave in ways consistent with their policy objectives, new regulatory frameworks have evolved (Henry *et al.* 1999; Marginson 1999). A more flexible regulatory environment could characterize such a restructuring; thereby public policy formulation is reoriented toward a smaller and more business-oriented state machine. This paradigm shift, manifested by a more individualistic, competitive, and entrepreneurial approach, has become increasingly prominent in public management (Robertson and Dale 2000).

With changes in governance, especially when the newer tools of public action now increasingly exercise discretion over the use of public authority, come issues related to how regulatory frameworks should be set up. More specifically, issues of how we understand the notion of "regulation" and to what extent nonstate funded and nonstate run education institutions could have autonomy and flexibility in governing their education services are raised. Moreover, whether a "self-regulatory" framework could be developed in assuring education quality/academic standards is open for further discussion. Most important of all, the power-money dimension is anticipated to become a major tension between the state and nonstate sectors, especially when funding sources and education services are diversified. The growing interdependence between the state (public) and nonstate (private, community, family, and individual contributions) and the exchange relationships between these sectors will render the conventional regulatory arrangements inappropriate. With more private contributions and donations or resources generated from the civil society to support education development, we anticipate there will be a decline in hierarchical forms of intervention from the state but other forms of regulatory arrangements will develop. When education financing and provision are no longer monopolized by the state, the conventional "interventionist regulation" framework (implying a hierarchical intervention of the state in imposing micro control of every aspect of education delivery) will be found to be problematic. The reduction of the state to a *regulatory state* can be clearly seen from the trends of decentralization, deregulation, privatization, marketization, and administrative reforms in education (Hood 1999; Robertson 1999).

With diversification of actors/coordination and institutions in education financing and provision, coupled with growing patterns of "coproduction," "co-arrangements," and "comanagement" in education services, we anticipate a new regulatory model: *regulated self-regulation* will evolve. Through regulated self-regulation, "the state plays a central and active role and disposes of powers and resources which are not available to societal actors" (Knill and Lehmkuhl 2002, p. 50). Although the state is held responsible for promoting quality education and meeting heightened expectations of education, the state cannot adopt the same interventionist regulatory framework to govern the relationship between the state and the nonstate/private actors, especially when education provision and financing are diversified. Special arrangements are to be made in allowing private/nonstate actors to participate in policy making and implementation. One of the ways is delegating power to these nonstate actors, particularly when these non-state actors are playing increasingly important roles in education. A self-regulatory framework should be established in governing these newly emerging private/nonstate education coordination institutions, provided the participating institutions still follow the overarching framework or directions set out by the state.

A regulated self-regulatory framework could be further developed in conceptualizing the relationship between the state and professional bodies. Unlike other private goods, it is believed the overall quality assurance responsibility in education still lies with the state. But state intervention somehow is filtered by professional influences. Taking professional qualifications, for instance, it is not the state that sets detailed requirements for approving professional credentials. Instead, professional bodies should have a very important role to play in governing professional standards. What the state has to do with maintaining high education quality is to liaise with professional organizations concerned to assure quality instead of specifying detailed requirements. The proliferation of private/nonstate actors in education will certainly pose challenges to the conventional regulatory framework, driving the state to move away from the "interventionist regulation" to the "regulated self-regulation" framework (with more emphasis given to "negotiated regulation"), especially when cooperative patterns of interaction between private and public actors in education delivery and "cooperative contracting" are becoming increasingly common in education provision and financing (see Table 1.3).

Contextual analysis of the mix of "Policy Instruments"

Against broad generalizations such as the growing diversity of instruments and trends toward "third party government" (Salomon 2002, pp. 1–3) are a number of findings showing the contingent nature of actual instrument choice. The mix of instruments used for delivering government policies varies widely for a number

Table 1.3 Different modes of governance

	Bureaucratic governance	*Deregulated governance*	*Societal-market governance*
Policy trend and style	Centralization State dominance	Decentralization Diversification Mobilization	Marketization Privatization Various social sources
Form of regulation	Interventionist regulation	Interfering regulation	Regulated self-regulation

of reasons (Linder and Peters 1989; Howlett and Ramesh 1995, pp. 157–63; Peters 2002). Paradoxes are likely to be observed; for example, so-called deregulation in fact often entails tough new forms of "reregulation" (Vogel 1996). Comparative research also suggests the extent to which national factors influence instrument choice (Vogel 1996; Ringeling 2002). The scope and impact of instrument change rests heavily on pre-existing patterns of administration and on the political context (for the case of privatization see Ramamurti 1999; Cheung 2001). Another complication is that instrument choice is not the end of the matter. The same instrument can be applied in very different ways—the distinctions made between types of instruments in the abstract can conceal important facts about their real character in practice. For example, important for understanding the case of privatization in Malaysia would be a detailed analysis of its implementation, including the importance of privatization for targeted support to particular entrepreneurs (Jomo *et al.* 1995). Therefore, researchers should pay additional attention to the particular policy context in which policy instruments are chosen and adopted.

When determining which policy instrument to adopt, one should pay heed to how and in what way the particular policy instrument chosen may come out with different consequences in terms of the four dimensions discussed earlier. What could be the best policy instruments or mix of different policy instruments is heavily dependent on the unique socioeconomic, sociopolitical, and historical backgrounds of individual societies. In addition, a country's unique legal, administrative, and political system will affect the particular institutional arrangements; hence we must pay attention to the institutional context in which policy instruments are chosen (Knill and Lehmkuhl 2002).

In addition, we must evaluate the four dimensions of policy instruments, especially when determining the mix of policy instruments. Different policy instruments or different actors involved in education financing, provision, and regulation may yield different consequences. A comprehensive contextual analysis is needed when examining and comparing changing education governance taking place in different societies. Therefore, careful empirical analysis is needed before jumping to conclusions about broad trends. For instance, it is particularly important to be cautious when transplanting observations about what is "new" in a European context to the conditions of East Asia. The history of East Asian developmental states may provide a somewhat different starting point from that in the mind of many new governance theorists: "old governance" in East Asia has its own features. Research has identified the importance of networks and third-party cooperative implementation as distinctive features. In industry policy, some of the common instruments are information sharing, close informal consultation, and strategic financial support for targeted, collaborative R&D. Heavy-handed regulation and high levels of public subsidy are less common (Evans 1999). At the same time, analysis of different developmental states in East Asia makes it clear that there are many differences in both the content and style of government action. For example, different patterns of social welfare provision combining different instrument mixes—social insurance schemes, tax-based entitlements, and directly produced services—have been observed (Holliday 2000).

Taking these points into account, the instruments approach opens the way to trying to test the existence both of broad trends and local variations. Whether or not we can identify some common trends in outcomes, as Jayasurya (2001) and other new governance theorists propose, is a key question for this book. This is largely a question of identification. But beyond identifying whether or not there are common trends in instrument adoption lies the task of explanation. The process by which new instruments are adopted needs investigating in detail in order to understand the causes of any observed trends. If there is an observable trend (whether "new governance" or not) there are three possible types of explanation: first, such outcomes may be the result of concurrent choices in the face of similar constraints; second, they may be formed as a result of international processes, such as imitation and emulation of ideas and practices; and third, they may be "transnationally formed" (Sahlin-Andersson 2001: 45), that is, the result of the influence of "transnational mediators" such as international consultants or organizations such as the World Bank, IMF, and OECD, in the context of globalization.

Discussions and conclusion

Our earlier discussions have shown how globalization processes have affected governance and management in education policy. One crucial point to note is that when talking about the impacts of globalization on education, I have no intention to overstate or underestimate the possible impacts of globalization. Rather, I take a more critical stand in reflecting upon the impacts of globalization on education policy and educational developments. No matter how we assess the impacts of globalization on education, we must admit the fact that the principles of structural adjustment, coupled with the ideologies of managerialism and economic rationalism, have become increasingly popular not only as a governance philosophy but also as an effective means for public administration (Hood 1991; Flynn 1997; Marginson 2000; Deem 2001). It is not surprising that corporatization, marketization, and privatization have become the most popular policy strategies for reforming public services, including educational institutions (Mok and Currie 2002). This chapter has attempted to explain recent changes and reforms in education by analyzing how educational governance is affected by globalization challenges, with particular reference to the analysis of education policy development using the "policy instruments" approach. The proposed "policy instruments approach" could serve as a useful public policy framework that may enable education researchers to engage in systematic and critical research into major educational governance activities and changing roles of the state and other non-state actors in education within the wider context of globalization and transforming societies. Therefore, education researchers could develop research to investigate the changing mix of policy instruments, particularly in the context of globalization and transforming societies. More specifically, attention should be given to examine issues related to changing relationships between state, society, and market in educational financing, provision, and regulation. When actors in education financing and provision are diversified, the traditional way of private-public distinction is rendered inappropriate. Therefore, education analysts can explore new research frontiers by investigating the changing mix of policy instruments and the way that various educational governance activities are transformed, with particular reference to formulating new regulatory frameworks in governing "coproduction" and "co-arrangement" in education.

Equally important, when talking about the changing mix of policy instruments in governing and managing education, we must be aware of the negative consequences associated with the practices of marketization, privatization, and commodification of education. Since a growing number of modern states have adhered to the principles recommended by UNSECO, the World Bank, OECD, and IMF to run modern schools and universities like private and business entities, the adoption of such ideas and practices has negative consequences. Modern states want to be economically competitive, but the question remains whether they are prepared to sacrifice their national autonomy in accepting measures imposed by the supranational bodies mentioned earlier. Despite the fact that there is a tendency for the modern state to reduce its role in the economy and move away from its present regulatory to a more facilitative stance, allowing businesses more space and creating more diversity and choice for people, are modern states prepared and ready to undertake such measures in becoming less effective national powers or less capable nation-states?

In addition, the stress on competition, diversity, choice, efficiency, and economy in education governance raises issues related to education disparities and inequality. The growing tendency of privatizing and marketizing education has caused increased social concerns about social restratification and marginalizing effects on social groups coming from lower socioeconomic strata (Brown *et al.* 2001). When framing debates about choices and diversity in education in line with globalization discourse, we easily find people with better financial means can enjoy far more choices and diversity while children from poorer families have difficulties in paying for education expenses. In this regard, we must carefully examine both the positive and negative consequences when education providers proliferater and policy instruments in education are diversified. We must guard against change processes that may lead to social inequalities and education disparities by privileging only a few but disadvantaging a larger proportion of the population.

2 Education systems and policy change in East Asia

Introduction

Globalization and the evolution of the knowledge-based economy have caused dramatic changes in the character and functions of education in most countries around the world. However, the impacts of globalization on schools and universities are not uniform even though similar business-like practices have been adopted to cope with competition in the global marketplace. The pressure for restructuring and reforming education is mainly derived from the growing expectations and demands of different stakeholders in society. In the past decade, government bureaucracy, public service institutions, and schools and universities have been significantly affected by the tidal wave of public sector reform around the world. Apart from the improvement of the efficiency and effectiveness of public services, schools and universities are confronted with a situation in which the principles of financial accountability and responsiveness to stakeholders prevail amidst the massification stage under the condition of global economic retrenchment.

In response to such pressing demands for change, policies and strategies of decentralization, privatization, and marketization are becoming increasingly popular measures in education governance. In the school sector, the principles of "diversity" and "choice" have become increasingly popular, curriculum reform and school management have been oriented toward a more "market-driven" approach. For universities, reform strategies and measures such as quality assurance, performance evaluation, financial audit, corporate management, and market competition are employed to reform and improve the performance of the higher education sector. The principal goal of this chapter is to examine recent education reforms and policy changes not only in the four Tiger economies (namely, Hong Kong, Singapore, Taiwan, and South Korea) but also in the other two major economic powers in the region, mainland China and Japan. The aim of this chapter is to set a wider policy context for this book, preparing readers for further discussion in the coming chapters. The first part of the chapter briefly introduces the education systems of these Asian societies. The second part of the chapter outlines and discusses the most recent education reforms and policy changes in these Asian societies.

Education systems of selected societies in East Asia

China

Since the economic reform started in the late-1970s, the Chinese Communist Party (CCP) has begun to put more emphasis on education. In 1985, the central government promulgated a "Decision on Reform of Educational System," introducing a new policy of decentralization in education to engage local governments in generating additional revenues to finance and provide basic education. In 1993, the government promulgated the "Outline for Reform and Development of Education in China," setting out the blueprint for education reform. In the mid- and late-1990s, "211 Projects" and "Facing the 21st Century" policy documents were published with the intention to promote the competitiveness of China's higher education. Believing that Chinese universities should have attained international standards, the Chinese government has attempted to introduce "internal competition" and "quality assurance" exercises to run and monitor its higher education institutions. All of these measures are aimed at creating more education opportunities for Chinese citizens by achieving the policy goal of state provision of nine years of education on the one hand and improving education quality on the other hand. Through the restructuring of the education system, the central government expects that human capital can be improved in terms of both quality and quantity. By the end of 2001, official statistics proved that such education reforms had significantly improved the education system and that student enrollment at all levels had greatly improved.

In China, the education system can be divided into three main categories, namely, basic, higher education, and vocational and adult education. Figure 2.1 shows the education system of China. For basic education, it comprises preschool education, primary education, and secondary education. Preschool education is mainly privately run and the term of study varies from one year to three years. In 2001, there were 111,700 kindergartens, 20,218,400 students, and 630,100 principals and teachers. Primary education takes six years, followed by three years of junior secondary school. These nine years of education were made compulsory in 1986. In 2001, there were 491,300 primary schools, 1,254,347,000 students, and 6,379,700 teachers. The ratio between teachers and students was about 1:22. In the same year, there were 66,600 junior secondary schools in China, recruiting 65,143,800 students and employing 3,385,700 teachers. The ratio between teachers and students was about 1:19. In addition to liberal arts courses such as politics, Chinese, foreign languages, history, geography, physical hygiene, physical education, music, and art, students in junior schools have to study a variety of science subjects as well (Luo and Wendel 1999). After finishing the nine years of basic education, students have to pass the Standardized Test organized by the Education Administrative Department in order to proceed to senior secondary school (Ministry of Education, PRC 2002b; 2004).

Senior secondary school education in China consists of regular secondary schools, technical schools, teacher training schools, and vocational schools. The diversified junior secondary schools provide different choices catering to the different education needs of students. In 2001, there were 34,210 junior high

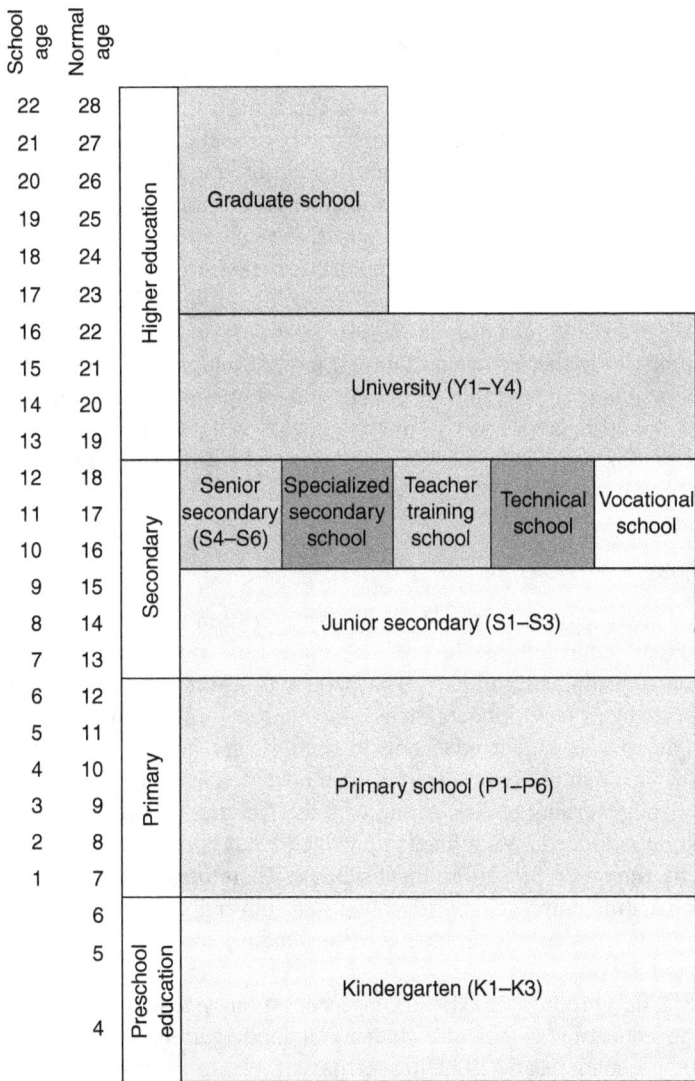

Figure 2.1 China's education system.

schools, enrolling 26,009,300 students and over 1,472,600 teachers engaged in the profession (Ministry of Education, PRC 2002a). For higher education, the pace of development has been fast in recent years. In 2001, there were 1,911 higher institutions, admitting 117,505,000 undergraduate students, 307,400 masters degree students, 393,300 masters degrees by research, and 85,900 doctoral students. Although the central government emphasizes the importance of higher education indefatigably, it is unrealistic and impossible for the central government to act as the sole agent to invest resources in higher education. Based on the central government's limited financial abilities, it is really difficult to hold the central government alone responsible for meeting the huge demand and increasing expectations for higher education of the public.

In order to diversify higher education financing sources, the central government has attempted to mobilize the community or social forces/nonstate actors to finance and provide higher education. In addition, the Chinese government has highly encouraged the private sector and other nonstate actors to establish *minban* or community colleges to create more learning opportunities in terms of higher studies. In 1995, the State Education Commission promulgated a policy document entitled "Suggestions on Deepening Higher Education Structural Reform," proposing changes in the orientation, financing, curriculum, and management of higher education through joint development (*gongjian*), restructuring (*huzahuan*), merging (*hebing*), and cooperation (*hexuo*) to initiate fundamental changes in order to improve the overall performance and competitiveness of universities on the Chinese mainland (Ministry of Education, PRC 2001; Mok 2004a).

Hong Kong

There are five major sectors in Hong Kong's education system: preschool education, general education, technical education and vocational training, higher education, and adult education (K.M. Cheng 1997). While preschool education is mainly run by private kindergartens, the majority of primary and secondary schools as well as higher education institutions are heavily subsidized by the government, although these government-funded schools/universities are run by independent governing bodies. Along with the fact that the government has been the most important education funding provider, it has taken up some responsibility in directly running a few government schools. Therefore, the education sector in Hong Kong (including school education and university education) is predominantly public, particularly as measured by funding sources (Y.C. Cheng 2000) (see Figure 2.2).

In 2002, the enrollment in Hong Kong's education system exceeded 1.2 million, providing education to 143,000 students at kindergarten, 483,000 at primary, 465,000 at secondary, and 142,000 at tertiary levels. In the same year, there were 2,200 schools and 1,200 of them were publicly funded. On the public expenditure front, approved recurrent public expenditure and total public expenditure on education in the financial year 2002–03 increased to HK$49.3 billion and HK$59.4 billion, respectively, taking away about 23.8 percent of the total recurrent government expenditure and total government expenditure (Information Services Department, HKSAR Government 2003, p. 144).

For early childhood education, all kindergartens are now required to employ no less than 60 percent professionally trained teachers. Since 2001, the teacher-pupil ratio in kindergartens has improved to 1:15. In addition, quality assurance inspection has been started in kindergartens and a set of performance indicators for

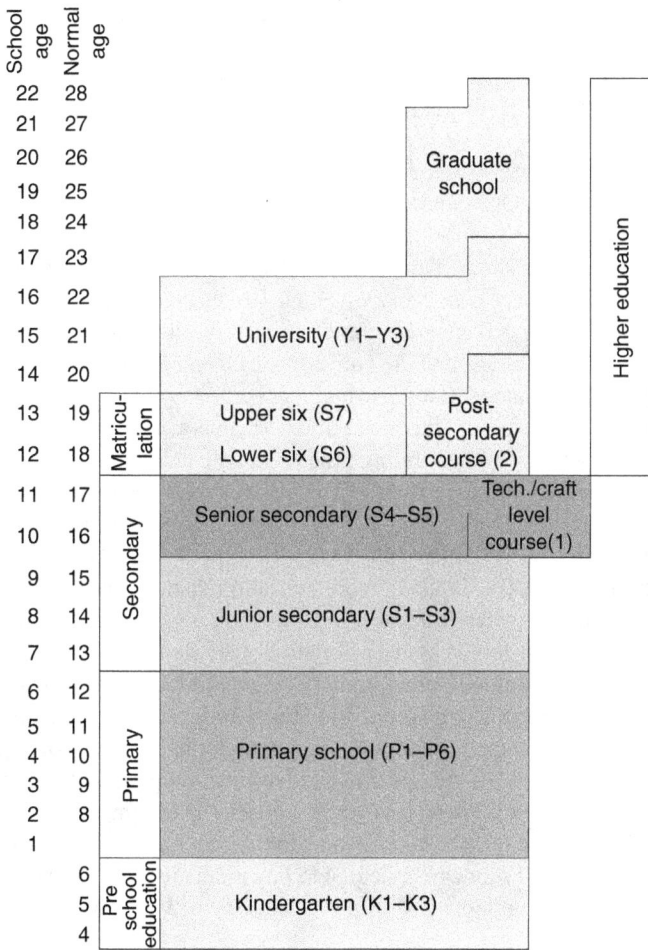

Figure 2.2 Hong Kong's education system.

Source: Education and Manpower Bureau, HKSAR Government 2004.

Notes
1 Including courses run by the Hong Kong Institute of Vocational Education (IVE).
2 Including associate degree, higher diplomo/certificate and diploma/certificate courses.

kindergartens was published in 2002 to assure education quality at the early state of schooling in Hong Kong (Information Services Department, HKSAR Government 2003, p. 146).

Hong Kong children aged 6–15 enjoy free and universal basic education from primary one to secondary three. For primary schools, the student-to-teacher ratio was about 20:1 in 2001–02 with 60 percent of the school places offered on a whole-day basis in 2002–03. As for secondary schools, the student-to-teacher ratio was about 18:1. Apart from government and aided schools, there has been a more rapid development of Direct Subsidy Scheme (DSS) schools and nonprofit-making private independent schools over the past few years. There were around 40 DSS schools offering 3 percent of school places, and it is projected that a total of 10 nonprofit-making private independent schools will be opened by 2007–08 (Information Services Department, HKSAR Government 2003, p. 147).

At present, 14,500 first-year first-degree places are offered by eight University Grants Committee (UGC)-funded higher education institutions with an admission rate of 18 percent of the 17–20 age cohort. The eight UGC-funded institutions are City University of Hong Kong, Hong Kong Baptist University, Lingnan University, the Chinese University of Hong Kong, the Hong Kong Institute of Education, the Hong Kong Polytechnic University, the Hong Kong University of Science and Technology, and the University of Hong Kong. Each of these institutions is an autonomous statutory body governed by its own ordinance and governing body. Moreover, there are three degree-awarding higher education institution that are not funded through the UGC: the publicly funded Hong Kong Academy for Performing Arts, the self-financing Open University of Hong Kong, and the Hong Kong Shue Yan College (Information Services Department, HKSAR Government 2003, pp. 149–51).

In addition to the UGC-funded higher education institutions, a number of non-government-funded higher education/post-secondary education institutions have developed in the past few years to offer subdegree training programs on a self-financing basis. For instance, a community college founded by Caritas, one of the charity organizations in Hong Kong, and Hong Kong Technical Training College currently provide associate degree or higher diploma prgrams for high school graduates. Similarly, UGC-funded universities also set up separate administrative entities undertaking activities related to subdegree training on a self-funded principle. For instance, SPACE, an extension of the University of Hong Kong, offers a wide range of subdegree, degree to postgraduate training in collaboration either with faculty members within the University or with overseas universities (Space, HKU 2003).

Japan

In Japan, the education system is well known for its keen competition and intense pressure. Figure 2.3 shows the education system of Japan. The 6–3–3–4 system of school education was adopted with the enactment of Fundamental Law of Education and the School Education Law in 1947. Before entering elementary education, there is preschool education for those children who are aged 3. Children aged between 6 and 15 have to attend 9 years of compulsory education, which includes 6 years of general elementary education and 3 years of general secondary education. After completing the lower secondary education, children have to pass the Examination for Granting Equivalency Certificate of Lower Secondary School Graduates before they can continue their upper secondary school education. Following the three years of upper secondary education,

School age Normal age

School age	Normal age	
18	24	
17	23	
16	22	
15	21	
14	20	
13	19	
12	18	
11	17	
10	16	
9	15	
8	14	
7	13	
6	12	
5	11	
4	10	
3	9	
2	8	
1	7	
	6	
	5	
	4	
	3	

Higher education

Secondary education

Elementary education

Preschool education

Graduate school

University

Miscellaneous school

Specialized training college general courses

Colleges of technology

STCUSC*

Upper secondary school

Unified secondary school (upper division and lower division)

Lower secondary school

Elementary schools

Kindergarten (K1–K3)

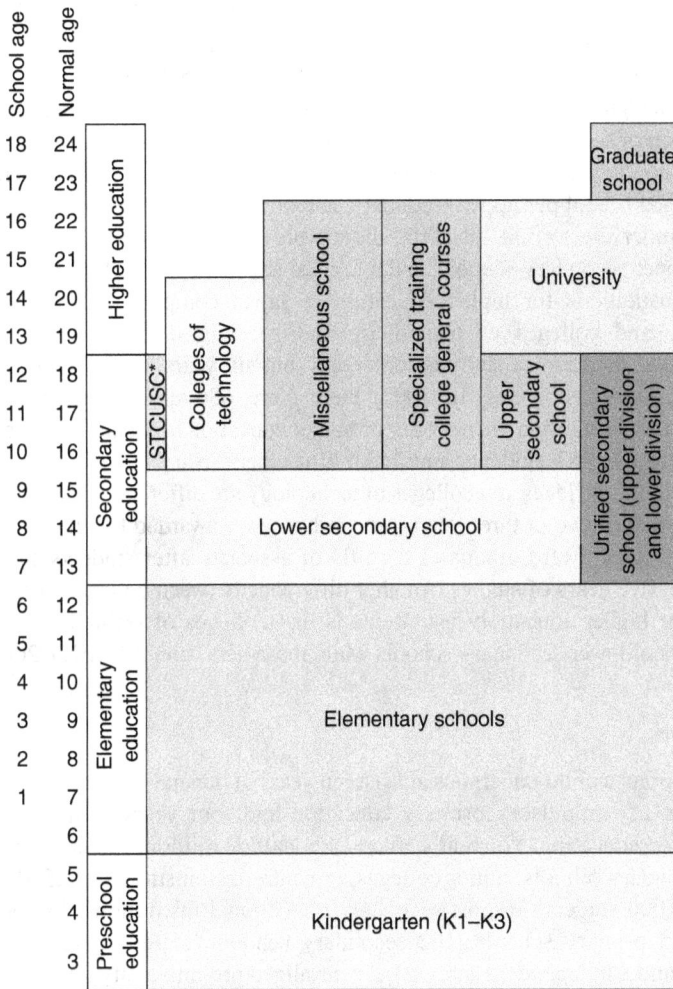

Figure 2.3 Japan's education system.

Source: MEXT, Japan 2004.

Note
* Represents Specialized Training College Upper Secondary Courses.

students have to attend the university entrance examination. The university system in Japan takes four years to complete (MEXT 2004a).

In 2002, there were 14,279 kindergartens, 1,769,096 students, and 108,051 teachers in preschool education. Most elementary schools, are public institutions. In 2002, the total numbers of elementary schools was 23,808, admitting 7,239,327 students and employing 410,505 teachers. Traditionally, secondary schools are composed of lower secondary schools and upper secondary schools. Yet, in April

1999, a unified lower and upper secondary school education was developed and became a part of the Japanese education system. The introduction of the unified secondary school aims at diversifying secondary school education to cater to the individual needs of Japanese students. The unified school system allows students and parents/guardians to select six-year consistent courses. Although the major proportion of secondary schools are still divided into lower secondary schools and upper secondary schools, the Japanese government is determined to open at least one unified school per upper secondary school district in order to make its school system more diversified. In 2002, there were 11,159 lower secondary schools, 5,472 upper secondary schools, and a unified secondary schools (MEXT 2004).

The institutions for higher education in Japan comprise universities, junior colleges, and colleges of technology and specialized training colleges. For universities, the term of study is four years (but six years for medicine, dentistry, and veterinary medicine). In 2002, there were 686 universities, with private universities constituting the majority of higher education in Japan. In the same year, there were 621,487 students and 155,050 teachers in universities. The terms of study in junior colleges and colleges of technology are different. For the former, the term of study is two or three years and graduates are awarded the title of associate, while the latter award graduates the title of associate after students successfully complete five years of studies. Another difference between colleges of technology and other higher education institutions is that colleges of technology can admit graduates of lower secondary schools while the others cannot (MEXT 2004a).

Singapore

In Singapore, a child undergoes at least ten years of general education, comprising six years of compulsory primary education and four years of noncompulsory secondary education. Currently, there are half a million students in primary and secondary schools, junior colleges, or centralized institutes, 24,500 teachers, and 104,000 students in post-secondary educational institutions. In 2003, there were 175 primary schools, 162 secondary schools (including 23 autonomous schools and 8 independent schools), 2 centralized pre-university institutes, and 16 junior colleges in Singapore.

There are two major stages in Singapore's primary education. In the foundation stage (primary one–four), the curriculum focuses on English, mother tongue, and mathematics. Pupils are assessed in these three subjects and recommended for a stream appropriate for their abilities. In the orientation stage (primary five–six), there are three language streams, EM1, EM2, and EM3. Pupils in the first two streams take English, mother tongue, mathematics, and science, with EM1 pupils studying their mother tongue at a higher level. As for EM3 pupils, they take foundation English, basic mother tongue, and foundation mathematics. The allocation of secondary school places is based on the academic results of the Primary School Leaving Examination (PSLE). It is not surprising that the primary education system in Singapore has a streaming effect, offering fast tracking for those high flyers in academic performance.

Similar to primary education, there are three streams in Singapore's secondary education system: Special, Express, and Normal (Academic/Technical). For the Special and Express courses, students take four years for the Singapore–Cambridge General Certificate of Education (GCE) "Ordinary" level examination. The major difference between these two streams is that the students in the Special stream study their mother tongue at a higher level. On the other hand, students in the "Normal" (Academic/Technical) stream take the GCE "N" level examination in their fourth

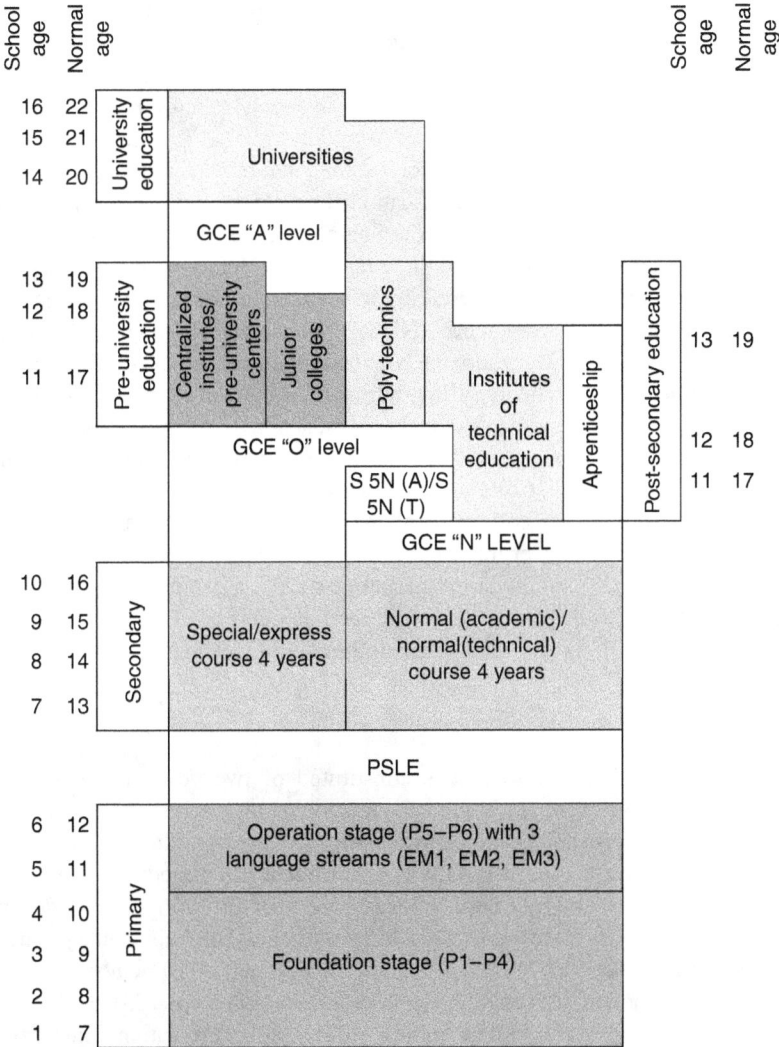

Figure 2.4 Singapore's education system.

Source: Ministry of Education, Singapore 2004.

year of study. Only those who do well in the "N" level examination can proceed to the fifth year of study for the GCE "O" level examination. Again, the streaming and screening effects are clearly found in Singapore's secondary education (see Figure 2.4).

Unlike Hong Kong, the Singapore government maintained a binary system in higher education, by which I refer to the divide between universities and poly-technics. In addition to this binary system high school students are provided with different types of post-secondary education, comprising "A" level preuniversity courses, Institute of Technical Education (ITE) courses, polytechnic education, and university education. Secondary school graduates can enter a junior college for a two-year course or a centralized institute for a three-year course for the GCE "A" level examination. As an alternative, they can go to study in an ITE specializing in technical skills and knowledge. There are five polytechnics in the city-state, namely Singapore Polytechnic, Ngee Ann Polytechnic, Tamesak Polytechnic, Nanyang Polytechnic, and Republic Polytechnic, that provide training for students with "O" and "A" level or ITE qualifications in diploma courses in areas such as engineering, business studies, mass communication, nursing, and product design.

On the university front, there are three universities offering undergraduate and postgraduate courses, and undertaking research and development, including National University of Singapore (NUS), Nanyang Technological University (NTU), and Singapore Management University (SMU). NUS offers courses in sciences, engineering, technology, law, humanities, medicine, and social sciences. NTU offers courses in engineering, technology, accountancy, business, communi-cation studies, and education. SMU specializes in business and management (Ministry of Information, Communications and The Arts 2003, pp. 212–17). The divide between technical colleges, polytechnics, and universities in Singapore satisfies different manpower training needs. At the same time, this higher educa-tion system reveals the fundamental belief of the Singapore government in "meritocracy," rewarding those who work hard, and one can easily feel the strati-fication effect resulting from this education system (Mok and Tan 2004).

Taiwan

In Taiwan, the education system is constituted of two years at kindergarten, six years at primary school, three years at a junior high school, three years at a high or vocational school, and various periods of higher education (Shan and Chang 2000, p. 186). Since the Taiwan government has put education in a very important position, children have enjoyed nine years of compulsory education since 1968. In 2003, there were 3,275 kindergartens, 2,627 elementary schools, 716 junior high schools, 302 senior high schools, and 170 senior vocational schools (Government Information Service, Taiwan 2003, p. 285). In the same census period, there were 70 universities, 32 of which were national institutions, and 73 independent colleges offering bachelor's degree programs (Department of Statistics, Taiwan 2003, 2004; Government Information Service, Taiwan 2003, pp. 290–91).

There have been two main purposes of schooling in Taiwan since the Nationalist Government moved to the island province in 1949. The first purpose of education is to institutionalize a compulsory education system of "National Education" in order to solidify national sentiment and to incite national consciousness among the people in Taiwan. Like other developing economies in the early 1950s, formal education was adopted as a policy tool by the nationalist government in Taiwan to meet the manpower needs for economic development. Attaching significant weight to education, Taiwan experienced a rapid education expansion from the 1950s to

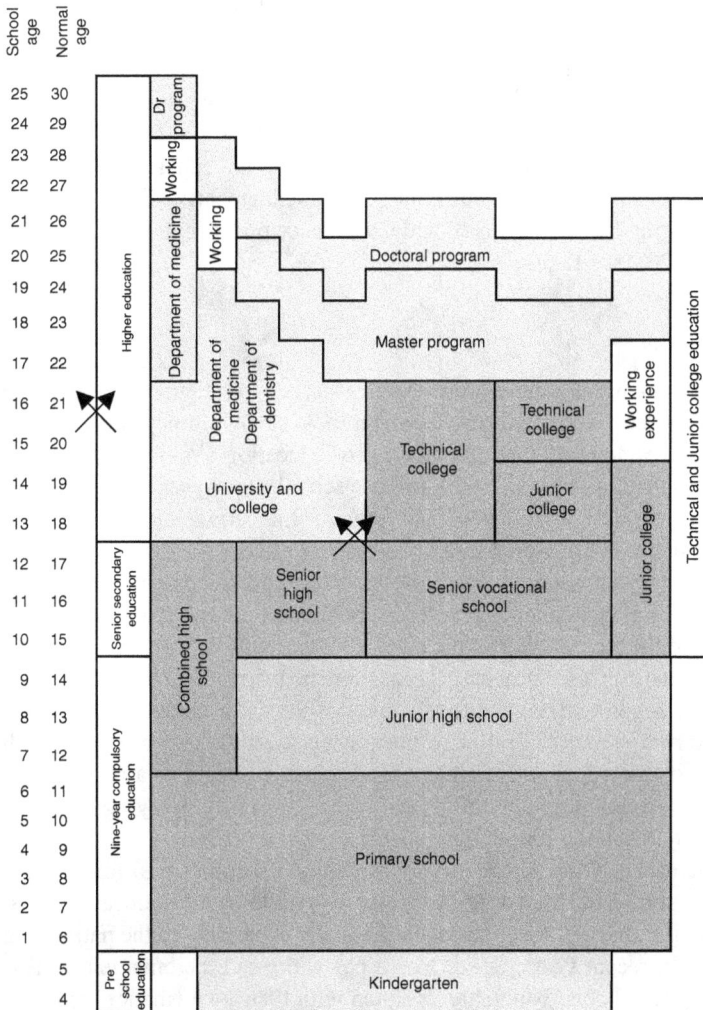

Figure 2.5 Taiwan's education system.

Source: Ministry of Education, Taiwan 2004.

the 1980s. The implementation of nine years of compulsory education from primary to junior secondary levels in 1968 was the watershed of educational development in Taiwan. Nonselective "National Junior High Schools" were created in the same year in response to the compulsory education policy. Apart from the normal schooling system, the Taiwanese government also put emphasis on the development of technical-vocational education for junior high school leavers, particularly for the manpower needs during a period of rapid economic growth and fast industrialization (Shan and Chang 2000).

Another milestone in Taiwan education was the lifting of the curfew and abandonment of martial law in 1987, after which Taiwanese society has experienced a genuine liberalization. Schools and universities have been given more autonomy and flexibility in running their activities, particularly since the policy of decentralization was implemented in the 1990s (Law 2003; Weng 2003). In the post-martial law era, a significant number of private colleges and universities have emerged and developed since the 1990s to meet the pressing higher education needs. Envisaging greater pressure on reforming the education system from the civil society and pressure groups, the government embarked on education reforms by sponsoring the Seventh National Conference on Education in 1994 (Shan and Chang 2000) (see Figure 2.5).

South Korea

South Korea has a single-track 6–3–3–4 school system, which comprises six years of primary school, three years of middle school, three years of high school, and four years of college and university education (Young 2000). The higher education institutions consist of graduate schools, four-year universities, and two- or three-year junior colleges (Ministry of Education and Human Resources Development, South Korea 2002, p. 36).

Elementary schooling in South Korea is free and compulsory. At the age of six, children are allocated an elementary school based on the principle of vicinity. At the end of the Korean War in the early 1950s, South Korea witnessed the quantitative expansion of elementary education in response to the rapid process of industrialization and the sudden increase of the urban population with urbanization and rural–urban migration, especially between the 1970s and 1980s. In order to expand foreign language education, English is taught as a part of the regular curriculum beginning with the primary three level by employing native speaking teachers to teach the foreign language.

In the earlier years, there was no limitation on entrance to middle schools. It was not until 1985 that free compulsory middle school education was put in place, at first in rural areas and then gradually expanding to the nation as a whole in 2002. In recent years, South Korea has witnessed the emergence of independent private schools, which are operated with their own finances and tuition fee incomes and empowered to select students. For high schools, there are four major types: general high schools, vocational high schools, science high schools, and special high schools. General high schools offer common subjects including humanities, natural sciences, and vocational training. Vocational high schools provide advanced general education and vocational training in agriculture, tech-nology, commerce, fishery, industry, and home economics. Science high schools cater to scientifically gifted students, who can be admitted to the bachelor's program at the Korea Advanced Institute for Science and Technology. Special high schools specialize in areas such as foreign languages, arts, and sports to provide more opportunities for gifted students to develop further in those fields (Ministry of Education and Human Resources Development, Korea 2002, pp. 46–50).

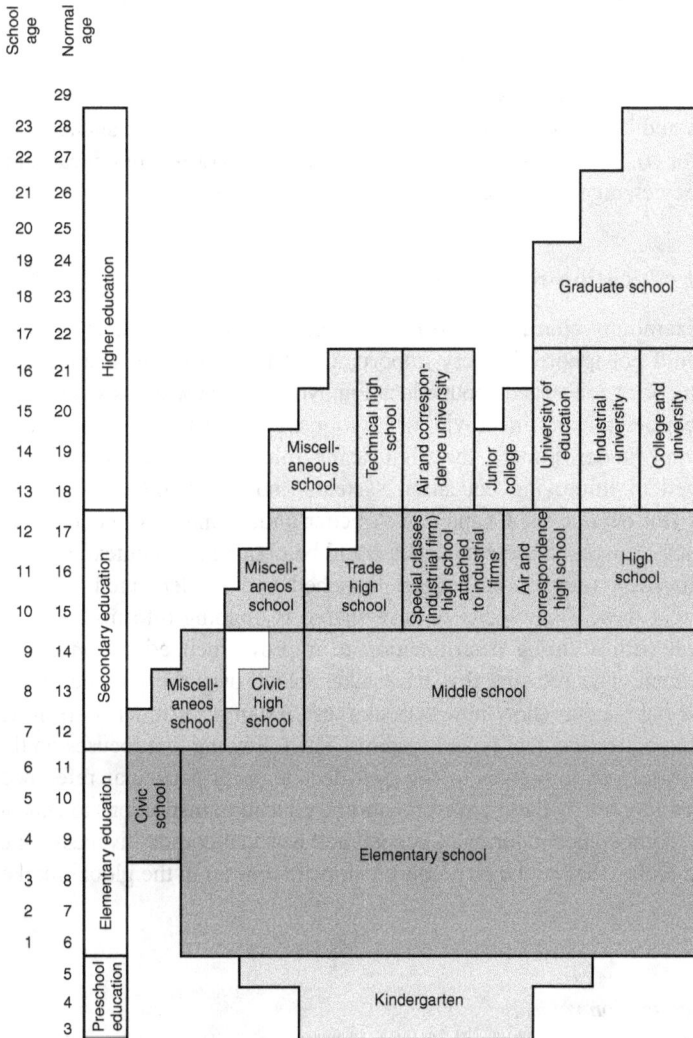

Figure 2.6 Korea's education system.

Source: Ministry of Education, Korea 2004.

On the higher education front, there are seven types of institutions: colleges and universities, industrial universities, universities of education, junior colleges, the Air and Correspondence University, technical colleges, and other miscellaneous institutions (Ministry of Education and Human Resources Development, Korea 2002, p. 51).

Comparing the higher education systems of the Tiger economies, we may discover the differences among them. For Hong Kong and Singapore, the higher education systems are more predominantly public, while there is a clearer mix of private and public higher education institutions in Taiwan and South Korea. One point that deserves our attention here is that the private sector has performed a more significant role in meeting people's higher education needs in Taiwan and South Korea, while the role of the state is more prominent in higher education financing in Hong Kong and Singapore. In response to the growing impact of globalization, all these Asian governments have started to review their education systems and different kinds of education reforms have been launched in the past decade or so. The following section discusses the most recent education reforms and policy changes in these Asian societies (see Figure 2.6).

Recent education reforms and policy changes

When examining education reforms and policy changes in the Tiger economies, one should not ignore the very important fact that all these Asian governments have long been concerned about education. No matter how we assess the intentions of these governments in providing high-quality education to their citizens, we should not underestimate the significant role that these governments have performed in improving education systems and education quality in the past decades (for details, see Chapter 3). A better understanding of education reforms and policy changes in these societies could be obtained by contextually analyzing how education reforms have been launched and implemented. One common feature that these Tiger societies have shared is ongoing reforms and changes in education with a strong determination to improve their education delivery and management. The reforms that have taken place over the past decade in these societies once again show how serious these Asian governments are in terms of improving education quality and systems. The following text focuses on the major education reform initiatives of the past decade, with particular reference to the strategies adopted by these governments and education institutions to enhance their citizens' competence in terms of general and national competitiveness (in the case of Hong Kong, that is, the city-state's competitiveness) in the global marketplace.

China

School education reform

Since the central government promulgated a "Decision on Reform of Educational Reforms" to engage local governments in providing basic education in 1985, school education in China has made a significant progress. This is particularly true in the coastal areas. In the coming years, the central government will continue its efforts to implement nine years of compulsory education, especially investing additional resources to support educational development in the western part of China and provinces with poorer socioeconomic conditions in order to reduce the illiteracy rate. The central government is also concerned about the quality of school education. Therefore, in the "2003–2007 Revitalizing Education Plan," the Ministry of Education (MOE) implemented a "New Century Quality Education Project." First, the MOE attempted to reinforce and improve moral education in schools by initiating an "Outline to Propagate and Cultivate the Nationality Education" and implementing an "Outline of Morality Construction" to cultivate in students a higher sense of national unity, national identity, and integrity through education. Moreover, the MOE will continue to reform the curriculum for basic education. The MOE probes into the teaching materials and teaching methods in order to improve the quality of school education on the one hand and to reinforce the monitoring mechanism of school education on the other. In addition, the MOE pursues quality education as a goal and is quickening the reform of the examination system. The MOE will investigate the recruiting methods of senior secondary schools to further develop standardization but also introduce diversified elements into examinations and to develop the information system to enable senior secondary students to register and take examinations through the Internet. Furthermore, the MOE promotes the development of preschool and secondary education actively via diversified channels (Ministry of Education, PRC 2004).

In 2001, the MOE reformed the syllabus of senior secondary school examinations. In order to help senior secondary schools to select potential students and to increase their autonomy, a system of "3+X" subjects has been implemented. The number "3" represents Chinese language, mathematics, and foreign language. "X" represents politics, history, geography, physics, chemistry, biology, and integrated test. These "X" subjects are elective subjects (China Education 2000; Ministry of Education, PRC 2002b). Students can choose elective subjects according to their interests and preferences. With such changes in place, students will enjoy more choices in learning subjects, while senior secondary schools can enjoy more autonomy in selecting their students in the light of their own criteria.

Higher education reform

In 1995, the State Education Commission promulgated "Suggestions on Deepening Higher Education Structural Reform," proposing fundamental changes in the orientation, financing, curriculum, and management of higher education through joint development (*gongjian*), restructuring (*huzahuan*), merging (*hebing*), and cooperation (*hexuo*) in order to improve the overall performance of universities in China (Ministry of Education 2001; Mok 2004a). In the past decade, 556 higher institutions were merged to become 232 higher institutions. Of those universities undergoing the restructuring process, many of them have become top-universities in China. For example, with the mergers between the Zhejian University, Hangzhou University, Zhejian Agriculture University, and Zhejiang Medical University, the Chinese government was able to establish a new Zhejiang University in 1998. After the mergers, the new Zhejiang University is now ranked amongst the top five in China's university league table. With such success, the MOE continues to encourage higher institutions in China to form deeper collaborations and engage in more cooperation where suitable and practicable (Mok 2004a).

The "2003–2007 Revitalizing Education Plan" "Project 985" and "Project 211" policies continue to be adopted by the Central government to create world-class universities and key academic disciplines in China. "Project 985" aims at facilitating a target university to become a world-class research university in the near future. Since 2000, "Project 985" has expanded its scale to identify 21 universities as key universities to be developed as world-class universities. These key universities receive additional funding from both the central and local governments in order to get sufficient resources to develop these designated institutions into internationally renowned universities. For instance, Peking and Tsinghua University received 1.8 billion RMB yuan each from the national construction fund from 1999 to 2001. With additional resources, these universities can be equipped with better facilities and they are able to recruit top scholars in different fields to teach and research at their institutions. "Project 211" it aims at improving the quality of higher education, scientific research, administration, and institutional efficiency as a base for training high-level professional manpower for China. In 1998, the State Planning Commission (SPC) identified 387 key disciplinary areas. Obviously, the central government is keen to invest in the key universities and discipline areas so they can become world-class universities and internationally famous (Yang 2004).

Hong Kong

School education reform

Education reform has never been a new "vocabulary" in Hong Kong's education. Over the past three decades, the Hong Kong government has implemented education reforms of various kinds. The watershed of educational development in Hong Kong lies in the introduction and implementation of nine-years' free and compulsory education from primary to junior secondary (Form one–three) levels during the 1970s (Morris and Scott 2003). The policy of compulsory education was introduced after the publication of the white paper on Education Policy in 1965. In line with the education reform proposed in the mid-1960s, six-year primary compulsory education was realized in Hong Kong (Hong Kong Government 1965). After the successful launch of compulsory primary education, the second stage of three-year compulsory junior secondary education was started in 1978 (Hong Kong Government 1974). The launch of compulsory education resulted in a sharp rise in the demands of basic education in Hong Kong and led to a fundamental change from an elitist education system to a massified system.

With the implementation of the compulsory education policy, public expenditure on education was increased drastically to ensure the provision of enough school places by opening more new primary and secondary schools and purchasing school places from private schools under the Bought Place Scheme from the late 1970s. Moreover, the availability of qualified and trained teachers for the expansion of educational opportunities had become even more critical for the compulsory education policy. On the other hand, compulsory education changed the developmental landscape of education in Hong Kong in a sense that the existing education policies such as medium of instruction and examination system might not be able to cope with needs and problems induced by the universalization of basic education. Therefore, a comprehensive review of the education system and policy was deemed necessary by the early 1980s, when the government invited a visiting panel from the Paris-based Organization for Economic Cooperation and Development (OECD) to conduct such a review exercise.

In 1982, the OECD panel released its review report entitled *A Perspective on Education in Hong Kong*, in which it recommended the setting up of an education commission (EC) for defining overall educational objectives, formulating education policy and priorities, coordinating and monitoring the planning and development of education, and initiating educational research (Y.C. Cheng 2000, p. 23). Subsequently, from 1984–96, the EC published six reports with a variety of foci covering the areas of language teaching and learning, teacher quality, private sector school improvements, curriculum development, teaching and learning conditions, and special education. As Y.C. Cheng (2000) argued, these reports revealed the EC's assumption that policymakers could identify best practices to enhance effectiveness to solve the major problems of schools. Best practices are characterized by a "top-down approach" to drive schools and universities to perform. Efficiency and effectiveness measures and quality assurance exercises have been introduced in the school sector. In the meantime, most education policy efforts during that time period assumed high homogeneity among schools and ignored their unique features and needs. Therefore, the policy effects were limited in terms of motivating school teachers, improving performance for enhancing effective achievement of planned goals, and satisfying stakeholders' needs and expectations (pp. 23–29).

Apart from the main policies for educational change and development formulated by the EC, there were other forms of reform and improvement efforts initiated in the 1990s by the government, such as the School Management Initiative (SMI) emphasizing school-based initiatives and process improvement at the school level. Most important of all, a new stage of educational change and development was marked by the release of *Education Commission Report No. 7* on quality school education in 1997, and the government of the HKSAR adopted new education policy initiatives. The most significant feature of the education reform introduced at this time was a paradigm shift from the traditional external intervention to a school-based approach focusing on school-based initiatives and making the school the unit of change and improvement (Y.C. Cheng 2000, p. 29).

SMI, which was a movement to give more autonomy in management (K.M. Cheng 2002), was intended to build up a new management framework among all public sector schools with the aim of enhancing the effectiveness and quality of school education. The four major aims of SMI are

1   to clearly define the roles of sponsors, managers, supervisors, and principals and, consequently, to ensure greater effectiveness and accountability;
2   to provide for greater participation of teachers, parents, and alumni in school decision making and management;
3   to encourage more systematic planning and evaluation of schools' programs of activities and reporting their performance; and
4   to give schools more flexibility in the use of resources in meeting their own needs.

(Education and Manpower Branch and Education Department 1991, cited in Y.C. Cheng 2000, pp. 30–31)

It was expected that the SMI policy would increase teachers' participation in school decision making and improve the quality of decision making and thus provide better opportunities and conditions for serving school-based needs. In return, schools are more motivated to develop their own effective practices in managing, teaching, and learning activities (Y.C. Cheng 2000, p. 32). The policy of school-based management was eventually recognized by the EC in its *Report No. 7*, in which it was recommended that

1   schools should be helped to set goals and indicators for monitoring and evaluating quality education;
2   all schools should have school-based management in place as the internal quality assurance mechanism, in the spirit of SMI, by the year 2000;
3   the education department should adopt a whole-school approach to quality assurance inspection and set up a quality assurance resource corner;
4   all schools which have put in place school-based management should enjoy the management and funding flexibility of SMI;
5   the government should set aside a substantial amount of money to establish a "Quality Education Development Fund" to fund one-off projects for the improvement of education quality on a competitive basis; and
6   the government should raise the professional standards of principals and teachers through providing coherent preservice and inservice training and setting up a general teaching council, and all schools should be required to put in place a fair and open performance appraisal system for principals and teachers.

(EC 1997 cited in Y.C. Cheng *et al.* 2002, p. 12)

After the ideas and practices of SMI were implemented, school-based management was treated as the major approach to enhance effectiveness and quality assurance in education (Y.C. Cheng 2000, p. 35). According to the schedule, all public sector schools were required to adopt school-based management in 2000. The shift from the external interventionist to the school-based approach reveals a trend of decision making and managerial power decentralization from the central education authorities to individual schools.

Since the inception of the HKSAR government in 1997, Chief Executive Tung Chee-Hwa has highlighted the importance of education as a major element in transforming Hong Kong into an international city in terms of providing educated manpower and professionals for the economy and enhancing the competitiveness of Hong Kong in the global economy. Public expenditure on education has been conceived as an item of social investment, so that the largest proportion of public expenditure has gone to education policy every year since then. Apart from pledging to increase public expenditure on education, the HKSAR has introduced a number of policy initiatives and even launched a comprehensive review of the education system in Hong Kong in recent years.

Apart from endorsing the policy recommendations made by the EC in its *Report No. 7*, the government has set up a HK$5 billion Quality Education Fund for encouraging educational innovations and initiatives among different educational institutions within the territory. Other new policy initiatives include upgrading primary teachers as graduate teachers, improving training and facilities for the teaching profession, enhancing the professionalism of the teaching force, implementing a long-term information technology education strategy, and working toward the target of whole-day schooling for all primary students (Education and Manpower Bureau 1997, cited in Y.C. Cheng 2000, pp. 35–36).

Education reform was in the limelight when the EC carried out a comprehensive review of the education system in 1998–2000. The review was conducted in three stages. The first stage was to establish the aims of education and identify the responsibilities of relevant people and organizations in enhancing the quality of education. The second stage focused on the academic system, in which it examined the divisions between learning stages, the curricula, the assessment process, the duration of study, and the interface between stages. In the final stage, the EC would finalize its recommendations taking in account public views through the previous rounds of consultation.

The EC formulated the overall aims of education thus:

> To enable every person to attain all-round development in the domains of ethics, intellect, physique, social skills and aesthetics according to his/her own attributes so that he/she is capable of life-long learning, critical and exploratory thinking, innovating and adapting to change; filled with self-confidence and a team spirit; willing to put forward continuing effort for the prosperity, progress, freedom and democracy of their society, and contribute to the future well-being of the nation and the world at large.
>
> (2000a, p. 4)

As stated clearly by the EC, the review aimed to transform the education system in Hong Kong to be more student oriented by enabling students to enjoy learning, enhance their effectiveness in communication, and develop their creativity and sense of commitment (Education Commission 2000, p. 4). In response, the review focused on the academic structure, the curricula, the assessment mechanism of various stages of education, and the interface between different stages. In terms of the academic structure, although there would be no fundamental change in the duration of primary and junior secondary education in Hong Kong, the government was advised to encourage primary and secondary schools to link up in light of the principle of "through-train schools" for ensuring consistency in curricula, teaching methodology, and personal development of students in those schools. For senior secondary education, the development of a diversified and multi-channeled system would be facilitated, and senior secondary and matriculation education would be combined into three-year senior secondary education in order to leave more room for local universities to reform their academic and admission systems.

Another area of major concern for the review was the amendment of the curriculum for different education subsectors. The emphasis of basic education would be to pave a good foundation for lifelong learning and all-round development on top of developing students' basic knowledge and abilities. What is more important at this stage is to teach students how to learn. As for senior secondary education, students should be allowed opportunities to choose between curricula according to their own aptitudes for further study or employment. In the meantime, universities were advised to review the functions, contents, focuses, and modes of teaching of their first-degree programs so that students would be helped to master the necessary knowledge and skills for specific professions or disciplines and develop a sense of integrity, a positive attitude, a broad vision, and important generic skills (Education Commission 2000a, p. 9).

Higher education reform

In the 1970s, the expansion of educational opportunities was confined to primary and junior secondary levels, while tertiary education largely remained an elitist system with no more than 2 percent of the relevant age cohort being admitted in to higher education institutions. Although the government proposed to increase the enrollment of tertiary education by 3 percent every year as a response to the white paper on The Development of Senior Secondary and Tertiary Education published in 1978 (Hong Kong Government 1978), the majority of young people did not enjoy higher education opportunities in the 1980s. From the late 1980s onward higher education has begun to change from an elitist system to mass education, particularly after the government started to expand higher education enrollment in the early 1990s (Mok and Lee 2002).

In recent years, higher education in Hong Kong has experienced significant changes. Core to such changes is the emphasis being placed on a diversified, multi-channel and flexible system for higher education to allow credit units to be freely transferable. In response to a three-year system for senior secondary education, it would be necessary for universities to study the need to adjust the length of study for most of their undergraduate programs (Education Commission 2000a, pp. 7–8). Most recently, the chief executive stated the government's intention to call for public consultation on education structure reform from a 5–2 secondary education and three years' university education system to a 3–3–4 secondary and higher education system in order to enhance the competitiveness of the education system in Hong Kong (Tung 2004).

In the past decade, higher education institutions have confronted intensified demands for quality assurance through various kinds of performance assessment exercises. Academics nowadays have to prove themselves worthy of their positions in higher education by showing their strengths in terms of research output and teaching quality. More measurements have evolved to evaluate university performance. The Research Assessment Exercise (RAE), Teaching and Learning Quality Process Review (TLQPR), Management Review (MR), and University Governance Review are becoming increasingly popular in the university sector. Most important, all these reviews have significant financial and funding implications. Most recently, the UGC conducted a role differentiation exercise among all universities to renegotiate the specific roles and missions for every UGC-funded university. The future funding of universities will be closely tied to whether activities taking place in individual universities are role consistent (Mok 2005b).

Japan

School education reform

From 2002, all elementary and secondary education in Japan has used New Courses of Study as the standard for educational courses. The aim of New Courses of Study is to foster the "zest of living," aiming to encourage students to learn and think independently. Moreover, it reinforces students' rudiments of education, especially hoping to improve students' problem-solving skills and skills such as reading, writing, and arithmetic. According to MEXT, the purposes of New Courses of Study are

1   to firm up the rudiments and basics with the aid of in-depth and elaborate instructions, responding to an individual as well as the careful and strict selection of educational content;
2   to enrich education to develop personalities by widening the scope of selective courses;
3   to enrich the experiential and problem-solving learning of each course subject to cultivate the ability to learn and think voluntarily;
4   to create a "period of integrated study" to cultivate ways of learning and thinking and an attitude of trying to solve or pursue problems independently and creatively; and
5   to upgrade ethical education to strongly equip children with the judgment of good and evil and norm consciousness.

(MEXT 2004a)

In order to better equip Japanese students, MEXT has promoted efforts in schools to secure improvements in "academic ability;" reform measures have been introduced such as

1   an increase in the number of teachers so as to enable small group teaching in line with the degree of attainment;
2   the "Frontier Project to Improve Scholastic Competence," which is to designate one or more base schools to research trial practices for the improvement of teaching in line with a child's personality and to spread the results of the research to all other schools in Japan; and
3   the announcement of "Exhortation toward Learning" in January 2002, a package of comprehensive measures issued to secure improvement in academic ability, such as "the enhancement of individual-oriented instruction," increasing the desire to learn and academic ability, "the growth of character and ability," and "the improvement of English and foreign language skills".

(MEXT 2004a)

All of the above measures are aimed at developing and enhancing students' problem-solving and independent thinking abilities. As information technology has become increasingly important in this fast-changing world, it is desirable for students to be able to use computers and information technology to communicate with others. On the basis of the "e-Japan Priority Policy Program Plan," all classrooms can use computers and significant Internet facilities were to be put in place by 2005. Currently, MEXT is proceeding with the plan to install computers and Internet connections as well as intraschool LAN. In order to comply with the policy of promoting information literacy among children, MEXT is developing educational content that can be used in classrooms and enhancing the functions of the National Information Centre for Education Resources. Besides hardware, MEXT is also concerned about "software," hence extra efforts are being made to promote teachers' instructing ability (MEXT 2004a).

Higher education reform

Entering the twenty-first century, the Japanese government was keen to reform its higher education to become a place to cultivate talented human resources and to make its university graduates more creative in science and technology. In order to build distinctive universities that are internationally competitive, the Japanese government has introduced a series of higher education reforms.

On January 25, 2001, MEXT published its "Education Reform Plan for the 21st Century," which was based on the final report of the "National Commission on Education Reform" in 2000, to initiate measures and issues of educational reforms. MEXT has set out "Seven Priority Strategies":

1   improve students' basic scholastic proficiency in 'easy-to-understand classes';
2   nurture open and warm-hearted Japanese through participation in community and various programs;

3   improve the learning environment to one which is enjoyable and free of worries;
4   promote the creation of schools trusted by parents and communities;
5   train teachers as "education professionals";
6   promote the establishment of world-class universities; and
7   establish a new educational vision for the new century and improve the
    foundations of education.

(cited in MEXT 2004a)

The main framework of the "Seven Priority Strategies" is to encourage more diversification and respect for individuality in higher education. In order to further develop the universities in Japan to achieve the highest international standards, the National University Corporation Law, together with five other related laws, were implemented from July to October 2003. All national universities became national university corporations and independent from the government as of April 1, 2004 (Oba 2003; MEXT 2004a). According to MEXT, the incorporation of national universities is one of the most dramatic reforms of university since the Meiji era. The six key directions of the university incorporatization process are as follows:

1   incorporation respectively of each national university;
2   introducing management techniques based on "private-sector concepts";
3   people from outside the university participating in the management of
    universities;
4   improvement in the process of selection of the president;
5   the assigning non-civil servant status to personnel; and
6   through disclosure of information and evaluation.

(MEXT 2003a)

Through the incorporatization process, the Japanese government hopes to run its national university system more like a corporate, giving more autonomy to the national universities, which are currently held accountable to the public. The national university system has been too reliant on the state funding and now it has difficulties in adapting to the ever-changing socioeconomic context of the globalization era; in this context the Japanese government is keen to introduce market principles and practices to run the national university system in order to make it more responsive and flexible to cope with globalization challenges. With the intention of pushing the national universities toward self-improvement and changes for good, the Japanese government also introduced the Principle of Competition by using Third Party Evaluation in 2002. Now, all national, public, and private universities in Japan have to perform well and all of them are now subject to external evaluations. Universities without good performance and continual improvements will suffer from financial consequences of budget and resource cuts (Amano and Poople 2004; MEXT 2004a).

In order to strengthen the foundation of education and research, it is beneficial for universities to reorganize and consolidate with each other so that resources can be used efficiently. Currently, as in other Asian societies, the Japanese government has considered seriously the adoption of university merging to make its higher education system become globally competitive. In 2003, 20 universities were scheduled to be consolidated into 10. Besides, three universities reached agreements to be consolidated into one in October 2005 (MEXT 2004a). All of these reforms and initiatives are aimed at the Japanese universities becoming more internationally competitive, improving quality, and ensuring that resources are efficiently used (Yonezawa 2003a).

Singapore

School education reform

The Singapore government is well known for its determination and commitment in promoting high-quality education. In order to improve its education systems and enhance its citizens' global competence, the Singapore government has consistently engaged in launching different kinds of education reforms. There were three major education policy initiatives in Singapore during 1979–91 (Gopinathan 2001a). These policy initiatives included the introduction of ability-based streaming as proposed in the *Report on the Ministry of Education* in 1979, the establishment of independent schools following the *Towards Excellence in Schools* report in 1987, and the provision of ten years of general education as recommended by the *Improving Primary School Education* report in 1991.

In the late 1970s, the Singapore government advocated the policy of bilingualism, with the use of English as the common link language alongside ethnic languages in its multiracial society. However, there were about 20–30 percent of students who were unable to meet the bilingualism requirements, especially when most of them dropped out from the schooling system at the end of primary six. The high dropout rate caused widespread social concerns about the wastage of resources on education. In order to tackle this problem, the *Report on the Ministry of Education* was released in 1979, proposing an ability-based streaming system at the end of primary three with the development of an ability-differentiated curriculum in order to resolve the problem of school dropout rate. According to Gopinathan (2001), the introduction of the school streaming policy heralded the "efficiency-driven" phase of educational development in Singapore.

In the mid-1980s, the government intended to give selected top schools more autonomy to set fees, hire and fire teachers, and plan for curriculum enrichment. The report *Towards Excellence in Schools*, which was published after an overseas visit to the United States and the United Kingdom to observe high-quality schools, recommended the establishment of independent schools in Singapore's schooling system. The proposed independent schools would be managed by a board of governors who would have the power to appoint the principal, determine teachers' salaries, set fees, decide on admission policies, approve major financial projects, and ensure a challenging and enriched curriculum. In 1988, three government and aided schools went independent. Now there are eight independent schools. On the other hand, more than 20 autonomous secondary schools have been formed since the early 1990s to provide high-quality education while charging more affordable fees than the independent schools. Looking into the policy change intention of independent schools, it becomes clear that the reform is to induce more flexibility and diversity in Singapore's education system (Mok and Tan 2004).

The government published a report entitled *Improving Primary School Education* in 1991 after a review of its primary education system, recommending the postponement of streaming by one year to primary four, changing PSLE from a pass–fail to a placement examination, and allowing almost all students to go on to secondary schools to complete an additional four to five years of secondary education. Moreover, the report proposed the introduction of the normal technical curriculum so that secondary school leavers can continue their studies in institutes of technical education.

More recently, education reform reached its climax when Prime Minister Goh Chok Tong laid out the comprehensive review of the education system, ranging from preschool education to university admission criteria and curriculum, under the umbrella of "Thinking Schools, Learning Nation" (TSLN) in 1997. There are four major thrusts of TSLN: emphasis on critical and creative thinking, the use of information technology in education, national or citizenship education, and administrative excellence (Gopinathan 2001a, pp. 11–12).

A total of six major education initiatives were introduced after the announcement of TSLN in 1997. In summary, these education initiatives include

1 a S$2 billion initiative to introduce information technology in the schools and to have pupils spend 30 percent of curriculum time learning with computers within five years;
2 a commitment to reduce content coverage and to introduce new ways of assessing achievement;
3 increased autonomy for school principals, in part through the cluster schools model;
4 a re-emphasis on citizenship education through the "National Education" program;
5 infusing critical and creative thinking into the school curriculum; and
6 a new school appraisal system—the School Excellence Model (SEM).

(Gopinathan and Ho 2000, p. 171; Ng 2003)

It is noteworthy that since 2000, it has been compulsory for a school to carry out self-appraisal under the SEM policy. SEM aims to provide a means to identify and measure schools' strengths and areas for improvement. It is driven by a set of core values emphasizing the importance of having a purposeful school leadership, putting students first, and seeing teachers as the key to making quality education happen. SEM comprises nine quality criteria: leadership, strategic planning, staff management, resources, student-focused processes, administrative and operational results, staff results, partnership and society results, and key performance results (Ng 2003, pp. 28–29).

Most recently, the government has launched two major reform programs for the school sector. One is focusing on junior college and upper secondary education and the other is about university sector restructuring. In 2002, the government completed the review of junior college and upper secondary education. It was recommended that a broader and more flexible junior college curriculum should be put in place. Major recommendations were

1   integrated programs (IPs) to provide a seamless upper secondary and junior college education;
2   specialized schools to cater to exceptional talents in the arts, mathematics, and science;
3   adoption by some schools of alternative curricula and qualifications that are internationally recognized; and
4   the setting up of a few privately run and privately funded schools.

(Ministry of Information, Communications and The Arts, Singapore 2003, p. 215)

Higher education reform

Apart from school education reforms, the government addressed the importance of transforming the two public universities, NUS and NTU, into world-class institutions in the 1990s. After reviewing its higher education system, university reform was initiated with a fundamental change of the admission system and university curriculum. Major initiatives are

1   the adoption of the American Scholastic Aptitude Test (SAT) scores;
2   the introduction of open-book examinations for up to 30 percent of university examinations;
3   trimming the curriculum to reduce memory work and encourage thinking and reflection;
4   offering better incentives to encourage more of the well-known scholars to work in both universities; and
5   stimulating a greater inflow of some of the brightest students from other countries to study in Singapore in order to create an "intellectual critical mass".

(Gopinathan and Ho 2000, p. 175)

Furthermore, the government has played a proactive role to strengthen the linkage between local and top universities around the world in order to achieve the ultimate goal of having world-class universities in the city-state. In 1998, it was announced that at least ten world-class universities would be invited to set up their own branch campuses in Singapore or form alliances with local universities to offer special programs. For instance, INSEAD, Johns Hopkins University, Chicago School of Business, Pennsylvania's Wharton School of Business, and the Massachusetts Institute of Technology have been invited to join the world-class universities program by the Singapore government over the past few years. The development of world-class universities does not impede further expansion of tertiary education in Singapore because the government has set the targets of having 20 percent of its school cohort each year receive technical-vocational education at an ITE, 40 percent polytechnic education, and 25 percent university education by the year 2010 (Gopinathan and Ho 2000, p. 176).

In 2002, a review of the university sector and graduate manpower planning was launched. The review was completed in early 2003. Regarding university sector restructuring, there were two major recommendations. First of all was the recommendation to establish a university sector structure comprising two large comprehensive universities and three "niche" institutions. NUS could be transformed into a multi-campus university. One new campus could be a research-intensive institution focusing on engineering, info-communications, and the sciences. The other reform strategy is to focus on graduate medical and health sciences education. NTU could expand into a full-fledged comprehensive university, with disciplines in the physical sciences, humanities, and design and media. Believing in the importance of nurturing an environment that is conducive to diversity and institutional excellence in different niches, three recommendations were made:

1   fine-tuning the university admissions system to allow universities/campuses more flexibility in choosing those who can benefit from and contribute to the institution;
2   providing flexibility to the public universities to adjust their fees and respond to industry needs in the provision of places for the different disciplines; and
3   encouraging a focused approach to funding postgraduate education and setting up graduate schools to facilitate multidisciplinary postgraduate studies.

(Ministry of Information, Communications and The Arts, Singapore 2003, p. 216)

All the reform strategies discussed here once again show the Singapore government's strong commitment to making its education systems more competitive in the global marketplace. Intending to position Singapore as a regional hub of higher education and professional training, the government has attempted to adopt various reform strategies to strengthen its leading role in higher education in the region.

Taiwan

After the lifting of the martial law in 1987, there has been a general consensus among the public in Taiwan on the need for education reform. Criticizing the education system for being inflexible and unable to cope with rapid social and economic changes, education reform measures introduced since the 1990s have focused on establishing a more comprehensive and compulsory education system and creating a more universal preschool education system. In addition, other major areas for education reforms relate closely to improving the higher education system; diversifying and refining the vocational education system; setting up a system of lifelong learning and information education; and offering additional channels for continuing studies (Government Information Service, Taiwan 2003, p. 283).

School education reform

In order to improve the education system in Taiwan, the government set up a special commission, the Commission on Educational Reform, headed by Nobel laureate Lee Yuan-tesh in late 1994 to analyze the problems of the education system and propose reform recommendations. After a comprehensive review, the education reform report was published in 1996, proposing to allow more flexibility in the higher education admissions system by diversifying channels for assessing students' performance not only on their academic scores in public examinations but also on other aspects of students' talents. The reform commission also stressed the notion of quality education and professionalism. Major reform measures included lowering the student-teacher ratio, increasing the number of professional personnel in compulsory education, improving professional education standards, strengthening preschool education, promoting computerization, enhancing nine-year compulsory education, cooperating with enterprises, strengthening higher education, and caring for disadvantaged groups (Government Information Service, Taiwan 2003, p. 294). On the school education front, two major reforms were initiated. One is the reform of the senior high school and university admission system and the other is the introduction of the First through Ninth Grades Curriculum Alignment for Elementary and Junior High Education.

The latter has been in the limelight of education reform. The new curriculum is claimed to be a more comprehensive and thorough curriculum designed for compulsory education in Taiwan. Five basic areas are emphasized in the new nine-year curriculum, namely,

1   developing a humanitarian attitude (self-understanding and respect for others and different cultures);
2   harmonizing different human qualities (sense and sensibility, theory and practice, and human sciences and technology);
3   establishing a democratic attitude (self-expression, independent thinking, social communication, tolerance of different opinions, team work, social service, and a respect for the rule of law);
4   fostering nationalist and patriotic worldviews (both cultural and ecological); and
5   fostering a habit of lifelong learning.

In response to the growing dissatisfaction with the emphasis on examinations and the university entrance examination system, a new multiroute promotion program for entering senior high schools was implemented in 2001, replacing the Joint Public Senior High School Entrance Examination. The Basic Achievement, a test for assessing students' abilities in languages, sciences and mathematics replaced the entrance examination, and social science for all junior high school graduates in 2002. As for university admission, a multi-route promotion program comprising application, selection by recommendation, or a new version of the entrance examination modified the Joint Universities Entrance Examination, which had been in use for 48 years. The application method requires students to pass the general Scholastic Attainment Test and then apply individually to the universities and colleges they wish to attend. Each senior high school has been assigned a quota of students it can recommend for students' applications to universities and colleges. In 2002, while the application and selection by recommendation methods covered a fourth of the total students admitted into universities and colleges, the current entrance examination still accounted for 40 percent of students (Government Information Service, Taiwan 2003, p. 296).

In order to prepare students for challenges generated from internationalization and globalization, English has been made a compulsory subject from primary five. Textbooks were rewritten to cope with the new curriculum and could be edited and published either by the government or private publishers approved by the government authorities. Elementary schools were entitled freely to select their textbooks and form their own curriculum development committees to review teaching materials and pedagogical methods (Government Information Service, Taiwan 2003, p. 297).

Higher education reform

In the past decade or so, Taiwan's higher education has moved from elitism toward universality, from controlled toward open systems, and from monolithic toward a pluralist culture. The massification of higher education has forced the government to attach far more weight to raising quality in research and enhancing teaching effectiveness among the local universities (Ministry of Education, Taiwan 2001). Regarding the development of higher education in Taiwan, the government published a white paper in 2001 setting out new directions for higher education. Attempting to strengthen Taiwan's global competitiveness, universities are expected to create knowledge and raise international competitiveness in order to compete with the world's best higher education institutions. The white paper recommends a total of seven goals of higher education reform in Taiwan, which are stated as follows:

1 To establish open and competitive educational opportunities. The increase of university numbers has already reached saturation point. Universities should not be overly numerous. Excessive growth of universities and undesirable competition, which would lead to unnecessary resource wastage, should be avoided. Nor should the government exercise undue control over personnel matters. In principle, the market mechanism of free competition should be respected.
2 To enhance operational capacity of institutional self-governance. Institutional operations should enjoy greater freedom so that individual institutions can develop their own special characteristics in order to meet the needs for specialized functions and shoulder the responsibility of success and failure of their own survival.
3 To establish flexible paths to cultivate the workforce. The curriculum design and cultivation of personnel must have greater flexibility to meet the rapidly changing demands of industry and the human resource needs created by industrial development.

4   To strengthen development of personnel in science and technology. In the era of the knowledge-based economy, there is a major direction for the future development of higher education: the creation, deployment, and expansion of new knowledge. In particular, the cultivation of science and technological knowledge is of vital importance to raise Taiwan's national competitiveness in the global marketplace.
5   To increase opportunities for adult education. This goal corresponds to the call for lifelong learning such that universities have to bear the responsibility to provide opportunities in adult education and enable adults to enrich their knowledge and elevate their living standards.
6   To regulate the disbursement and deployment of educational resources. The national universities relied too much on government subvention and tuition fees as their main income sources. In order to solve this problem, the universities are encouraged to increase their sources of educational revenues and raise the efficiency of expenditures in relation to the distribution and deployment of resources.
7   To pursue the development of academic excellence. The educational system in the past had overly stressed equality in development and was under a monolithic system which could not reflect the special characteristics of diverse higher education institutions. As a result, it lacked the pressure of competition among the universities. In response to the trend of internationalization and globalization, the development of higher education should be dedicated to the pursuit of excellence and the cultivation of the capacity for global competition.

(Ministry of Education, Taiwan 2001)

As in other Asian societies, teachers, principals, and university academics have experienced waves of education reforms in Taiwan. Strategies along the lines of marketization, privatization, and corporatization are adopted to make higher education more efficient and sensitive to changing social and market needs (Weng 2003). Most recently, academics in Taiwan have engaged heavily in debating how to make Taiwan's higher education more internationalized. In addition, a growing number of education practitioners and scholars have become less patient about the education reforms introduced by the new government. Many interviewees and academic friends that I met in Taiwan complained about the confusion resulting from the education reforms implemented in the past few years, criticizing the existing reforms for leading Taiwan's education development in no clear directions.

South Korea

School education reform

As early as the mid-1980s, the Korean government considered the launch of education reform in response to changes resulting from the expansion of basic and higher education. A Presidential Commission for Education Reform (PCER) was formed in 1985–87 to prepare a national plan for a comprehensive education reform. Ten years later, the former president Kim Young Sam commissioned another PCER to carry out, between 1995 and 1997, education reform for the twenty-first century. The commission produced a series of "Education Reform Proposals for the Establishment of a New Education System." While primary and secondary education in the new education system was conceived as developing such characteristics as morality, sociability, aesthetic appreciation, and creativity, universities would be given full autonomy with necessary financial support for conducting high-quality research.

According to Young, the New Education System involves eight major policy changes:

1   creation of an "autonomous school community";
2   reform of the student evaluation system;
3   construction of a curriculum which considers individual differences;
4   introduction of open classroom education;
5   reform of the secondary school entrance system;
6   introduction of the school and university evaluation system;
7   introduction of information technology in education; and
8   increasing the education budget to 5 percent of gross national product (GNP).

(2000, pp. 91–92)

In order to promote autonomy in individual schools and enable them to provide diverse educational programs reflecting the needs of the individual communities, the Korean government required public and private schools to set up school councils consisting of the principal, teachers, parents, community leaders, alumni, and educational specialists in 1995. The school council has the function of decision making and deliberation and consultation in the following areas:

1   budget and the settlement of accounts;
2   determination of elective courses and extracurricular programs;
3   formulation and implementation of regulations;
4   the constitution and management of "committees to recommend nominations for principal" or "committees to recommend nominations for teachers";
5   raising and using funds for school development;
6   collection and management of community contributions; and
7   operation of after-school activities and their expenses.

(Young 2000, pp. 92–93)

Regarding student evaluation, the Ministry of Education introduced a new "Student School Record" system in 1996. Instead of assessing the academic performance of students, nonacademic aspects such as extracurricular activities, voluntary services, and moral development have been taken into account in student evaluations in schools (Young 2000, pp. 93–94).

On the curriculum front, the Korean government launched a new school curriculum in 2000. The new curriculum comprises two parts: a basic common curriculum from the first year of primary school to the first year of high school and optional courses for the second and third years of high school. In the new curriculum, the total amount of learning content would be reduced by 30 percent in order to facilitate more self-initiated studies. Students would be allowed to choose the streamed curriculum for particular subjects such as English, Korean language, mathematics, and science according to their ability (Young 2000, pp. 94–95). In terms of pedagogy, the practices of open classroom education were introduced. Open classroom education means the promotion of students' active participation and spontaneous learning by adopting diversified instructional techniques such as team teaching with less direct instruction in classroom activities. The open classroom education movement has been implemented on a voluntary basis and it has become popular among both primary and secondary schools (Young 2000, pp. 95–96).

Another major change relates to the secondary school entrance system, which has been equipped with a preliminary examination and lottery assignments since 1974. That system has been criticized because it brought students from academically heterogeneous backgrounds together in classrooms and thus produced mediocrity. As an admission mechanism, the lottery assignment was criticized for depriving the right of students and parents to choose. In order to diversify school systems and ensure students and parents school choice, local education authorities have been empowered to adopt appropriate measures to reform the secondary school entrance system. For instance, in Seoul, applicants for academic high schools have become eligible to apply to several academic high schools of their own choice within a common school district since 1996. In the meantime, the Korean government has encouraged the establishment of more specialized high schools or alternative schools to cater to diverse students' needs. In addition, private high schools have been encouraged if they have clear goals and are able to be independent from governmental financial support. In turn, they can select their own students and decide tuition fees (Young 2000, pp. 96–97).

The importance of the use of information technology in education has been emphasized in the New Education System. The government provided schools in Korea with hardware and with Internet access for the three-year plan in 1997–99. It was expected that electronic networking and Internet linkage would be installed in all primary and secondary schools by 2000. Apart from providing the hardware, the government has encouraged the development of high-quality software and databases for teaching and learning in order to facilitate more interactive teaching and learning methods in classrooms. About one-fourth of primary and secondary school teachers received in-service training for information technology in education between 1997 and 2000 (Young 2000, pp. 99–102). In response to the call for achieving quality education, primary schools, secondary schools, and universities should be evaluated periodically. As in the other Asian societies discussed, resource allocation to schools and universities is linked with their performance.

Higher education reform

On the university education front, the Korean government formulated a total of six policy directions for the sector. First of all, the excellence of higher education is to be achieved through the diversification and specialization of universities. In a diversified system of higher education, each university would be encouraged to specialize in its own areas of excellence. Brain Korea 21 is a project initiated by the Ministry of Education to make local universities compete with foreign universities rather than focusing on local competition. Individual universities are required to establish and implement their own development plans based on their strengths of institutional specialization and capacity for sustainable growth (Ministry of Education and Human Resources Development, Korean 2002, pp. 52–53).

Second, the strengthening of autonomy and accountability simultaneously ensures the quality of university education. It is believed that creativity is positively related to autonomy. In addition, universities are required to preserve their accountability with the decentralization of decision-making power from the state authorities down to individual institutions. Therefore, the universities can make decisions independently and thus cope with societal changes actively and flexibly (Ministry of Education and Human Resources Development, Korea 2002, p. 53).

Third, the Korean government has attached more weight to the importance of raising efficiency in the higher education sector, particularly trying to improve institutional management and governance. In so doing, the role of national universities would be redefined as distinctive from the private universities in the process of university restructuring. The restructuring involves exchange of academic departments between different universities and the improvement of the universities' management systems. Moreover, universities have been required to submit their self-development plans since 2001 for future performance and governance review purposes (Ministry of Education and Human Resources Development, Korea 2002, p. 54).

In order to provide a favorable atmosphere for universities to achieve excellence in research and teaching, the government pledges to increase public investment in higher education. In Korea, universities are guaranteed full autonomy in recruiting professors so long as the standard and procedure of recruitment and contract renewal are clearly defined. The contract-based hiring of professors became effective in 2002, thereby securing a fair and competitive human resource management system in the universities (Ministry of Education and Human Resources Development, Korea 2002, pp. 54–55).

Fifth, the scope of university education has been expanded to cope with the development of a lifelong learning society in South Korea. Closer linkage between universities and industry has been emphasized, with the government taking a proactive role in helping universities to develop applied research in response to the demands of industry and the local community (Ministry of Education and Human Resources Development, Korea 2002, p. 55).

Finally, recognizing the impact of globalization, university education is urged to become more internationalized; thus universities are required to adapt to international benchmarks and global academic standards. Moreover, the selection of a language as the medium of instruction in universities is a major issue to be considered in the university reform (Ministry of Education and Human Resources Development, Korea 2002, pp. 55–56). Encouraging academics to become internationally renowned, the PCER even recommended the government provide financial support to academics for publishing in international journals and setting up qualified research centers and collaborations with international scholars. By doing so, it is expected that the quality of Korean scholars' research will be raised to international standards (Park 2000a, p. 173).

Conclusion

In this chapter, I have discussed briefly the education systems, followed by outlining and examining education reforms and policy changes that have taken place in the past decade in the selected Asian societies. The discussions in this chapter have suggested that these societies have some common reform agendas, namely, improving their existing education systems and struggling to enhance students' competence in the globalizing context. When reflecting upon the significance of globalization in shaping local education reforms, we should not underestimate the driving forces of globalization in local policy formulation. Having said that, we must also turn to examine how local and regional variables and forces may have acted as determining factors influencing local education policy formulation. This chapter is an attempt to set out a brief background to prepare readers to better engage in the discussion in the coming chapters. The discussions in Chapter 3 focus on three major educational governance issues, regulation, provision, and funding, the discussion of which is closely related to the policy context and reform background set out in this chapter.

3 Education in East Asian Tigers

Regulation, provision, and funding

Introduction

One explanation for the economic success of the East Asian Tigers is the role their governments have played in education (Morris 1996; H.J. Kwon 1997; White and Goodman 1998). In order to strengthen their competitiveness and to secure the economic development needed to establish and consolidate their legitimacy, these governments put education in a very strategic position. The education systems of these "purposive governments" were thus characterized by a centralized, standardized, top-down approach, which created educational opportunities and raised the education level of citizens (Morris and Sweeting 1995; Bray and Lee 2001). All these Tiger governments believe that only through a high level of education can they keep pace with rapid social and economic change.

With the rise of the knowledge-based economy and the growing impact of globalization, people in these societies have begun to question whether such a centralized governance model adopted in the education sector can really sustain socioeconomic development (Stromquist 2002). The growing challenges and competition generated from processes of globalization, coupled with rapid technological innovation and knowledge reinvention, as well as the rise of the knowledge-based economy, have driven these East Asian societies to reform and reinvent their education systems (Cheng and Townsend 2000; Jarvis 2000; Mok 2001a). Comprehensive reviews of educational systems and fundamental education reforms have thus been introduced in the past decade, in the belief that radical educational restructuring is necessary to create a more autonomous, flexible, and innovative education system and a labor force to compete in the international marketplace (Sharpe and Gopinathan 2002).

This chapter sets out to examine and compare similarities and differences in educational developments and governance in the four Asian Tigers, with particular reference to educational regulation, provision, and funding. The chapter is divided into five major sections. The first section is an overview of the basic orientation and history of education policy. The next three sections examine issues related to regulation, provision, and funding in education, followed by an assessment of the four systems and a comparison to synthesize their similarities and differences. The chapter concludes by pointing out the similarities and differences in education regulation, provision, and financing in these Asian economies.

History and basic orientation

A number of key factors have shaped the basic orientation of education policy in the Asian Tigers. All were colonies of either Japan or Britain and obviously the education systems initially were affected by their colonial history. After gaining independence from colonial rule (before in the case of Hong Kong), these Tiger governments gave education a very important role in social and economic development (Bray 1997; Tilak 2000). Second, despite the fact that these governments are primarily antiwelfarist in public discourse and public policy, they all conceive of education as an exception (Asher and Newman 2001). Instead of treating education simply as a necessary public expenditure item, the Tiger governments have put strong emphasis on developing education as an investment for providing their economies with a high-quality labor force and well-educated professionals. These East Asian governments' emphasis on education is often cited as one of the main reasons underlying their economic dynamism (Applebaum and Henderson 1992; World Bank 1993; Morris 1996). The third factor shaping educational developments in these societies is social and psychological, focusing more on those values and attitudes perceived to be prerequisites for development. Central to the legacy of Confucianism and neo-Confucianism is an emphasis on education and cultural enhancement (Rozman 1992; Morris and Sweeting 1995; So and Chiu 1995).

The fourth factor is the significance attributed to education as an instrument, direct and indirect, of nation building in Singapore, South Korea, and Taiwan or society building in Hong Kong. Education has helped to create a sense of belonging and nationhood and so has been important in political legitimation in these societies. It has also contributed to that legitimation through the economic opportunities it has offered and the contribution it has made to economic growth (Bray and Lee 2001; Gopinathan 2001b). Fifth, education policies in these societies are increasingly shaped by external socioeconomic and sociopolitical changes. In response to the latest challenges posed by either globalization or the development of the knowledge-based economy, these Tiger economies have started reforms and initiated measures such as decentralizing managerial power from the state to the higher education level, reviewing curriculum and examination systems and revamping university admission mechanisms. All these reform measures suggest that these governments are keen to launch education reforms to enhance their competitiveness in regional and global markets (Goh 1997; Green 1997, 1999; Mok 2001a). Finally, educational developments and reforms have also been shaped by the impact of public sector reform. In recent years, notions such as quality education, accountability, choice, competition, quality assurance, efficiency, effectiveness, value for money, and responsiveness have become increasingly popular among education policymakers and such ideas have been translated into measures to reform the existing systems in response to changing beliefs and understandings (Lim 1998; Kwak 2002; Mok and Welch 2002; Weng 2002).

Analyzing, comparing, and contrasting educational developments in the East Asian Tigers from a historical perspective, three major shared patterns emerge. First, apart from the case of Hong Kong, the former colonial administrations never made a serious effort to develop education. When independent status was obtained in Singapore, Taiwan, and South Korea, education began to be recognized as one of the important policy agendas (Cheng and Townsend 2000; Tilak 2000; Bray and Lee 2001). Second, real change in the education sector came largely because of the role that education was believed to play in economic development, which encouraged governments in the Tiger economies to allocate additional resources to expand schooling opportunities. The 1970s and 1980s can be seen as golden periods of rapid expansion in education, especially when free and/or compulsory education was introduced (Morris and Sweeting 1995). After a period of rapid growth, the 1990s witnessed a tidal wave of education reform, and comprehensive reviews of education systems were conducted in all four societies. Fundamental reforms can be characterized as the most central feature of educational developments in the East Asian Tigers in the new century (Y.S. Cheng 2002; Mok 2002c).

Hong Kong

The colonial government of Hong Kong had almost no involvement in education until 1860. In 1854, the government was providing grants to only five schools, which enrolled 150 students out of a child population of 8,800 (Tse 1998). After the formation of the People's Republic of China in 1949, and a flood of refugees from mainland China, the government's attitude toward education began to change. In response to the *Report of the Education Commission* published in 1963, an education department was set up to open government schools and to offer subsidized places in private schools. With rapid economic growth in the late 1960s and the early 1970s, the government realized the need for more educated manpower and six years of free and compulsory education was established in 1971 (Tse 1998).

In the 1970s and 1980s, the government assumed an increasingly active role in educational provision and financing, with the extension of six years of free and compulsory education to nine years. Between 1984 and 1997, the government launched a series of wide-ranging reforms in early childhood education, primary, secondary, and tertiary education, special education, student assessment methods, teacher education, and the private school system and in funding systems (Tsang 1998, p. 11).

In 1997, when the Hong Kong Special Administrative Region (HKSAR) was established, Chief Executive Tung Chee-Hwa promised to increase public spending on education. A comprehensive review was launched in early 1999. The release of the reform proposals entitled *Learning for Life, Learning through Life* in September 2000 set out a blueprint for education reform. Four major areas were covered: academic structure, the curriculum, assessment mechanisms, and the interface between different education stages. Entering the twenty-first century, the HKSAR has placed education at the top of its political agenda. Fundamental reforms have been initiated not only in the school sector but also in the university sector (Chan 2002; Y.S. Cheng 2002; Mok and Chan 2002).

In 2002, the University Grants Committee (UGC) published a review report entitled *Higher Education in Hong Kong*, outlining the reform directions and discussing the major reform strategies recommended to the HKSAR. Most recently, the UGC has published a few reports setting out directions for future higher education reforms. Core to the reform proposals is to uphold principles of "selectivity," "competition," "diversity," and "choice." Universities in Hong Kong are subjected to further public scrutiny and they are urged to redefine their roles and missions. The "role differentiation" exercise, which was orchestrated by the UGC toward the end of 2003, intends to renegotiate a new set of roles and missions for individual universities. Parts of the future funding will very much depend upon how far activities taking place in universities are consistent with their designated roles and missions. Again, such a "role differentiation" review has clearly indicated that universities in Hong Kong are under greater pressure for change and reform (Mok 2004b).

Singapore

Like Hong Kong, Singapore was a British colony and the colonial government paid little attention to education until the end of the Second World War. It was not until 1946 that substantial change came about when the government announced a ten-year plan for free primary education (Tan 1997). Since the foundation of the Republic of Singapore, the ruling People's Action Party has held the firm belief that education is an agent for social change. The government strongly believes that education can serve the purposes of nation building. National cohesiveness, racial harmony, and meritocracy are the core themes of education in a multiracial society (Quah 2001). In 1966, the goal of universal primary education was accomplished. It was followed by a stage of qualitative consolidation, in which greater attention was paid to quality. The policy of bilingualism was introduced to ensure students' proficiency in English as well as in their own mother tongue (Yip *et al.* 1997).

In the late 1970s, the Singapore government began to refine the education system on the basis of improving quality. Identifying problems such as resource wastage, low literacy rates, ineffective bilingualism, and variations in school performance, the government response was a radical restructuring of the education system into a system of ability-based streaming at both the primary and secondary levels. The government searched for viable ways to make its citizens more competitive and to stimulate economic growth. One major strategy was to raise the educational level of the population by the expansion of educational institutions, especially by creating more learning opportunities in universities in order to give a competitive edge to the Singaporean economy. At the school level, the government began to diversify the school systems by establishing independent and autonomous schools, which would be flexible in staff deployment and salaries, finance, management, and the curriculum, while conforming to national education policies (Yip *et al.* 1997; Gopinathan and Ho 2000; Tan 2002).

In the mid-1990s, the Singapore government proposed the notion of "Thinking Schools, Learning Nation" to enhance the capacity of its citizens to learn and to be more innovative and entrepreneurial (Goh 1997). The Ministry of Education formulated a set of desired outcomes to serve as the aims and ultimate goals of education (MOES 1998). At the same time, the government contributed more than $1 billion for a master plan to promote information technology in education. The school curriculum was cut by 30 percent to leave more room to develop creative and independent thinking. Following the trend of decentralization of school administration and management, a cluster system was introduced in 1997 to achieve greater efficiency in decision making without involving the Ministry of Education in financial and staffing matters. In 1999, the government introduced the School Excellence Model, which forms a new self-appraisal system for schools to judge their own effectiveness (Gopinathan and Ho 2000).

During the Teachers' Day Rally in 2001, Prime Minister Goh Chok Tong even spoke of allowing some private schools to be set up to encourage a more diverse and innovative schooling system (Goh 2001). Universities also have to reform their admissions system and curriculum. They are given more autonomy in making decisions regarding staff and salary matters, funding allocation, and strategic development in exchange for a higher degree of financial accountability and market relevance and responsiveness. Most recently, the Singapore government has allowed overseas universities to set up their offshore campuses in the city-state to offer undergraduate education not only for Singaporeans but also for other nationals in the region. The "partnership" strategy adopted by the Singapore government is primarily to deal with the government's commitment to make Singapore a regional hub of higher education and professional training (Lee 2003a). Most recently, the Singapore government has decided to change the statutory status of national universities, making them into independent legal/judiciary entities and hoping the change in governance model can make national universities more entrepreneurial.

South Korea

Many of the features of the contemporary education system in Korea go back to the Chosun dynasty (1312–1910), when one of the main purposes of education was to select a political and social elite to support the ruling class (Chung 1999). In the late 1950s, the policy of free compulsory education was implemented in South Korea. The following decade witnessed a stage of quantitative expansion, symbolized by the universalization of secondary education and a rapid expansion in higher education.

Systematic reform dates back to the 1970s, when the aim was stated as being to produce self-directed and future-oriented Koreans. There was a scheme to make elementary and secondary education opportunities as wide as possible. There was a diversification of higher education institutions, including universities and junior colleges, to provide tertiary education. In the 1980s, with more emphasis on qualitative improvement and lifelong education, the Korean government set up the Commission for Education Reform to determine the pattern of change (Moon 1998).

Reform gained momentum when the South Korean government set up the Presidential Commission on Education Reform in February 1994 to submit reform proposals (MOEROK 2000). In May 1995, the presidential commission submitted its proposal to develop a New Education System for "Edutopia" or a utopia of education, to assure lifelong educational opportunities for every citizen. The five governing principles of the New Education System are equity, excellence, diversification, learner-oriented education, and autonomous school operation. In 1998, the Ministry of Education launched a campaign for a New School Culture with the aim of transforming the traditional school culture into a more flexible and liberal one (Moon 1998; MOEROK 2000; Kwak 2001).

Generally speaking, the latest developments in South Korea indicate a paradigm shift from supplier-oriented to learner/consumer-oriented education in the elementary school sector. Diversification, specialization, autonomy, and open competition have become the central themes of higher education. Open to both local and foreign competition, universities have been striving hard to improve their quality (Moon 1998). In higher education, the Ministry of Education in 1999 launched the "Brain Korea 21" reform to foster world-class research to provide creative ideas and innovative technology, to promote competition among local universities, and to strengthen their international competitiveness (MOEROK 2000).

Taiwan

The contemporary educational system in Taiwan resembles the one established in mainland China in the 1920s, which itself was heavily influenced by the American system (W.H. Cheng 1995). Educational development in Taiwan can be divided into two major periods: between 1945 and 1987, and from 1987 onward. The education system in pre-1987 Taiwan was characterized by centralization under an authoritarian regime. Education was treated as a means to solidify national sentiment under the Kuomintang (Chinese Nationalist Party) regime and to meet the manpower needs of economic development (Weng 2000b).

Since the late 1980s there has been a sharp turn from authoritarianism to pluralism, which shaped the development of education reform in the 1990s. In contrast to the top-down monopolistic control of school management, parents' and teachers' associations have been set up to share power in school decision making. Enactment of the University Law in 1993 provided a legal basis for these institutions to enjoy institutional autonomy and academic freedom. University heads were to be elected by faculty members. To assure more financial autonomy for public higher education institutions, the Ministry of Education set up the University Development Fund System to provide more flexibility in the use of revenues generated from tuition fees, university–industry cooperation, and research grants. In order to generate extra nonstate funding, public universities have carry out fund-raising activities and compete for research grants with other institutions (Shan and Chang 2000).

As in the other three East Asian Tigers, the Taiwanese government has published a number of documents on education reform over the past few years. The most important one, which focused on the overall development of education, is *Towards an Educational Vision for the 21st Century* (1995), which argued for the need to establish a lifelong learning society. In another document entitled *Towards a Learning Society: The Promotion of Lifelong Education*, released in 1998, the government called upon all stakeholders to share responsibility for lifelong learning. In 2001, a white paper on higher education was published, setting out new principles for the sector (MOEROC 2001a).

After a period of rapid expansion of student numbers in the past few decades, educational development in the East Asian Tigers has entered a phase of consolidation. In order to maintain high academic standards, these governments have conducted comprehensive reviews of their education systems and education reforms of various kinds have been initiated.

Regulation

The Tiger governments have imposed considerable central control on the regulation of educational affairs in their societies since the 1950s. In recent years, however, they have begun to follow the global trends of decentralization and diversification in educational governance, as well as the pursuit of marketization to provide more choice for consumers and introduce competition between education institutions to improve the quality of education (Cheng and Townsend 2000; Mok and Tan 2004). Here, regulation is broadly understood as the legal, political, and policy framework within which education services are delivered. As all four societies have adopted a centralized system of regulating education service delivery, they all have an education bureau, department, ministry, or special advisory committees to oversee policy development and policy implementation. Professional associations or other educational bodies perform only advisory functions rather than being part of the formal regulatory framework.

Hong Kong

Having long adopted a centralized governance model, the government has set up both executive and advisory bodies for the regulation of education in Hong Kong. On the one hand, there are executive bodies such as the Bureau of Education and Manpower and the Education Department. On the other, there are various advisory bodies such as the Education Commission, the Board of Education for school education, the Vocational Training Council for technical education and vocational training, and the UGC for higher education. In the whole governance process, public consultation is an essential means to win legitimacy for the government and improve communication with its citizens (K.M. Cheng 1992).

Education policymaking power is still retained in the hands of the government, with the dominant role played by the Bureau of Education and Manpower and the Education Commission. In the past, the underlying assumption of policymaking was that progress would be best achieved by top-down policymaking without much consideration for the uniqueness of different education institutions (Cheng 2000). A number of controversial policies such as the school management initiative, the target-oriented curriculum, and the medium of instruction were criticized as not giving serious consideration to the concerns of school management, teachers, and parents.

Two major areas relating to regulation in education are how the school curriculum is developed and how the performance of schools is best assessed. For curriculum design, the Curriculum Development Institute (CDI) was set up in May 1992. The major role of the CDI is to advise the HKSAR government through the director of the education department on all matters relating to school curriculum development and to give support to schools in the implementation of curriculum changes. Analyzing the relationship between the CDI and the education department, it is clear that the government regulates curriculum design in Hong Kong by steering from a distance with the CDI as the key steering/regulating mechanism.

Another means whereby government regulates schools in Hong Kong is through quality assurance inspections. In the 2000–01 academic year, quality assurance inspections were conducted in 50 primary and secondary schools, while 20 kindergartens were also selected for inspection. When schools are inspected, four major domains are under scrutiny: management and organization, learning and teaching, support for pupils and school ethos, and attainment and achievement. In each domain, there are elaborate performance indicators. During quality assurance inspections, review panels gather evidence from observation of lessons and other school activities, discussion with members of the school community, scrutiny of samples of students' work, and conducting surveys of school staff, students, and parents. The implementation of quality assurance inspection across the whole school sector suggests that even though the government of Hong Kong closely monitors and regulates school education, more autonomy has been allowed to individual schools with decentralization and school-based management (Leung 2001).

In addition, educational regulation is clearly visible in teacher training and the monitoring of the teaching profession. In Hong Kong, while all preservice training courses are now provided by the publicly funded Hong Kong Institute of Education for primary and secondary school teachers at subdegree and degree levels, the government and other local higher education institutions also provide in-service professional development programs for teacher training. Similar to other higher education institutions, the quality of teacher training is closely monitored by both internal quality assurance mechanisms and external reviews. In order to maintain a high language standard, the government also sets language proficiency requirements for teachers of English and Mandarin Chinese, and language teachers have to sit for language benchmark examinations (HKSAR Government 2002, pp. 156–57). The Education Ordinance also stipulates that school teachers need to apply for registration as teachers through the education department.

Another aspect of regulation is the role that the education department plays in school building. The education department in HKSAR oversees the allocation of school sites for different kinds of schools at all levels. The government also controls the design of school buildings. The School Building Design Committee, which comprises practicing architects and representatives of the school sector, was established under the education department to explore innovations in school building design. Since 1994, with the launch of a school improvement program, improvement works for 367 schools have been undertaken. The aim is to complete the program by covering about 900 schools by the 2004–05 school year (HKSAR Government 2002, pp. 149–50).

Moreover, the government also centrally directs student admission policies. Admission to primary one in aided and government schools is through a centralized system, which aims to avoid intense competition among children for entry to popular schools. At the end of primary six, all pupils in schools participating in the Secondary School Places Allocation System are provided with free secondary one places. The allocation is based on parental choice and internal school assessments. Starting from the 2002–03 school year, all secondary three students from public schools (government schools and aided schools) were guaranteed the opportunity to receive subsidized secondary four education or vocational training (HKSAR Government 2002, pp. 148–49).

Although the university sector traditionally expects to be immune from the influence of government, there are examples demonstrating that the government has attempted to intervene in university affairs. The most noteworthy case is the Chinese University of Hong Kong, which was forced to switch from its original four-year to three-year degree programs following a recommendation made by the Education Commission in 1988. Although there is the UGC to act as a buffer between the government and higher education institutions, this case demonstrates that the government can bypass the UGC to interfere in university matters without obtaining consent from university management, academics, or students (Cheng 2000; Tse 2002). Quality assurance exercises initiated by the UGC are designed to monitor teaching quality, academic standards, research performance, and governance in universities. Academics generally feel that the university sector is under public scrutiny and stringent regulation (Mok and Lee 2002).

Until recently, the government worked to decentralize more decision-making power to individual schools in financial and personnel matters on the basis of the school-based management policy. The government has changed not by handing over control but by steering from a distance by empowering institutional leaders and giving management a higher degree of autonomy and responsibility while setting up a range of performance measurement mechanisms. Strategic development planning and performance appraisal have become the norm for the education sector amidst the global trend of public sector reform (Mok and Lee 2000; Mok 2001a).

Singapore

Since achieving independence in the mid-1960s, the Singapore government has played a decisive role, dominating education developments through top-down policymaking. The core body responsible for education policymaking is the

Ministry of Education, via the Prime Minister's Office, in consultation with Parliament. As an example of the top-down approach, the implementation of streaming according to student ability was adopted centrally to reduce an alleged wastage of resources in education. Concern about maximizing value for money through action by central government is a feature of such an economically driven developmental state (Low 1998).

As in Hong Kong, curriculum design is centrally regulated with the ministry taking primary responsibility in designing, reviewing, and revising syllabuses, and monitoring their implementation. It is also the ministry's function to provide assistance in the teaching of core subjects, provide training in the effective use of instructional materials, disseminate information regarding teaching strategies, and act as change agent and facilitator of effective and innovative ideas. In addition, the ministry takes charge of special curriculum programs such as international science, promoting the integration of information technology, thinking skills, and national education into the curriculum. Furthermore, the ministry inspects textbooks and supplementary materials, and it develops and monitors media resource libraries and reading programs. Judging from the responsibilities of the ministry in curriculum design and textbook or media resource monitoring, we can argue that the Singapore government stringently regulates school education.

As in Hong Kong, the Singapore government has adopted a self-assessment model for schools, adapted from the various quality models used by business organizations. The School Excellence Model (SEM) was developed and modified from the European Foundation of Quality Management to set out criteria for assessing school performance. The SEM has a very comprehensive assessment framework, examining areas such as leadership, staff management, strategic planning, and resource use (MOES 2002a). In order to encourage schools to engage in deeper reflection about their work, the SEM allows individual schools to conduct their own self-assessment every five years. Once schools are ready for validation, review teams visit the schools and gather evidence. Even though the SEM is meant to be a self-appraisal exercise, the Singapore government can still make schools perform according to the standards set by the Singapore Quality Board. Seen in this light, quality assurance systems introduced in the school system in Singapore are a key element in the regulatory framework (Mok 2002c).

However, recently there has been an emerging trend to devolve more autonomy to individual schools to handle financial, personnel, and educational matters. Allowing more autonomy for well-established and well-performing schools is a means to greater self-governance. Moreover, the introduction of the school excellence model was based on the assumption that more autonomy is given in exchange for more transparent public accountability in terms of both performance and resource utilization. As a consequence, new internal and external assessment mechanisms have been installed (Tan 2002).

Another means that the Singapore government adopts in regulating education quality is to oversee teacher training. In Singapore, the National Institute of Education (NIE), an institute of the Nanyang Technological University, provides teacher education training courses and postgraduate programs. After graduation, the Ministry of Education recruits students and teachers who are appointed by the government to serve as general education officers (MOES 2002b). In terms of school building and development projects, the ministry initiated the Program for Rebuilding and Improving Existing Schools (PRIME) in 1999, in which about 290 schools were to be upgraded or rebuilt by 2005. Moreover, schools constructed before 1997 will be upgraded or rebuilt. PRIME is to be achieved through three measures, namely, on-site rebuilding and upgrading, relocation, and mergers (MOES 2002c).

Another quality assurance mechanism in Singapore is related to student admission policies. At the end of primary four, pupils are assessed in English, the mother tongue, and mathematics to determine a stream appropriate to their abilities for primary five and six. At the end of primary six, students need to take the Primary School Leaving Examination, by which pupils are placed in secondary school courses according to their learning pace and aptitude. There is a division between the Special, Express, and Normal courses for secondary education. University admission depends on students' examination results, Scholastic Assessment Test scores, and performance in cocurricular activities (Ministry of Information, Communications and The Arts, Singapore 2002, pp. 223–34).

As for the university sector, there is a history of state intervention in university affairs. On two occasions cabinet members were appointed as university heads in Singapore in the 1960s and the 1980s. Staff associations were banned in universities. There was pressure to make teaching and research more relevant to economic needs. A performance-based salary system and competition for research grants have been introduced with more stringent quality assurance and performance evaluation mechanisms. The government can therefore steer universities from a distance by different means. The government intends to rely increasingly on market forces and mechanisms to encourage competition between local and world-class institutions from overseas to improve the quality of education (Lee and Gopinathan 2001; Mok and Tan 2004).

South Korea

As in Singapore and Hong Kong, the South Korean government adopted a centralized model of educational governance. The Ministry of Education and Human Resources Development (formerly the Ministry of Education) is held responsible for the formulation and implementation of education policies, covering basic and tertiary education, textbook approvals, administrative and financial support to education institutions, universities and local educational agencies, teacher training, and lifelong education (Adams and Gottlieb 1993). Kim argues that "centralized administration, far from playing a service role, dominates the main sectors of education...The school has been in a subservient position, serving its master, the administrators" (Kim 2000, p. 89). Similarly, the OECD stresses the "highly regulated and centralized governing system" in education in Korea (OECD 2000, p. 57).

One indicator that clearly shows South Korea's highly regulated and centralized model is the way that curriculum design and textbooks are organized. The ministry is responsible for developing a national curriculum. Education Law 155 prescribes the curriculum for each school level and the criteria for the development of textbooks and instructional materials. Although flexibility is given to individual schools, the ministry sets out very clear guidelines to govern curriculum design. At the same time, textbooks and teachers' manuals are developed within the framework of the national curriculum. Only three types of textbooks are allowed to be published in South Korea, and all are tightly controlled.

Centralized governance is clearly revealed in teacher training in South Korea since teacher education is mainly provided by universities of education for elementary school teachers, by colleges or departments of education at universities for secondary school teachers, and by colleges and junior colleges for kindergarten teachers. The ministry and the superintendents of regional offices of the ministry authorize the establishment of teacher training institutes (MOEROK 2000, pp. 104–11). The ministry closely monitors academic standards of teacher training in South Korea.

Another means to regulate education is related to student admissions. In South Korea, elementary education is free and compulsory. Children automatically advance to the next grade each year. Since 1969, there has been no limitation on entrance to middle school and pupils have been assigned to schools based on the principle of vicinity. Middle school graduates may enter high schools subject to the grades attained in a selection examination. With the education reform of May 31, 1995, general high schools have selected students through a multiple application lottery system in each school district since 1996. As for university education, in April 1994, a new entrance examination system was put in force. The system made obligatory the 40 percent inclusion of the high school achievement scores and allowed the college to decide the recognition ratio or selection between the scholastic achievement test and the college's own test (MOEROK 2000, p. 70).

With power concentrated in the hands of the central administration, local initiatives and autonomy have been weakened, and individual institutions have lacked the enthusiasm for a creative approach to their operations. Under strict orders and directives, teachers and academics have had little autonomy while the participation of parents in school education is very limited. Similarly, students have little opportunity to develop their own interests, talents, or creativity (Kim 2000; Mok 2001a). In spite of its remarkable achievements in education, the South Korean government has realized that globalization has rendered the conventional centralized governance model inappropriate. The past decade has witnessed, therefore, a trend of decentralization in relation to budget planning and administration (Kwak 2002).

In order to make schools more creative and innovative, the South Korean government has initiated a reform project "Vision for Education Beyond 2002: Creating a New School Culture." Central to this project is a move away from the centralized model to the mobilization of individual schools and local communities to initiate reforms. Five major reform areas are proposed to promote a New

School Culture: creating an autonomous school community, implementing a student-centered curriculum, cherishing the value of students' life experiences, diversifying the methods of evaluating students, and emphasizing the professionalization of teachers (MOEROK 2000). This reform proposal indicates that the South Korean government has tried to move away from the centralized to a more decentralized approach.

As for higher education, universities and colleges have been encouraged to formulate their own plans for diversification and specialization with management and financial support provided by the government. The government also eased the criteria for founding private higher education institutions. Before the reform, the MOEROK officially controlled all aspects of higher education management as well as the number of student enrollments. That situation has changed since 1994, when the government granted decision-making power on student quotas to individual institutions. Individual institutions are required to undertake an annual self-evaluation and a more comprehensive evaluation of research and teaching every three to four years. Government funding is now closely linked to research performance. Higher education institutions are therefore motivated to engage in more research-oriented activities to secure government funding (Kwak 2000).

Taiwan

Education development in Taiwan is closely linked to sociopolitical change. Before the mid-1980s, the Taiwanese lived under an authoritarian regime and education was under rigid government control (Tsai 1996a). In order to preserve the cultural and national identity rooted in mainland China, the ruling Kuomintang adopted a centralist model of governance (Knowles 1978; Husen and Postlethwaite 1985). Education, being a very important means of social and ideological control, was tightly organized (Law 1998a). Under this governance model, the ministry was responsible for the appointment of school principals and university presidents, the allocation of finance, the design of curricula, the adoption of textbooks, and the procedures for student admission and graduation, tuition fees, and even examination and certification standards. Academic publications were assessed and screened by the ministry, leaving very little room for intellectual freedom for teachers and academics (Law 1996b; Morris 1996). Even after Taiwan was politically and socially liberated in the late 1980s, the ministry still compiled, published, and provided textbooks and teaching materials for elementary and secondary schools. Despite the fact that teachers and academics now enjoy more autonomy, any proposed changes in teaching materials must go through the screening process of the ministry and the National Institute for Compilation and Translation (MOEROC 2002).

As in the other three East Asian Tigers, the government plays a significant role in monitoring academic standards and the administrative efficiency of schools and universities. For school systems, education supervision is divided into two main aspects, namely, administrative review and education review. Schools are divided into different districts and in each district inspectors are appointed to review performance (MOEROC 2002). In recent years, the ministry has started a quality assurance exercise to monitor academic standards, teaching quality, and research performance in the university sector. Putting education inspection at school level and the university quality assurance movement together, the state has imposed a systematic regulatory framework on educational institutions.

The sociopolitical and socioeconomic changes that have taken place since the revocation of martial law in 1987 have led to significant changes in the education sector. With moves toward democratization, the state has begun to reduce its control over educational affairs. The notion of *song-bang* or "deregulation" was introduced in the late 1980s in order to resolve problems resulting from over-centralization in the prereform period (Chu and Tai 1996). Since then schools and higher education institutions in Taiwan have experienced a change in governance from a centralized to a more market-oriented model (Mok 2002d).

With the introduction of reforms in the education sector, coupled with a far more liberal sociopolitical environment, Taiwan's education system has experienced processes of diversification in provision and financing, and the nonstate sector, especially the private sector, has become a significant actor (Mok 2002d; Weng 2002; Law 2003). Before the lifting of martial law, the development of private schools, colleges, and universities was stagnant since education provision was virtually monopolized by the public sector. There is now a consensus between the government and education practitioners that private schools should supplement state provision.

Despite the fact that the ministry remains the key regulator in education, the level and extent of state control have fallen significantly. Public opinion in Taiwan believes it is necessary to create a more favorable environment for interest groups and organizations to run private schools by providing public subsidies, improving teaching and learning facilities, adjusting tuition fees levied by private schools, and encouraging social donations for private schooling (Weng 2000b). On the other hand, the ideas of school-based management and campus autonomy have been promoted among all schools to enable different stakeholders, including headmasters, teachers, and parents, to be involved in school administration and management. It is in the context of the "deregulation of education" (*jiaoyu song-bang*) and decentralization of power that school managerial efficiency has been emphasized with the shift toward school-based management (National Institute of Educational Resources and Research 1999, 2000).

In addition, the Law of Teacher Training enacted in 1994 stipulates the importance of teacher training. Teacher training courses are offered by normal universities (universities for teacher training) and universities which have departments or colleges for teacher training (for secondary school teachers) and nine colleges of education (for kindergarten and primary school teachers). In order to assure academic quality, the government has paid more attention in recent years to strengthening quality assurance and evaluation for teacher training institutions by means of external evaluation and peer evaluation by a singular national accreditation body for teacher training. After graduation, teachers have to apply for registration through the ministry to become certified teachers (National Institute of

Educational Resources and Research 2000). With the rapid growth of private schools and universities, the government has therefore formulated a set of rules and regulations to control development.

More recently, the government has developed a multi-route promotion program for senior high schools. In 2001, the Joint Public Senior High School Entrance Examinations were eliminated, allowing junior high graduates to enter senior high schools through assignment, application, or selection by recommendation, provided that they passed the Basic Achievement Test for Junior High Students. Meanwhile, the Joint University Entrance Examination, which had been in use for 48 years, was replaced by a new system that requires students to pass the general Scholastic Attainment Test for College-Bound Seniors and they apply individually to the institutions they wish to join (Government Information Office, Republic of China 2002, pp. 302–03).

As in schools, the higher education sector has been experiencing a process of deregulation. The revision of the University Law in 1994 reduced the control of central government over higher education institutions. While the law provides legal guidelines for the restructuring of the university sector in Taiwan, decision-making power in relation to institutional structure, finance, and curriculum has been devolved downward to individual institutions. Tai argues that Taiwanese universities are moving from a state-control model to a state-supervised model (Tai 2000a, p. 112). While universities enjoy more autonomy in various aspects of institutional management, the concept of professorial university governance (*jiaoshou zhixiao*) has become a fad in the academic profession in Taiwan.

State regulation has also been replaced by market competition designed to improve the quality of education. A performance-based staff remuneration and reward system has been adopted. Public and private universities have to compete for research grants. The introduction of market forces and mechanisms in higher education can be understood as devolution not only of decision-making power but also of responsibility for universities to improve their ability to compete in attracting resources derived from student enrollment and research grants (Law 1998a, 2003; Mok 2002d).

Putting the four Tigers' education regulatory frameworks into perspective, we can argue that they have gone through a process of centralization in educational regulation. With the adoption of a centralized model, the education systems have been shaped by central government while other professional associations or educational bodies perform an advisory role rather than exercising regulatory functions. Despite the growing trend toward decentralization and marketization in recent years, these governments still remain the decisive regulatory force in education, while other nonstate bodies only perform advisory functions. Seen in this light, the state still orchestrates educational policy developments, even though the role of direct service regulator and controller may have declined in recent decades (Mok 2002c). Putting all the mentioned observations into perspective, we may argue that these four Tiger economies have experienced "centralized decentralization," reflected by the coexisting trends of "centralization" and "decentralization" in education governance.

Provision

Despite the fact that all four East Asian Tigers have been well aware of the importance of education for social and economic development, the pattern of educational provision varies in these societies. When comparing and contrasting educational provision, it is noted that the major differences relate to the roles that the public and private sectors play. While the majority of schools in Hong Kong and Singapore are either run by government or financially aided by government, there is a clearer private–public mix in Korea and Taiwan. This section reviews the pattern of educational provision in the Tigers.

Hong Kong

There are four major types of school in Hong Kong: government schools, aided or subsidized schools, schools in the direct subsidy scheme, and private schools. Despite the government's large expenditure on education, only a small proportion of schools in Hong Kong are actually government schools. In 2001, there were 41 government primary schools and 37 government secondary schools, constituting only 5.63 percent and 9.14 percent of the total public primary and secondary school sectors, respectively (Census and Statistics Department, Hong Kong 2001a, p. 244). In 2000, however, 89 percent of primary schools were either run or subsidized by the government, while the genuinely private ones constituted only 11 percent. At the secondary level, 77 percent were effectively public schools (either government schools or aided schools), and 23 percent were privately owned. Nonetheless, one point must be noted. Aided schools and schools under the direct subsidy scheme are subsidized or primarily financed by government, while being given more autonomy in running their affairs. Seen in this light, aided schools in all aspects but actual ownership are effectively government schools since the government provides almost all the funds and controls whom they admit, what they teach, and what students have to do to graduate (Post 1996).

At primary and secondary levels, the genuinely private school sector is relatively small. The only exception is kindergartens, all of which are privately owned. The government has recently encouraged some existing subsidized schools to join the quasi-private school scheme, known as the direct subsidy scheme, by which schools are granted more autonomy regarding student admission, curriculum design, and tuition fees on top of public subsidies for each student enrolled. In fact, the number of such schools remains small, capped at no more than 40 for the academic years 2001–03 (Education Department, Hong Kong 2002).

In terms of actual services offered by government and subsidized schools in Hong Kong, all share a similar curriculum issued by the education department and students have to sit for public examination or assessment, so the syllabus is the same. What really differs among schools could be the way that the principals and teachers present the teaching materials. Since a school-based management model was adopted by the education department, individual schools can choose their own ways to run classes. Some may adopt a more creative and active way of teaching while others may still maintain the traditional form of education delivery (Adamson and Li 1999; Leung 2001). When comparing government and subsidized schools with privately run schools, what really differentiates them is that the latter have far more flexibility and autonomy in curriculum design, less pressure from examinations and varied ways of governance. The private school sector in Hong Kong comprises a growing number of international schools. This increase indicates that these schools no longer only serve various foreign populations but increasingly serve the local population, especially when parents are not happy with the local public school system. They believe the international school sector can make their children become more active learners (Yamato and Bray 2002).

As regards university education, there are not yet any private universities and all the eight higher education institutions are funded by the government through the UGC (Mok 2001a). This situation may change as the Education Commission suggested in its education reform proposals that private universities should be encouraged to produce a more diversified system of higher education to allow students more choice. There has been a rapid development of associate degree programs by community colleges, which are not supported financially by the government. A growth of private higher education, both associate and degree programs, can be expected in the coming ten years with a long-term goal of achieving a 60 percent student enrollment rate in higher education (Tung 2001; Mok and Lo 2002).

Singapore

As in Hong Kong, the state has long dominated the provision of education. There are four major types of school in Singapore: government schools, government-aided schools, independent schools, and autonomous schools. Nonetheless, it is difficult to differentiate between them, particularly in terms of educational financing, since the government primarily funds them all. The overwhelming dominance of the state can be explained by the belief that education needs to be kept in the hands of the state to ensure that educational institutions conform to national policies for socioeconomic development and nation building. This is especially important in an island-state comprising four racial groups. Although independent schools now enjoy greater autonomy in decision making, they are still required to conform to national education policies designed to serve political, social, and economic needs (Gopinathan 2001b; Quah 2001).

What really differentiates schools of various types in Singapore is the extent of autonomy exercised by principals at the school level. In independent and autonomous schools, they are allowed more flexibility and autonomy in running their schools under the guidelines of the ministry. Despite the fact that the ministry has set out clear requirements for the curriculum, independent and autonomous schools can enjoy autonomy in student enrollments and the number of teachers employed since they are given additional resources. Given abundant resources, students in these independent and autonomous schools enjoy not only more and better facilities but also a more rounded education especially with these schools having more resources to engage students in different out-of-class activities. As a consequence, students from ordinary neighborhood schools may find themselves in a less advantageous position since their schools are less competitive in academic results, facilities and activities when compared with autonomous and independent schools (Tan 1998; Tan 2003).

Similarly, the university sector is also state dominated with originally two state universities, the National University of Singapore and Nanyang Technological University. A new "private" university, the Singapore Management University, was opened in August 2000. It is private in the sense that the university administrators enjoy more autonomy in financial, personnel, and curriculum matters. With substantial physical capital support in terms of land and campus building, the university is a joint venture comanaged with the Wharton School of Business of the University of Pennsylvania in the United States. It is essentially a publicly funded, privately run university. Most recently, with the invitation from the Singapore Economic Development Board to world-class overseas universities to run their offshore campuses in Singapore, an internal competitive market of public, "private," and overseas institutions has been formed (Mok and Lee 2001; Lee and Gopinathan 2002).

South Korea

Unlike Hong Kong and Singapore, the private sector in educational provision has played a significant role in South Korea. Despite the fact that the majority of citizens in South Korea go to public primary, junior, and senior secondary schools, this pattern is reversed later on since in the higher education sector private institutions outnumber public or national ones (Chung 1999; Park 2000c).

Statistics show that the state or the public sector dominates the provision of elementary and middle school education. For instance, 99 percent of students at primary level, 75 percent at junior high level, and 84 percent at senior high level attended public schools in 1999 (KEDI 2000). The extremely large public sector in elementary school education is a result of the policy of free and compulsory education in South Korea. The student enrollment rate for elementary schools has soared to 99.9 percent. All children are provided with elementary education, with the state dominating provision (MOEROK 2001).

A central goal is to promote whole-person development. Since primary and secondary schools are state dominated, the ministry can actually shape curriculum design. Considering education to be part of the nation-building project, the ministry keeps the core values of traditional culture and Western science and technology in the school curriculum. Rationality in problem solving and decision making, scientific method in new discovery, and efficiency in management are preferred learning values. In actual educational delivery, scientific knowledge and technology occupy a central place in primary education, with more than 30 percent of instructional hours allocated to it in secondary education. More recently, importance has been attached to skills efficiency and work knowledge, training students to be adaptive to changes in the globalizing world, nurturing students with entrepreneurial ability, and preparing them to be more responsive to external changes (Kwak 2002).

In contrast, only 10 percent of students at the junior college and 17 percent at the university and college levels attend public educational institutions; the majority of students attend privately run high schools (KEDI 2000). Such figures suggest that the higher the educational level, the greater the number of privately run education institutions. In higher education, for instance, the publicly run and publicly funded institutions constitute a small number concentrating on teacher training and professional development. In order to create more higher education opportunities, the government has allowed the private sector to engage in educational provision rather than expanding the number of public institutions. The rapid growth of private colleges and universities has shifted the financial burden from the government to the private sector (Park 2000c).

Taiwan

As in South Korea, the state dominates the provision of elementary and junior high school education in Taiwan. As in the other Asian Tigers, the ministry sets out a very clear framework for school governance. In terms of actual delivery, individual schools may exercise a degree of autonomy and flexibility. All students in Taiwan have to study the same curriculum outlined by the ministry and they have to sit for public examinations before graduation. Under the Nine-Year Coherent Curriculum, schools have to develop students' basic competence, and they are now adopting an intergrated school-based curriculum. With more autonomy under the school-based management model, individual schools may exercise discretion in developing curricula (Weng 2002). But since the majority of schools are funded by the government, there are not significant differences between them, except that individual schools may choose varied teaching strategies or different emphases to achieve their missions or to meet the needs of their students (Doong 2002).

The private sector plays a more significant role in senior high school and university education. As for vocational schools, the number of private institutions exceeds the number of public ones. Even though the government enacted the Private School Law in 1998 to promote private education, the number of private elementary and junior high schools has remained stable. The dominance of the private sector is more obvious in higher education, which is comprised of junior colleges (*zhuanke xuexiao*), colleges (*duli xueyuan*), and universities. The private sector had already assumed a very significant role in educational provision at the junior college and college levels as early as the 1960s. Between 1965 and 1970, there was a rapid growth in the number of private junior colleges from 20 to 50. The growth was at a slower rate thereafter, but the number increased rapidly in the 1990s. It is noticeable that the number of private colleges jumped from 23 to 36 between 1998 and 1999.

The rapid expansion can be explained by the upgrading of a number of junior colleges to the status of colleges, which meant there was a sudden drop in the

Table 3.1 Education provision in the four East Asian Tigers, 2000 (%)

	Primary		Secondary		Tertiary	
	Public	*Private*	*Public*	*Private*	*Public*	*Private*
Hong Kong	89.2	9.56	77.1	22.9	90.9[a]	9.1[b]
Singapore	100	0	100	0	85.7[c]	14.29[d]
South Korea	98.6	1.4	67.1[e]	32.9[e]	16.3[f]	83.7[f]
Taiwan	99.0	1.0	86.6[g]	13.4[g]	35.3[h]	64.7[h]

Sources: Census and Statistics Department, Hong Kong 2001a, p. 244; MOES 2001, p. 5; MOEROK 2003; MOEROC 2001b, pp. 6–7.

Notes

a Eight out of eleven degree-awarding higher education institutions are funded through the UGC in Hong Kong. Hong Kong Academy for Performing Arts is funded by the government whilst the Open University of Hong Kong is operated on a self-financing basis.

b Hong Kong Shue Yan College is the only private degree-awarding institution in Hong Kong.

c Includes polytechnics and universities.

d The percentage indicates that SMU was set up as a "private" university in 2000.

e Includes middle schools, academic high schools, and vocational high schools.

f Includes junior colleges, universities of education, colleges, and universities.

g Includes junior high schools and senior high schools.

h Includes junior colleges, colleges, and universities.

number of private junior colleges in 1999. Moreover, there has been a growth of both public and private universities in recent years. While the total number of universities grew rapidly from 24 to 44 between 1996 and 1999, the number of private universities grew from 8 to 23. In 1999 the number of private universities exceeded that of public universities for the first time. The rapid expansion of privately run higher education institutions was an important development, in that higher education is no longer monopolized by the state. Well aware that it alone cannot afford the necessary expenditure on higher education without the involvement of the private sector, the government has encouraged private higher education. In 1999, 64 percent of institutions, including junior colleges, colleges, and universities, were privately run (Tai 2001; MOEROC 2002; Mok and Lo 2002; Weng 2002).

Comparing and contrasting educational provision in the four Tigers, Hong Kong and Singapore, the two city-states, can be grouped into one category characterized by strong state dominance with a tiny private sector. In contrast, there is a clearer public-private mix in South Korea and Taiwan, where the private sector plays a greater role particularly in senior and tertiary education (Table 3.1). With increasing demands for learning opportunities, the state alone cannot sustain the cost of rapid educational expansion, and nonstate actors and the private market are becoming more active in educational provision. Taiwan and South Korea have also been significantly influenced by United States, where the private sector is a key player.

Funding

The four East Asian Tigers have devoted a considerable amount of public money to education. Total public expenditure on education now ranges between 3.5 and

Table 3.2 Public expenditure on education as a percentage of
GDP in the four East Asian Tigers, 1998–2003

	1998–99	1999–2000	2000–01
Hong Kong	3.8	4.2	4
Singapore	3.5	3.3	3.6
South Korea	NA	4.3	NA
Taiwan	4.9	4.9	4.1

Sources: HKSAR Government 2001, p. 506; EMB 2004; Goh 2001;
MOES 2003; MOEROK 2000, pp. 48–49; MOEROC 2001c, p. 48.

4.5 percent of GDP (Table 3.2). Although the GDP ratio in the four East Asian
Tigers is relatively low when compared with Western countries, education is one
of the most important and high-spending policy areas. Public expenditure on
education is about 20 percent of the total budget in the four Tigers. The state is
still the dominant funder of education in these societies.

Hong Kong

The Hong Kong government has long been the major provider of funds for education. Education is the largest public policy area in terms of public expenditure.
In 2000–01, approved public recurrent and total spending on education was
23 percent of the government's recurrent expenditure and 22 percent of total
public expenditure (Census and Statistics Department, Hong Kong 2002, p. 18;
HKSAR Government 2002, p. 150). While primary and secondary education
account for more than half of the education budget, the ratio for tertiary education is above 30 percent, even though it has declined since 1998–99, when the
government decided to cut back the budget for tertiary education by 10 percent
over the triennium 1998–2001 (UGC 2000).

From 1996 to 2001, public expenditure on education increased by 53 percent
in real terms (Census and Statistics Department, Hong Kong 2002, p. 18). In
recent years, Tung Chee Hwa, ex-chief executive of the HKSAR, has promised to
continue pumping public money into the education sector. However, the increase
of investment in education does not necessarily mean that the government
will bear the sole responsibility in the longer term. Educational institutions are
expected to search for nongovernment sources of revenue such as tuition fees,
social donations, and partnerships with business. Performance-based funding
mechanisms have been installed in the university sector to replace the old funding method based on the number of students enrolled. Market mechanisms
have been introduced to encourage intra- and interinstitutional competition for
performance-linked grants and thus allow more choice for students. Although
recurrent public expenditure on primary and secondary schools has been increasing continuously despite economic depression and budget deficits, the eight
publicly funded higher education institutions have suffered a decline in their
recurrent grants over the past three years (Mok and Chan 2002).

Even in the midst of economic downturn since 1997, the government has maintained a steady growth in educational expenditure. Although other sectors such as the market, employers, NGOs, family, and individuals have begun to play an increasing role, the government is still the most significant source of funding (Education Department, Hong Kong 2001).

Singapore

As in Hong Kong, the majority of schools and higher education institutions receive funding from the government. Despite the fact that there are different types of schools in Singapore, all of them are dependent upon state financial support. Government-aided schools and junior colleges are given financial aid of up to 90 percent of the cost for development projects. Substantial grants are also made for technical training and tertiary education. The government subsidizes between 75 and 84 percent of the cost of university education as well as 83 percent of the cost of polytechnic education (Ministry of Information and the Arts, Singapore 2001, p. 231).

Public expenditure on all levels of education in Singapore has increased substantially as the government has set about developing and reforming the education system. In 2000–01, as in Hong Kong, more than half of government recurrent expenditure on education was spent on primary, secondary, and junior college education. For the higher education sector, counting both polytechnics and universities, expenditure was about a third of government recurrent expenditure on education (MOES 2001, p. 49). Although there is basically no resource problem in education in Singapore (Gopinathan 2001b), the government is trying to enable higher education institutions to depend less on government as the sole funding supplier. The government has set up a matching fund for universities to attract social donations for their long-term strategic development. It has promised to give the three universities $3 for each $1 raised in their fund-raising campaigns. What the government is attempting to do is to cultivate a culture of social donation for the university sector (Lee and Gopinathan 2002).

In short, the government has been the chief education funder in Singapore. The private sector remains tiny and despite the fact that it has begun to grow it seems probable that the government will continue to be the largest and most important education fund provider.

South Korea

Funding for education in South Korea comes from central and local government and the private sector. After a comprehensive review, the OECD concluded that "Korea has a unique education system characterized by a much larger private sector compared to other industrialized nations" (OECD 2000, p. 57). The state acts as the most important education funder, with about 85 percent of funding for schools coming from central government. Nonstate financial sources, however, make up a significant share in total education expenditure. This is particularly true when preschool education and higher education are taken into consideration (MOEROK 2001).

A close scrutiny of education financing in South Korea shows that there are three main sources: central government, local government, and the private sector. Central government, which secures its funding by levying an education tax, provides funding for local educational offices which supervise elementary and secondary schools, for national universities with some support for private universities, and for administrative and research organizations. Local government funding supports elementary and secondary schools, of which 85 percent is derived from central government while the remaining 15 percent is generated from parents and local government. As for private education, about 80 percent of junior colleges and universities are privately run institutions which depend on tuition fees from parents, support from national and regional entities, and resources from the schools' foundations (MOEROK 2000, p. 48).

While the central government has increased the budget for elementary and secondary education, the financial input to higher education has been declining. Such a decline suggests that the private sector has become more active in the provision of education at higher levels. Even though private education has flourished over the years, the sector has begun to receive subsidies from the government. Data also show high schools are the most prosperous sector in private education, since the majority of their income is derived from tuition fees, together with grants from the government through local educational authorities (MOEROK 2000, p. 51).

The private sector performs a clear role in education financing in South Korea. The increasing private expenditure on education is mostly accounted for by out-of-school and out-of-pocket expenditure. Despite the fact that the government has committed more resources to education, the private sector and other nonstate sources form a very important part of education funding.

Taiwan

As in Hong Kong and Singapore, the government has been very important in education funding in Taiwan. Over the past 50 years, education has grown significantly, with a substantial input of public money. Between 1988 and 1999, for example, government expenditure on education nearly doubled, and now constitutes about 19 percent of total government expenditure. However, the government is no longer the sole funder for education with the rise of private-sector provision. Although educational expenditure as a percentage of government expenditure remains stable at around 18–19 percent, there has been a decline of public educational expenditure as a percentage of GDP over the past few years (MOEROC 2001c, p. 48).

It is noteworthy that private contributions to education funding continue to grow alongside a relatively weakened funding role of the state especially in higher education, which is no longer treated as a free public service. Universities have been searching for alternative sources of funding other than government. The most common nongovernment sources of income include tuition fees, incomes from partnership with business, and social donations; NGOs, local communities, families, and individuals are additional potential financial sources (MOEROC 2000).

Table 3.3 Distribution of public expenditure between different education sectors in the four East Asian Tigers, 2000–01 (%)

	Public expenditure on education	Recurrent public educational expenditure		
		Primary education	Secondary education	Tertiary education
Hong Kong	18.9	22.4	33.7	31.9
Singapore	20.8	24.2	24.3	33.1
South Korea	19.5	83.4[a]	4.8[a]	
Taiwan	18.0	44.4	33.5	10.9

Sources: HKSAR Government 2002, p. 523; Department of Statistics, Singapore 2002, p. 49; MOEROK 2000, pp. 47–49; MOEROC 2001b, p. 46; MOEROC 2001c, p. 48.

Note

a Percentage of total public educational expenditure for combined elementary (primary) and secondary education, and for tertiary education.

In this section, we have compared and contrasted education funding in the East Asian Tigers. One major feature that emerges is the important role that the state performs in education financing. Although the governments of these societies have begun to diversify education financing by revitalizing the nonstate sector, these Asian governments still act as the key funding providers and education still remains the largest single area of government expenditure (Table 3.3).

Conclusion

In this chapter, we have examined the orientation of education, conducting a brief historical review and closely scrutinizing three major aspects namely, education regulation, provision, and financing in the Asian Tiger economies. When comparing and contrasting the education development experiences of these Tiger economies, we have discovered that we can further classify the four Tigers into two major categories. Hong Kong and Singapore, the two small city-states, have shared more similarities in education regulation, provision, and financing. The state role in these aspects is more prominent or even dominant when compared with the other two Tiger societies, South Korea and Taiwan. As Hong Kong and Singapore are far more state driven or public dominant in education regulation, provision, and financing, the state role in South Korea and Taiwan is less important, particularly in tertiary education provision and financing. In addition, our discussion has also indicated that the public and private distinction is clearer in South Korea and Taiwan, especially when the private sector has played an increasingly important role in postsecondary and higher education in these two Tiger economies. In conclusion, this chapter has offered an overview of education regulation, provision, and financing in these Tiger economies; the following chapter will examine common challenges and emerging trends of higher education in East Asia.

4 Higher education in East Asia

Common challenges and emerging trends

Introduction

Higher education systems almost everywhere are in a constant state of change. In particular, the changes in the socioeconomic context resulting from the globalized economy have inevitably led to changes in the university sector. The rise of the knowledge economy has developed new global infrastructures in which information technology has played an increasingly important role. The popularity and prominence of information technology has unquestionably changed the nature of knowledge and is currently restructuring higher education, research, and learning. It is within this wider policy context that an increasing number of institutions of higher learning are being established with new missions and innovative configurations of training, serving populations that previously had little access to higher education. In addition, the rapid expansion of higher education in the past few decades in many countries has also created the need for reform. Apart from accommodating a larger number of students, higher education institutions are required to improve their administrative efficiency and accountability in response to the demands of different stakeholders such as government, business, industry, and labor organizations, students and parents as well.

This chapter reflects upon the effects of globalization on national policy, with particular reference to how the selected East Asian societies—the four Tigers (Hong Kong, Singapore, Taiwan, and South Korea) and, Japan and mainland China—have transformed their higher education systems. More specifically, this chapter identifies and discusses common challenges and emerging trends in higher education by examining how the selected East Asian governments have reformed their higher education systems to cope with the growing impact of the global tide of marketization and decentralization.

Common challenges for higher education in East Asia

Seeing globalization as very complicated and complex processes of economic transactions and worldwide telecommunications (Waters 1995; Sklair 1999), sociologists generally believe that the impact of globalization is profound, as it is restructuring the ways in which we live (Rodrik 1997; Giddens 1999) and creating a new hybridity of cultural styles and mixes (Robertson 1995). Hyperglobalists argue that the increasing connections and interactions between different nation-states and the freer and quicker interchanges and movements of capital, goods, services, people, technologies, information, ideas, etc. have inevitably transcended national borders, thus suggesting an inevitable convergence of human activities and the receding role of nation-states (Ohmae 1990; Fukuyama 1992). On the contrary, scholars who oppose to the convergence thesis criticize the hyperglobalists for overstating and overgeneralizing or even overselling the convergence tenets of globalization. Instead, they point out the importance of nation-states and heterogenization in terms of national, regional, and local responses to global processes or imperatives (Hirst and Thompson 1999; Held 2000; Waters 2001). No matter how we assess the positive or negative impacts of globalization (Ratinoff 1995; Ekong and Cloete 1997), it is undeniable that modern states are not entirely immune from the prominent global forces (Held *et al.* 1999; Giddens 2000). Like their Western counterparts, the selected East Asian societies are confronted with a few major challenges caused as a result of the growing impact of globalization. Central to such challenges are changing governance philosophy and practices, which may eventually generate pressure to change the way higher education is delivered and managed.

Globalization and changing governance in public management

According to sociologists of globalization, the liberalization of national economies, the dominance of supranational institutions, the disempowerment of nation-states, the prevalence of the system and culture of liberal democracy, as well as the formation of a consumer culture across the globe have made the whole world in many ways more homogeneous (Ohmae 1990; Fukuyama 1992; Waters 1995; Sklair 1999). As social, economic, and political issues have become increasingly complicated in the context of globalization, it is argued that the capacity of nation-states has weakened or been constrained in managing the public domain. Instead of assuming the role of driver for change, modern states have to take a backseat within the framework of rising regional economies and a global marketplace (Ohmae 1999; Fualks 2000). As for the public policy domain, the impact of globalization is evident as revealed by the change in the philosophy of governance and the way public sector is managed (Baltodano 1997; Flynn 1997; Rhodes 1997). Living in the era of the globalization, individual states have to change their roles and their constitutions in order to accommodate, and not just adapt to, the demands and pressures generated from external environments. Therefore, notions such as "reinventing government" (Osborne and Gaebler 1992) and "entrepreneurial government" (Ferlie *et al.* 1996) have become fashionable, and the concomitant consequence is the initiation of reforms in public sector management. In order to improve the efficiency and effectiveness of public service delivery, new ways to maximize productivity and effectiveness comparable to those of the private sector are sought (Dale 1997).

More significantly, the politics of retrenchment in selected social programs and the reshaping of the private sector have caused the form of state intervention to be refined and the principles and practices of the market to be adopted in managing the public sector. Therefore, the role of the government/nation-state has undergone a fundamental change from "provider of welfare benefits" to "builder of market," whereby the state actively builds markets, shapes them in different ways, and regulates them (Sbragia 2000). Introducing market principles and practices to manage the public sector, together with the heavy weight being attached to quality control and "value for money" considerations, has inevitably transformed societies into "audit societies" and "performative societies" as Power (1997) and Ball (2000) suggested, respectively. The same processes are also turning traditional welfare states into "competitive states" (Cerny 1996) or "evaluative states," which attach importance to effectiveness, efficiency, and economy in public sector management (Henkel 1998; Kogan and Hanney 2000).

The changing governance and the major shift of national politics from maximizing welfare to promoting entrepreneurial culture, innovation, and profitability in both the private and public sectors have led modern states to adopt the techniques of steering from a distance through the means of regulation, incentive, and sanctions to make autonomous individuals and quasi-governmental and nongovernmental institutions such as universities behave in ways consistent with their policy objectives (Henry *et al.* 1999; Marginson 1999). Such a restructuring could be characterized by a more flexible regulatory environment, whereby public policy formulation is reoriented toward a smaller and more business-oriented state machine (Marrow and Torres 2000, p. 37). In short, globalization represents a new and distinct shift in the relationship between the state/government and universities, while the world is in the process of becoming commodified simultaneously through the recommodification of the provision of public services and the decommodification of the welfare state (Marginson and Rhodes 2002). Such a paradigm shift is manifested by a more individualistic, competitive, and entrepreneurial approach, and the new type of competitive contractual state settlement has become increasingly prominent in public management (Robertson and Dale 2000).

The rise of the knowledge economy and the changing university

The changes in the socioeconomic context resulting from the rise of the knowledge economy have inevitably caused transformations in the university sector. The fundamental challenge to the old paradigm of higher education concerns whether education and research should be defined or solely dominated by universities. The answer is definitely not, because other than higher education institutions, the market, the private sector, other organizations, and even individuals have engaged in different types of research and teaching (Jarvis 2000). Similarly, Castells (1996) also argues that information technology (IT) plays an increasingly significant role in influencing the processes of socioeconomic restructuring in modern societies. The control of IT and the communications system has proved that advanced capitalism has found its own way to accumulate additional capital. Living in such a wider socioeconomic context, the knowledge-based economy has a very different demand for labor. By categorizing labor into four main types, Castells highlights the predominant role of the producers of high value (knowledge workers). The importance of creating entrepreneurial culture to induce innovations and creativity in the knowledge economy context, together with the call for lifelong learning in the knowledge-based economy, has undoubtedly imposed pressures on the higher education sector to reform its curricula, mission, and vision, as well as to reflect deeply about the role of higher education in the new century (Green 1999; Jarvis 2000; Yang 2000).

Massification of higher education and the need for quality control

During the past few decades, most countries have successfully expanded their higher education systems, transforming from an elite higher education system to a mass or even a universal system in both developed and developing countries (Trow 1975, cited in Altbach 1998). The rapid expansion of higher education has resulted not only in massification of higher education but also in differentiation of academic systems. Despite the fact that the traditional research university is still the pinnacle of most academic systems, it is no longer the sole model for postsecondary education (Altbach 2000).

Similar to the experiences of the higher education systems moving from massification to postmassification in other Western countries as well as countries in this part of the world, such as Japan, there has been a massive expansion of higher education in these selected East Asian societies in the past two decades. At the time of writing this book, about 30 percent of the age group 18–21 are admitted to colleges and universities in Hong Kong, about 21 percent for universities and 36 percent for polytechnics in Singapore, 49 percent for colleges and universities in Taiwan, 89 percent for tertiary education in South Korea, and 13 percent in urban China (Bray 2000; Mok 2001c). The rapid expansion of higher education within a relatively short span of time (around 10 years or so) may lead to the problems of lowering academic standards, hence causing concern about quality assurance (see, for example, Williams and Fry 1994; Tan 1999; Mok 2000d; Weng 2000a). In times of economic constraints, universities experience immense pressures from governments, the main provider of higher education, to demonstrate maximum outputs from their budgetary allocations. In line with the global monetarist doctrine of cutback in public expenditures, stringency in university funding is an inexorable phenomenon (Currie and Newson 1998b; Biggs 1999). With emphasis given to notions such as "efficiency," "effectiveness," "accountability," and "curbing extravagance," the importance of quality assurance is repeatedly stressed by university governing bodies, while output-based schemes and quality control mechanisms are introduced in the university sector (Mok 2000d). Hence, devolution, efficiency, and accountability are becoming the most prominent themes for higher education reforms, whereby the four regulatory mechanisms including managerialism, auditing, markets, and community governance are introduced within the framework of competitive contractualism (Robertson and Dale 2000).

The contextual factors that we have just discussed earlier can be seen as common contextual variables shaping educational reforms and higher education policies in these Asian societies. In addition to these common challenges, the recent educational restructuring in these societies is also affected the unique socioeconomic and socio-historical-political environments of these societies, especially those shaped by the reforms started in the public sector management and public policy domain under the context of "reengineering of governments" (for details, see the section that follows). It is even argued that regional organizations such as the European Union, the North American Free Trade Agreement, and the Asian Pacific Economic Cooperation have varying effects on the formulation of education policies and the shaping of educational developments (Dale and Robertson 2002). Hence, a better understanding of higher education reforms in these societies can be obtained by analyzing the interactions between the global, regional, and local forces/factors instead of treating recent educational changes primarily as the "byproducts" of globalization challenges. Let us now turn to the reform measures adopted by the governments of these societies in transforming their higher education systems.

Similar trends in higher education reforms in East Asia

Comprehensive review of education systems and the fundamental reforms

One of the approaches accounting for the success in these East Asian societies is closely related to the purposeful governments. Similar to the field of comparative social security in East Asia, state-centric accounts are powerful explanations for the success of developments in these societies (Kwon 1997; White and Goodman 1998). Of course, the prominent weight given to education in the traditional/ cultural thought of these societies (may help in reinforcing) the role of education and, subsequently, give the impetus for the states/governments in these societies to promote education (Morris and Sweeting 1995). More interestingly, these East Asian governments are very "instrumental" in raising the quality of education and in promoting learning society with the intention of maintaining the competitiveness of their countries/places in both regional and global markets, particularly preparing people for the future knowledge-based economy. Seen in this light, education developments in these societies are significantly affected by both local and external socioeconomic and sociopolitical changes (Gopinathan 1999; Green 1999; Mok 2000e, 2001c).

Corresponding to the latest challenges posed by globalization or the knowledge-based economy, the governments of the selected East Asian societies, Hong Kong, Singapore, Taiwan, South Korea, Japan, and mainland China, have conducted comprehensive reviews of their higher education systems. In Hong Kong, the University Grants Committee reviewed its higher education system in 1996 (UGC 1996) while another comprehensive review of Hong Kong's overall education systems was completed in 2000 (EC 2000b). The Hong Kong Government of Special Administrative Region (HKSAR) conducted another round of comprehensive review of the higher education system in 2002. After these comprehensive reviews, education reform strategies have been formulated and introduced by the HKSAR government (EC 2000b; UGC 2002b). Similarly, the Singapore government has long been conscious about the importance to make/maintain the city-state's competitiveness in regional and global markets (Tan 2000). With the move to a knowledge economy, universities have to serve as engines of innovation and entrepreneurship and thus position themselves for the new economy (Quah 1999). The Singapore government therefore has conducted a comprehensive review of its higher education system and has already formulated new funding, management, and regulation policies to govern higher education development. Drawing comparative insights from other developed economies, the Singapore government has adopted a policy of decentralization to allow more autonomy and flexibility for universities in order to induce creativity and innovation (Goh 2000; Teo 2000; Mok and Lee 2003).

In Taiwan, the government has started to review and reform its higher education since the lifting of martial law in 1987. The review of the education system was started in the mid-1990s. After the review, the government is keen to internationalize Taiwan's higher education; universities are therefore encouraged to establish links and academic exchanges with universities overseas. In addition, the Taiwan government has introduced reform measures in terms of funding methodology, modes of provision, and new management strategies to improve the efficiency and effectiveness of its higher education (Mok 2000c; Tai 2000b; Weng 2001). Higher education reform was also started in South Korea with the intention of making its higher education system more responsive to the changing socioeconomic environments in the global economy context. Following the quantitative expansion of higher education in the 1980s, the reform measures introduced in the 1990s were to enhance the quality of higher education. In 1999, the Ministry of Education launched a reform project known as the "Brain Korea 21 Project" (BK21 Project) to nurture world-class scholars in research and to promote creativity and the advanced knowledge base necessary for the twenty-first century (Ministry of Education, Korea 2000). Acknowledging the importance of creativity and innovation in the new economy, the South Korean government is very keen to expose its universities to the external world by establishing more links with overseas institutions (Yoon 2001).

Similar observations can be made of mainland China. The higher education reform was started in the mid-1980s, when the Communist Party of China (CCP) attempted to create more opportunities for higher learning. Diversified higher education institutions have developed in the mainland, and the government has also adopted strategies appropriate for making its higher education system more comparable to other developed economies (Yin and White 1994; Christiansen

1996; Mok 2000a; Chan and Mok 2001). In addition, reform measures such as decentralizing managerial power from the state to the higher education level, reviewing curricula and examination systems, and revamping the university admission mechanisms are to be introduced in these countries. All these proposed reform measures have suggested that these governments are keen to launch "fundamental reform" rather than "incremental reform" to resolve the genuine problems inherited in the education systems as a whole.

Japan, like other East Asian societies, has engaged in various kinds of educational restructuring in the past decades. Realizing that the education system in Japan is not flexible and responsive to rapid social and economic changes, the Japanese government has introduced new reform measures along the lines of neoliberalism by injecting more competition into the education system. By incorporating national universities, the Japanese government has tried to make the national university system more proactive to address changes arising from domestic and global issues. One of the major reform directions is internationalization of the Japanese education system. Although there have been heated debates among academics, scholars, policymakers, and teaching professionals in Japan, reform strategies along the lines of marketization and corporatization have been adopted by the present government to restructure the rigidly sustained Japanese education system (Yonezawa 2003a; Oba 2004). All in all, the selected Asian societies have launched different forms of comprehensive reviews of their existing education systems, and thereafter these Asian governments have implemented various kinds of educational reforms and restructuring in order to make their education systems more globally competitive.

Policy of decentralization and educational governance

The discernible trend of restructuring the role of the state in running the public sector has undoubtedly affected the governance of education and eventually led to a fundamental change in state-education relationships. One of the changes common to these East Asian societies is the adoption of decentralization policy. Educational decentralization is a popular reform that governments around the world have adopted (Hanson 1998). In Hong Kong, the call for quality education and the launch of university-based management are initiated under the decentralization policy framework. Instead of "micro-control," individual universities are now given more autonomy and power in running and deciding their daily matters and affairs. Nonetheless, such a development does not necessarily mean deregulation and retrenchment of the state's control. Rather, the government can easily exercise its control through its executive arm, the UGC, to maintain a close watch on universities' performance. The approach to reforming the existing higher education system is a managerial or an executive-led model, attaching importance to the ideas of efficiency, effectiveness, and economy in education (Mok and Wilding 2003). Starting from the self-monitoring assessment exercise to a more formal quality assurance movement, together with the proposed education reform along the line of managerialism, one can easily imagine that the state's role as a regulator and overall coordinator will certainly be strengthened (Mok 2000a; Tse 2002). Such developments confirm Bottery's notion of "managerial globalization" to conceptualize recent reforms taking place in the public sector along the line of new public management (2000).

Similarly, the recent education reforms initiated by the Singapore government are not entirely new since the government has been very aware of the important role of education in national development and future modernization. In order to make its schools and citizens more competitive and competent to face future challenges, the government has taken a proactive approach to reform its higher education system by the introduction of far more formal quality assurance systems in universities. As Jason Tan suggested, the promotion of quality control definitely creates pressure for performance in the university sector. The adoption of decentralization policy in Singapore universities has indeed strengthened the state's role in governing these schools by introducing performance reviews and regular inspections. Benchmarking its university system with world-class universities, the Singapore government now grants more autonomy to individual universities in order to cultivate the spirit of entrepreneurialism and creativity among universities, academics, and students. Such measures are meant to promote the competitiveness of Singapore's citizens in the global economy (Tan 1999). Nonetheless, the "autonomization" process does not necessarily mean that the state's control and regulation have been reduced. Instead, the introduction of stringent measures to hold universities accountable to the public and the implementation of various kinds of quality assurance activities in Singapore's universities are clear indicators of recentralization (Lee 2000; Mok 2000a). Hence, it is not surprising that many university academics simply consider the policy of decentralization another process of re-regulation instead of a genuine policy of decentralization and deregulation (Lee 2003; Mok and Lee 2003).

The fundamental changes in Taiwan's higher education sector since processes of denationalization, decentralization, and autonomization conceptualize the late 1980s. By "denationalization," I mean that the state has begun to forsake its monopoly on higher education, hence allowing the nonstate sector and even the market to engage in higher education provision. By "decentralization," I refer to the shift from the "state control model" to the "state supervision model," whereby educational governance is decentralized from educational bureaucracies to create in their place devolved systems of schooling or universities, entailing significant degrees of institutional autonomy and a variety of forms of school-based/university-based management and administration. As for "autonomization," we mean that university academics now have more academic autonomy and they are empowered to do research projects of any kinds and they have far more discretion to manage and operate their institutions. The processes of "decentralization" and "autonomization," or processes of *song-bang* (liberalization), should not be understood as the total withdrawal of the state from the education domain. With the growth of private universities and colleges, the Taiwan government has tried to redefine the status of national higher education. The revised University Law stipulates that all national universities will become independent legal bodies and hence they are held accountable to the public; thus independent boards of directors will run all state universities and the state will gradually reduce its subsidy to these public universities. The proposed change will inevitably transform the way universities are financed, regulated, and managed (*United News* December 28, 1999; Weng 2001; Law 2003).

Realizing that the state has imposed too stringent a control and regulation on the university sector in the past few decades, the South Korean government has begun to implement a policy of decentralization to allow individual universities to have more flexibility and autonomy to run their businesses. In recent years, the Korean government has been focusing on building an institutional base that will enhance each university's autonomy. Power is particularly decentralized to individual universities in areas such as the size of student enrollment and the management of student affairs. In order to encourage diversification and specialization of universities, the government has played a supervisory role to assess performance of universities instead of imposing too strict a control on university governance (Yoon 2001). Similar developments can be easily found in mainland China. Starting from the mid-1980s, the CCP has adopted the policy of decentralization in education (Park 2000c). Like Taiwan and South Korea, the Chinese government admits the fact that the "centralized model" practiced before the economic reform in 1978 hindered higher education development in the mainland. Knowing that depending upon the state alone is never a way of meeting the pressing demands for higher education, the Chinese government has adopted a "macro-control" over higher education by giving policy directions and issuing policy principles since the mid-1980s (Wang 1988). Diversified education institutions of higher learning have emerged, while education financing has been sought from multiple channels; meanwhile major transformations have taken place in financing, provision, and regulation of China's higher education domain (Mok 1999, 2000d; Chan and Mok 2001). Nonetheless, we should not interpret educational decentralization in mainland China as an entire withdrawal of state control/regulation over the higher education sector. Rather, we must be aware that the relationship between the authoritarian state and the more autonomous university sector is an interactive one (Mok 2000d). As the center still keeps close watch on developments and changes that take place in the university sector, it is less likely that a genuine devolution of authority can take place in mainland China especially under a single dominant party retaining Maoist and Leninist traditions (Hawkins 1999).

Japan, like other Asian societies, has recognized the problems resulting from the state-driven and centralized governance model. With the present government adhering to the ideas of neoliberalism, policies along the line of decentralization have been introduced and implemented in the past decade to transform the Japanese education system. By allowing more autonomy and flexibility to education institutions, the Japanese government hopes to make its education systems more flexible and adaptive to rapid changes. One point that deserves attention here is that when talking about centralization and decentralization, they are processes of "-zation" rather than static situations. We must also note that the range of models for the governance of education is very wide. A scrutiny of the recent developments in these selected East Asian societies points to the fact that even though the policy of decentralization has been adopted in these societies, the state's role as a regulator and overall service coordinator has been strengthened rather than weakened.

Marketization and privatization of higher education

In addition to the trend of educational decentralization, higher education developments in these East Asian societies have been affected by the strong tide of marketization and privatization. Universities in these societies nowadays experience pressures from governments, the main providers of higher education, to demonstrate maximum outputs from the financial inputs they are given. In times of economic constraints, people begin to ask for better use of limited public money; thus more attention is given to the issue of "value for money" and how the investment in higher education can really facilitate social and economic developments (Lee 2000; Mok and Lo 2001; Law 2003). In order to make the delivery of higher education more efficient and effective, there has been an increasingly popular trend of marketization and privatization in the higher education sector in the region (Bray 2000; Kwong 2000).

Similar to the experiences in other countries, such changes are closely related to the "marketization" of education; hence private sector principles are adopted to run education (Whitty 1997). In order to reduce the state's increasing burden, different market-related strategies are adopted such as the increase of student tuition fees, reduction of the state's budget in higher education, strengthening the relationship between the university sector and the industrial and business sectors, and encouraging universities and academics to engage in business and market-like activities to generate more revenue/income (Su 1999; Bray 2000; Hawkins 2000; Mok 2000d, 2001). Contrasting and comparing the marketization and privatization projects of these societies, we may argue that for Hong Kong and Singapore, the reform strategies along the line of marketization are to improve the efficiency and performance of the university sector instead of purely resolving financial difficulties (Mok 2000a; Lee 2001), while the marketizing of higher education in mainland China is primarily intended to address the limited state capacity in higher education provision. Making use of market strategies and nonstate sources, the government can convince nonstate actors to resolve the problems that the state is now confronting (Mok 2000d; Chan and Mok 2001). In Taiwan, the market strategies adopted in the university sector are not only to explore additional nonstate resources to finance higher education but also to improve the performance and effectiveness of university education (Tai 2000b; Weng 2001). Japan, like other East Asian societies, has tried to introduce market forces and ideas in reforming its education systems. The implementation of the "corporatization" of national universities has clearly indicated the trend toward "market-oriented" reforms.

Rediscovering society in governance

Our previous comparative work has drawn us to another major observation that is closely related to the change in governance model in modern states. According to Rhodes (1997), the distinction between state and civil society, between public, private, and voluntary sectors, and even between government and market, is becoming increasingly blurred. Similarly, Rosenau also argues that "[g]iven a world where governance is increasingly operative without government, where lines of authority are increasingly more informal than formal, where legitimacy is increasingly marked by ambiguity, citizens are increasingly capable of holding their own by knowing when, where, and how to engage in collective action" (1992, p. 291). Kooiman, like Rhodes and Rosenau, conceptualizes the problems of governability in the post-welfare state Western democracies by the notion of "social-political governance" (Kooiman 1993). What's new to such new forms of governance is a "third way" between conventional systems of government which have reached the limits of their political and administrative capacities and those changes are to play down the need for governing (i.e., deregulation) or shifting such need (e.g., by privatization and marketization). As Cheung (2000) suggested, such changes signify a paradigm shift from *unilateral* (government or society separately) to an *interactionist* focus (government with society), with a growing realization of interdependencies.

As a society becomes more dynamic, volatile, and complex, the conventional notion of government in terms of using force, taking command, and imposing order, regulation, and control are rendered inappropriate. As Dunsire suggested, modern states have to search for new governance models by identifying any area of interest and examining

> what antagonistic forces already operate, what isotasy or stand-off configuration presently obtains, and what intervention would help to create a more desirable position...government with a minimum use of power and resources may shift a little weight, and in a time-honoured and ubiquitous but surprisingly untheorized way, steer the equilibrium.
>
> (Dunsire 1993, p. 34)

All these developments have pointed to the new governance model in modern state, particularly showing the importance of societal embeddedness, that is, the social and political interaction and networking in governance. As the capacity of the modern state declines, there is a strong need to reconnect domestic society to governance. In addition, new governance theory proposes a common trend in the pattern of instrument choice: the mix of instruments adopted by governments is changing in a more or less uniform manner. They are (on the whole) less direct, a less visible part of government, and less coercive (Peters 2002; Salomon 2002). At the same time, nonstate sources and nonstate actors including the market, the family, the community, individuals, and nongovernmental organizations are engaged in financing and providing social services or offering social/public policies (Mok 2003b).

The need for higher education expansion and the plan to establish their societies as "learning societies" obviously have driven these Asian societies to search for additional financing sources to support higher education development and lifelong learning initiatives (Mok *et al.* 2000; Yang 2000). Therefore, we can easily find that these East Asian governments have tried to make use of non-government (nonstate) resources and channels to engage in higher education provision. For instance, the Hong Kong government plans to double the number of higher education graduates in ten years' time by involving individual efforts, family support, community resources, and market forces into education provision (Tung 2001). Similarly, different societal forces are mobilized to engage in education provision in mainland China since the state alone cannot meet the pressing demands for higher education (Chan and Ngok 2000). The governments of South Korea, Singapore, and Taiwan have engaged the private sector to run higher education. In Taiwan and South Korea, for instance, the majority of higher education graduates are enrolled in private universities instead of public ones, while the Singapore and Hong Kong governments have attempted to recover recurrent costs from tuition fees and additional incomes generated by individual universities (Bray 2000; Tai 2000b; Mok 2001c; Law 2003). In Japan, national universities are now "incorporated" while the Singapore government has also announced a plan to change the statutory status of national universities into independent legal/judicial entities in order to make them less dependent on the government. All these developments have clearly indicated that these societies are experiencing a fundamental change in governance model shifting to an *interactionist* focus (government with society), with a growing realization of interdependence, as Kooiman (1993) rightly suggested.

Conclusion

This chapter has outlined a few major challenges that the selected East Asian societies are now commonly facing. The domestic socioeconomic and political changes, coupled with changes and transformations driven by regional and global forces, have inevitably changed the way that the education sector is managed and governed. This chapter has also examined a few major trends of education reforms and governance change in East Asia. With our earlier discussions setting out the wider policy context for education governance change in the selected East Asian societies, the discussions in Part II will focus primarily on how different Asian governments such as mainland China, Hong Kong, Taiwan, Singapore, South Korea, and Japan have reformed and restructured their education systems in coping with globalization challenges.

Part II

Globalization and national response

5 China's response to globalization

Educational decentralization and marketization in post-Mao China

Introduction

In the post-Mao period, higher education has been experiencing processes of decentralization and centralization, a "centralized decentralization" trend is becoming an increasingly popular trend shaping higher education governance in post-Mao China. In the past two decades, the Chinese government on the mainland has been confronted with difficulties in raising the education level and standards of its citizens. The Chinese government also faced a severe crunch in financial resources to finance higher education. In order to cope with the challenges of globalization, the urgent need to produce highly qualified and well-educated citizens, the post-Mao leaders have implemented the policy of decentralization in education to diversify the education systems. Departing from state monopoly of education provision, the post-Mao leaders have adopted not only market forces but also other social forces to provide and finance education, there by hoping to create more education opportunities. Therefore, higher education institutions and schools run by the nonstate sectors including the enterprises-run institutions, social-forces run institutions and other minban (people-run) school, and higher education institutions have become increasingly popular. The principal goal of this chapter is to examine how diverse the higher education systems are in the post-Mao China, with particular reference to how the policy of decentralization adopted by the Chinese government since the mid-1980s has affected higher education governance and management. The chapter reviews how complicated and diversified higher education institutions have developed since the economic reforms started in the late 1980s, especially with the growing prominence of minban education in the last two decades. In addition, this chapter will critically examine the politics of educational decentralization by showing how the Chinese state can still maintain its control over higher education institutions even though decentralization policy has been introduced and implemented in higher education.

Centralized governance model of higher education in Mao's China (1949–76)

Before the communists came to power in 1949, there was a coexistence of state-funded and nonstate (private/self-financed) universities, as well as a considerable number of universities run by overseas missionaries. A new structure of governance of universities began to take shape after the establishment of new China, and even more so after the Soviet model in higher education governance was adopted. Being influenced by the Soviet practices, higher education had become highly specialized in orientation and the state adopted a centralized model in managing and governing higher education developments (Hayhoe 1989, 1996). It is note-worthy that the Soviet influence was reflected not only on the organization and administration of schools and higher education institutions but also on the way in which textbooks, teaching methods, and classrooms were designed. The "central-ized" governance model did reinforce the tendencies toward the centralization of knowledge and uniformity of thought (Yang 2000).

In order to realize the ideals of socialism, in 1952, the Chinese government began to implement policies to nationalize all education institutions, including all public, private, and missionary universities and colleges in order to make all the schools and higher education institutions "state-run" or "publicly run" institu-tions. In addition, during the same period the higher education institutions experienced significant restructuring and readjusting. After the reorganization, all schools, colleges, and universities became state-run institutions. In particular, universities were made narrowly specialized according to the manpower planning derived from the central planning economy (Min 1994). In terms of higher education management and governance, a hierarchical, centralized, and well-organized network was developed (Agelasto and Adamson 1998, p. 31). The newly nationalized system was organized and restructured based on a "centralized model," characterized by the direct leadership of the government in implementing the unitary instructional plans, course syllabi, and textbooks in all the colleges and universities throughout the country. At that time, it was believed that such a "state control model" could best serve the centrally planned economy in general and national manpower needs in particular.

There is no doubt that the adoption of the "centralized" model in education governance had given the central government a relatively tight control over financing, provision, and management of education, especially under the reign of Mao Zedong from 1949 to 1976. Living in this policy context, Chinese citizens were accustomed to free education provided by the state (Yao 1984). As the top government agency in charge of educational policymaking, the Ministry of Education (MOE) was to provide general directions and guidance to all schools and higher education institutions. With such a governance framework in place, the MOE retained direct control over certain key universities, taking the responsibility for designing curricula and syllabi, designing textbooks, student admission, grad-uate job assignment, and exerted control over matters like budgets, salary scales, and personnel issues (Mok 1996, 2002a). With decision-making authority resting upon the central ministry, provincial and local education commissions and bureaus were just mediators to reinforce and implement national policy. It is within such a policy context that the enthusiasm of local governments and higher education institutions were jeopardized since the central ministry had absolute authority in deciding higher education development matters. More importantly, such a governance model was also notorious for the separation of the center and the locality, under which each higher education institution was directed by their departments in charge at the central and local levels, resulting in lack of coordination among these levels and inefficient administration and ineffective service delivery (Fan 1995, p. 43; Mok 2004).

Policy of decentralization and educational changes in post-Mao China (1976 to present)

Since the late 1970s, the modernization drive, the reform, and opening up to the outside world has transformed the highly centralized planning economy into a market-oriented and more dynamic economy. In the new market-economy context, the old way of higher education governance is rendered inappropriate. Acknowledging that over-centralization and stringent rules would kill the initiatives and enthusiasm of local educational institutions, the Chinese Communist Party (CCP) called for resolute steps to streamline administration, devolve powers to units at lower levels so as to allow them more flexibility to run education. Central to the reform, strategies are closely related to the policy of decentralization, whereby higher education institutions have been given more autonomy to run their own businesses (Min 1994; Mok 2002).

The promulgation of the *Decision on Reform of Educational System* (hereafter 1985 Decision) by the CCP Central Committee in 1985 marks the first comprehensive reform in Chinese higher education sector. The 1985 Decision stated that the key to restructuring higher education lies in eliminating excessive government control over schools and higher education institutions and, under guidance of the state policies and plans in education, extending the decision-making power of the colleges and universities and strengthening their ties with production units, scientific research institutions, and similar sectors, so that they will have the initiative and the ability to serve economic and social development (CCPCC 1985). The *Outline for Reform and Development of Education in China* issued by the Communist Party of China in 1993 identified the reduction of centralization and government control in general as the long-term goals of reform (CCPCC 1993). The government began to play the role of "macro-management through legislation, allocation of funding, planning, information service, policy guidance and essential administration."

Reshuffling the monopolistic role of the state in educational provision, reform in educational structure started in the mid-1980s and has manifested a mix of private and public consumption (K.M. Cheng 1995; Hayhoe 1996; Mok 1996). Diversification of education services began, especially when the Chinese state began to encourage all democratic parties, social organizations, retired cadres and intellectuals, collective economic organizations, and individuals actively and voluntarily to contribute to developing education by various means and methods (Wei and Zhang 1995). The education reform processes have also led to the diversification of education revenues and resources. More and more schools/higher education institutions now rely not only upon the state funding but also financial support from other sources such as social donations, students' tuition fees, and capital investment from enterprises, while different types of *minban* (nonstate run) schools, colleges, and universities have emerged to cater to the educational needs of the Chinese citizens. This chapter sets out in this wider policy context to examine how *minban* higher education has evolved and developed, along with discussing the policy implications and significance of the rise of *minban* education in post-Mao China.

Development of *minban* higher education: past and present

There were three waves of rapid growth of *minban* higher education in China. The *first wave* started in the late 1980s, especially when people from local community initiated self-learning schools, training schools, supplementary learning schools, and continuing learning colleges. In the early 1980s, *minban* higher education was initiated by a group of experienced professors, school principals, and educationalists in a "*sanwu*" (three-insufficient) condition. In March 1982, after around 36 years of the closure of private higher education in mainland China, the Zhonghua Zhehui University was inaugurated in Beijing, the national capital of China (China National Institute of Education Science Research 1995). In the same year, the National People's Congress, the national legislature in China, promulgated a new Constitution, stipulating that "the state encourages collective economic organizations, governmental enterprises and other social groups to initiate and administer various kinds of legal educational activities" (Article 19 of the Constitution of China 1982).

As discussed earlier, the decision issued by the central committee of the Chinese Communist Party in 1985 indicated the state's approving attitude toward the development of *minban* education, as over 100 higher education institutions of this kind were established and developed across the country despite the difficulties in mounting *minban* education. Due to lack of adequate financial and manpower resources, these *minban* higher education institutions were set up without campus, funding, and teachers. For example, Beijing Hridian Zoudu University and Zhejiang Shuren University were established with these poor conditions (Wei and Zhang 1995; Hu 1999). In 1987, the State Education Commission promulgated a document entitled "Provincial Regulations on the Social Forces Running Educational Establishments," attempting to rectify some of the disorders in the governance and management of *minban* schools and higher education institutions in China (Zhu 1994).

The *second wave* of *minban* education development began in the early 1990s. With the rise of *minban*/private higher education in the mainland, problems such as conferring of diplomas, status of students studying in these institutions when compared to the state-run counterparts, and other related issues came up. According to Wei and Zhang (1995), the first national conference on *minban* higher education was held in Wuhan, Hubei in January 1989. During the conference, more than 70 *minban* higher education institutions participated and the conference came up with a platform of five concrete suggestions on issues of importance, as well as a call for the central education ministry to take a more liberal approach in fostering *minban* education. Since 1992, a number of *minban* higher education institutions were established with the approval of the state and formed the second wave of growth.

The *third wave* of development began from the late 1990s and is currently ongoing. As of 1998, there were 1,277 *minban* (people-run or community-run) higher education institutions in China. In 2000, nearly 1 million students registered in the *minban* higher learning institutions in the whole country (Yang 2002). Table 5.1 shows the number of *minban* higher education institutions in mainland China from 1996 to 2001. Within a relatively short five-year period, *minban* higher education institutions already increased from 1,219 to 1,758; admitting 1,427.4 thousand students (see Table 5.2). In 2002 alone, there were around 133 degree-granting institutions in mainland China, admitting 311,200 students and constituting about 4.3 percent of regular higher education institutions' student enrollment. Another 1,202 nondegree awarding *minban* higher education institutions existed in China, recruiting about 1,403,500 students. With the enactment of the 2003 *Law on Private Education Promotion, minban* HEIs have been given legal rights and interests, as well as a reasonable return on investment (cited in Welch 2004, p. 16).

Table 5.1 Number of *minban* HEIs in mainland China

	1996	1997	1998	1999	2000	2001
Total	1,219	1,115	—	1,277	1,321	1,758
Minban HEIs authorized to issue academic qualification	21	20	22	37	43	89
Minban HEIs providing state-recognized credential programs	89	157	300	370	467	436
Other *Minban* HEIs	1,109	1,095	1,200	1,240	1,282	1,202

Source: State Committee of Education; MOE.

Table 5.2 Number of students enrolling in *minban* HEIs (Unit: Thousand people)

	1996	1997	1998	1999	2000	2001
Total	1,145.4	1,204	—	1,488	981.7	1,427.4
Minban HEIs authorized to issue academic qualification	12	16	—	40	68	140
Minban HEIs providing state-recognized credential programs	51.4	94	—	258	297	321
Other *Minban* HEIs	1,084	1,190	—	1,184	982	1,130

Source: State Committee of Education; MOE.

Diversity of *minban* higher education in post-Mao China

The continual increase in the number of enrollments in these *minban* higher education institutions has indeed shown that the market, nonstate sector, and other local forces have been revitalized and mobilized to finance and provide more learning opportunities for higher education (Mok 2001b, 2002a). All these nonstate funded or *minban* educational institutions adopt fee-paying principles and they offer diversified education services to Chinese citizens (Chan and Mok 2001b; Mok 2002a). The diversified education systems discussed here after demonstrates how China has been experiencing the proliferation of education provision in the post-Mao period. Education provision, seen in this light, has never been the state's business and state monopolization of education is over, especially when the nonstate sectors and actors are becoming increasingly prominent in education provision.

Table 5.3 indicates that higher education institutions (HEIs, hereafter) in China can be categorized into the public and private sectors in accordance to their provision and financing. Nonetheless, there is an overlapping area between the two sectors. Interestingly enough, many *minban* education institutions could be categorized in this particular domain known as "state-owned and people-run" (*guoyou minban*) education.

State-owned and people-run education

When examining these state-owned and people-run (*guoyou minban*) education institutions in China, we have found a diversity of schools/colleges and universities of this kind, ranging from affiliated schools/colleges to transformed schools/colleges/universities. Different kinds of governing models in other *minban/* private education institutions are adopted in China.

Affiliated higher education institutions (second-tier colleges)

This type of schools is established as an extension arm of a well-established public university with finances being generated from student tuition fees or other

Table 5.3 Typology of HEIs in post-Mao China

Financing \ Provision	Public	Private
Public	Public HEIs	—
Private	State-owned and people-run (*guoyou minban*) HEIs • Affiliated HEIs • Transformed HEIs (1)	Private HEIs • Education saving fund • Private individual/unit • Education conglomerate (2)

Notes
1 Both provision and financing of transformed school are held by the private sector; the school preserves its public natures in form of its ownership instead of provision.
2 Education conglomerate often participate as the "people" side in state-owned and people-run (*guoyou minban*) school.

nonstate sources. After setting up the second-tier colleges affiliated to public universities, the parent universities are responsible for running the colleges, while the private partners provide financial support (such as campus, infrastructure, and support services) in terms of investment. In some cases, affiliated colleges share facility and teaching staff with their parent universities in order to achieve the economy of scale. Affiliated HEIs have become popular in Zhejiang, Jiangsu, Liaoning, Shanxi, Shanghai, and Szechuan. Until 2000, there were 23 and 18 affiliated colleges in Zhejiang and in Jiangsu areas respectively. The establishment of these second-tier colleges can serve the national policy goal in higher education expansion. In short, there are four types of affiliated institutions, that is, (1) established by a single public university; collaboratively established by (2) a public university and an enterprise; (3) by a public university and a foreign education institution; and (4) by a public university and a local private university (Wu 2003, pp. 320–21).

Transformed universities (Wanli model)

Transformed universities are another form of *guoyou minban* (state-owned and people-run) HEIs. It is called "*Wanli* model" because Zhejiang Wanli University was the first institution in mainland China that adopted this model. Before the transformation, the university was a public institution facing acute financial crisis. With the approval of the MOE and Zhejiang provincial government, the university was transformed into a *guoyou minban* institution by separating its ownership and management. During the transformation process, Wanli Education Group, a private enterprise invested and took the responsibilities of running the institution while the state still preserved the ownership over the institution. With the new governance model in place, Zhejiang Wanli University, the newly established university, is run on a cost recovery model and the operation rests upon market principles and practices. As a member of a private conglomerate, the university enjoys relatively high degree of autonomy in student admission, personnel, teaching, and curriculum design. Nonetheless, the university is not entirely free from the government control. To uphold its "quasi public" nature, the university's finance is audited by the government auditing department despite the fact that the university is financially independent from the government (Xu 2002).

Minban/*private education*

Education saving fund (Guangdong model)

Education saving fund was seen as an efficient way to mobilize the investment for *minban* education from the society. By adopting this financing model, institutions require parents to deposit a lump-sum payment (debenture) into the college fund before admitting their children. Parents can get the deposit back when their children graduate or quit from the institution, while the fund generated from the debenture would be used for developing the infrastructure and facilities of the institutions concerned. Without other revenues, the operation cost of the institution relies on the interest generated from the fund. Such a model was widely adopted in Guangdong, especially in the Pearl River Delta region, where in the 1990s around 40 institutions were run by this model (DPBMOE and SAES 2003, p. 137). However, this governance model ran into difficulties. First, without other financial sources, the institutions' revenue decreased especially with the drop of interest rate. Second, many families could not afford to pay the lump-sum deposit and therefore it affected the number of students being admitted. Third, there were embezzlements of the fund. Therefore, Guangdong government ordered all the institutions running on education saving fund to restructure their financing model by refunding the deposit and charging tuition fees in 1999. Among 36 schools, 14 have been transformed into the new financing model successfully. Another 11 have been transformed with hardship and the remaining had to close down because of financial difficulties (DPBMOE and SAES 2003, p. 137).

Private individual/unit (Wenzhou model)

Private individual/unit here mainly refers to retired educators, intellectuals, entrepreneurs, and various nongovernment organizations (like trade unions and political parties) that are interested in investing in education by establishing *minban* schools/colleges. This kind of institution is particularly popular in Wenzhou, a municipal city in Jiangsu area that is very famous for private/*minban* enterprises. After the economic reform, the private/*minban* enterprises have developed very rapidly in Wenzhou. The business people in Wenzhou are keen to invest in *minban* education since they believe better and more higher education opportunities would facilitate further economic and social developments. With the decentralization policy framework in place, coupled with parents' willingness to pay for higher education in Wenzhou area, a number of individuals and units have engaged in running and financing HEIs (Hu 1997, p. 44).

Education conglomerate

Education conglomerates prefer private investments in education on a relatively large scale. They usually consist of schools at different levels in order to provide a "through train" mode of education. Different to the private individuals and units, the education conglomerates have substantial resources and hence they are able to develop proper physical environment and buildings, equipped with better facilities. However, they rarely establish an HEI individually. In many cases, they seek for well-established public universities/colleges as their partners and establish their higher education sections in a collaborative manner. This arrangement results in the affiliated schools mentioned earlier. In other cases, the education conglomerates take control of the universities/colleges from the public sector. This is the mode of school transformation in the name of *guoyou minban* (state-owned and people-run).

One point which deserves particular attention here is that we could make better sense of the vast diversity of *minban* higher education in mainland China only when we contextually analyze *minban* education developments with particular reference to the unique socioeconomic and sociopolitical environments of different localities in which different types of *minban* institutions have evolved and developed. In Zhejiang province, for instance, the private sector nearly dominates the economy. Comparing public education development of Zhejiang with other parts of the mainland, public education is not as well developed since *minban* education plays a relatively important role in education financing and provision in this area. Taking Wenzhou, a city in the Zhejiang province, as another example, over 90 percent of the enterprises and over 85 percent of the economy are privately run and owned. The local government therefore has taken a "deregulation" policy to encourage and mobilize the nonstate sectors and actors to be engaged in providing and financing education. It is under such a particular socioeconomic and policy context that diversified modes of *minban* education have emerged and flourished and are known as "Wenzhou model." The important role of *minban* education is confirmed by the following official statistics: the share of *minban* education in kindergarten is 85.75 percent, while it also constitutes a very significant proportion at other levels of education (senior secondary education; 29.79 percent, vocational secondary education; 37.80 percent, and adult education; 92.1 percent) (DPB-MOE and SEAS 2003, p. 20).

In Guangdong, the provincial government has adopted an "education saving fund model" in facilitating education development. Guangdong, being one of the most economically prosperous regions in China, many families in the province are willing to spend more on their children's education. In addition, as the "window" of trade and international exchanges in southern part of mainland China, the capitalist economic model has significantly affected social and economic developments in Guangdong. Such a unique socioeconomic and sociopolitical background has unquestionably created a conducive environment for the emergence of the education saving fund model, a financing model totally relying on parents' contribution with minimum government subsidy and intervention, to flourish in the province.

Unlike Zhejiang and Guangdong where local governments have allowed more flexibility for *minban* education to develop, in areas with strong state control, private participation in education tends to be in the form of collaboration. For example, in Beijing and Shanghai, local governments at county and township levels often engage in *minban* elementary and secondary education in the name of "people-run state-assisted" or "state-run people-assisted." In higher education, private education operators tend to establish their institutions by collaborating with an established public institution, as there are many famous and well-established universities in the two municipalities. Therefore, *minban* education is mostly in the form of an affiliated school or a transformed school in the two cities under stronger state political influence. Our earlier discussions have clearly indicated that education providers have proliferated and funding channels have diversified in post-Mao period. Different forces, including the market and private enterprises, are involved in education financing and provision. Such developments have confirmed that China's education has been experiencing processes of decentralization and marketization. Most important of all, the earlier observations have drawn our attention not only to the vast diversity of *minban* education developments but also to the politics of education decentralization in mainland China (for further details, see following discussion). Having discussed the recent developments and major features of *minban* higher education in post-Mao China, let us now turn to the significance of the rise of *minban* education in China.

Significance of the rise of *minban* education in China

The rise of *minban* higher education has significant social and political implications for post-Mao China. First, the diversification of higher education and the proliferation of higher education providers have rendered the conventional public/private boundary inappropriate. It is particularly true when China's higher education institutions are run by not only the public/state sector but also the nonstate sectors including different kinds of governing bodies. Second, the diversification of higher education has suggested that an "education market" has evolved in mainland China but such a market is never immune from the state's control. The best term for describing the emerging education market in China is "governed market". Third, the recent changes taking place in China's higher education sector has inevitably changed the state-education relationship, while the state still controls the higher education despite the fact that education provision has been proliferated in the post-Mao period. The following sections will discuss these aspects in detail.

Blurring public and private boundary of education

Although *minban* education is widely used to describe nongovernmental education in China, the term *minban* (people-run) is not clear and precise enough to conceptualize the complicated nature of all *minban* (nonstate run) education. Initiatively, the term *minban* education had a distinctively different meaning from private education. It originally refers to the elementary education run and financed by the village community with government assistance and has the connotations of mass and people (Tsang 2003, p. 168). Nonetheless, *minban* education has changed its nature since the introduction of economic reform in 1978. Owing to the scarcity of educational resources, the state has adopted a decentralization policy and therefore lessened its control on higher education provision (Bray 1999, p. 211). It is against this particular context that various nongovernmental bodies have begun to engage in running nonstate run/*minban* schools, colleges, and higher education institutions, resulting in the diversification of education financing in China. Currently, the "multiple channels" for educational financing include government subsidies, private (e.g., individuals, overseas Chinese, foreign businesses, and private corporations) donations and investments, state-owned and collective-owned enterprises' donation and investment, tuition fee, and revenue generated from school-run enterprises and research results (Chen and Li 2002).

On the one hand, the diversified educational financing has facilitated the growth and improvement of educational services. On the other, the same process has also made the boundary of public and private education blurred. The diversified modes of higher education financing and provision have made a simple distinction between public or state and private or *minban* education very difficult. Unlike the Western societies where there could be a clearer boundary between public or government schools and private schools, it is difficult to differentiate *minban* (people-run) and public schools in mainland China. This is even more so since these *minban* schools are not entirely private in nature.

Notwithstanding the definitional difficulties, some scholars have suggested that the sources of financing and provision of education is the major criteria for analyzing the public-private boundary in China's education (Yuan and Zhou 2003). In spite of adopting such criteria in examining the public and private/*minban* distinction in education, we still encounter a considerable extent of difficulties in resolving the definitional problems. Considering *minban* education institutions as an example, which are run by nonstate sectors and actors, including private enterprises/individuals or collectives (such as a democratic party or a legally approved group), how could we compose a clear definition for them? The problem arises in terming them as either "private" or "public." It is particularly difficult to make a clear distinction between public and *minban*/private education, especially when their funding comes both from public and private sources. In this regard, it is right to argue that they are somehow caught between public and private domains, thus suggesting that they are a mixed economy in higher education. What makes it difficult to differentiate public and *minban* education in mainland China is especially when people in the mainland use the terms of "*minban*" and "private" interchangeably when they are talking about these education institutions (Wang 2003).

Hence, the conventional public-private dichotomy is found to be inappropriate in conceptualizing the complicated relations between the private and public sectors in education governance in a transitional economy like China. It is particularly difficult to differentiate the public and private distinction in education financing when financial support from state-owned and collective-owned enterprises is neither a governmental resource nor a community one. It is particularly problematic to develop a clear public and private boundary when community-support schools, those schools run by the state-owned and collective-owned sector, also uphold the principle of nonprofit making, it can hardly embrace the concept of community (Bray 1997, p. 186). In fact, nonprofit making is a general principle for school administration in China. It seemingly cannot be used as a condition for drawing the public and private boundary. Within the Chinese context, such an overlapped area in education is thus termed *minban* (people-run) education (see Figure 5.1). Nonetheless, even for public education, it may have private elements. For example, government schools in China often receive nongovernmental financial support (Tsang 2003, p. 182). In some cases, the proportion of nongovernment financing may constitute a dominant part of school financial sources (Wang 2003, p. 8).

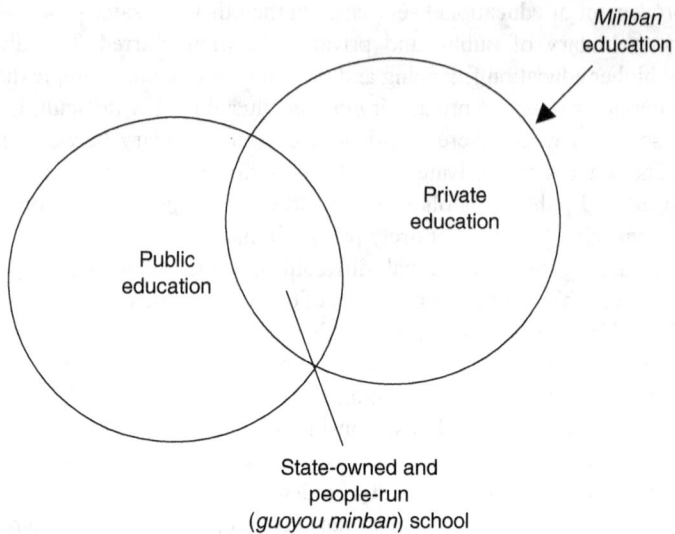

Figure 5.1 Public and private boundary of education.

Emerging "governed education market": second-tier colleges in China

It is claimed that the development of *minban* education in China is leading toward the diversification of financing and running model. However, the emergence of second-tier colleges as affiliated HEIs of public/national universities in mainland China has cast doubt on the real intention of the central ministry in diversifying higher education services. Before the establishment of these second-tier colleges as subsidiaries of public universities, *minban* higher education had indeed been performing certain roles in China's higher education. Despite the fact that many of these *minban* HEIs have not been granted self-accreditation status and many of them still cannot confer degrees to students, they have provided additional higher education opportunities for Chinese youth in the past decade or so. Nonetheless, since the state has begun to endorse the development of second-tier colleges based upon a self-funding basis, the conventional *minban* institutions have had to struggle for survival since they have to compete with the newly emerging second-tier colleges not on an equal basis.

The first of the second-tier (*minban*) colleges was formed by Zhejiang University in Jiangsu province. With the intention to set up a new Zhejiang University as one of the leading research universities in the mainland by means of university merging strategies, the central ministry therefore allowed Zhejiang University to set up a City College, a second-tier college of Zhejiang University, to run on a self-financing basis. Adopting the principles and practices of conventional *minban* colleges, City College has indeed got the blessings from both the central and provincial governments since it possessed the degree conferring authority from the beginning and thus could offer undergraduate degree programs. Having been granted the authority in offering undergraduate degree programs, City College had no difficulty in recruiting students, especially since the college has a strong affiliation with its mother institution, one of the top five universities in China's university league table. In my field interview with Prof. Zhou, executive director of City College, I was told that some of the graduates of his college could be directly admitted to Zhejiang University, while undergraduate students with outstanding academic performance during their studies with the college could also be transferred to Zhejiang University with the "fast track" in place (Field Interview April 2004 at City College, Zhejiang).

According to Lin,

> called City College of Zhejiang University, the college was jointly owned by Zhejiang University, which sent in its administrators and teachers; by the Postal University of Hangzhou, which offered its campus as the site of the college; and by the local government, which provided one-third of the funding
>
> (2004, p. 17)

Having such a close relationship with the local government and strong affiliations with local higher education institutions, City College can really gain the benefits from "two worlds." On the one hand, this college has been conferred with status and legitimacy in offering undergraduate training by the government. And on the other hand, the college also enjoys the flexibility in governing its institutional development like other *minban* colleges. What really makes City College out-weigh its *minban* counterparts is its "quasi-*minban* nature."

Believing in the establishment of second-tier colleges to create additional education opportunities as an effective way to meet the national policy targets in expanding higher education enrollment on the one hand and to make Zhejinag University more focused on research on the other, the City College experiment has been endorsed by the MOE and therefore more colleges of this kind have been developed across the country. In 2004, around 300 second-tier colleges were functioning in the mainland. Criticizing the conventional type of *minban* colleges for "manipulating official policy in the interest of profit making, in the process damaging or undermining the rights of students and parents," the MOE believes the launch of these second-tier colleges can fulfill a very important mission in this particular juncture of history (Interview with Officials January 2004, Beijing). As Lin has also commented, Chinese officials also complain of *minban* colleges lacking in "self-discipline" (2004, p. 18).

Viewing the issue from the *minban* institutions' perspective, we may appreciate the difficulties that these conventional *minban* are now encountering. During a public forum organized by a *minban* education organization in Beijing, many presidents of these conventional *minban* HEIs openly criticized the government for confusing its policies. They complained about the confusing role of these newly established *guoyau minban* colleges, arguing that their quasi-*minban* nature and special treatments by the government have indeed put the conventional *minban* institutions in a very disadvantageous position (Field Observations January

2004, Beijing). Most significantly of all, the development of these "quasi-*minban*" second-tier colleges has created an unfair competition between the former and the other conventional *minban* education institutions since both of them are competing not on the same level. Attached to their parent institutions with famous brand names, it is obvious that students in China normally prefer to apply for these second-tier colleges when compared to conventional *minban* institutions.

In the past three years, public universities have begun to expand student enrollment by setting up their second-tier colleges. In order to meet the national policy goal of the expansion of higher education learning opportunities, these second-tier colleges are aspiring to increase their enrollment from 20,000 to 30,000 students, matching the size of a "comprehensive university" as outlined by the MOE in the future model university (Lin and Yu 2004). When these second-tier colleges are attempting to expand their enrollment, it is not surprising that the conventional *minban* colleges are running into difficulties in recruiting sufficient students. According to Lin, "students are so heatedly competed for that private [*minban*] universities have to spend 20 per cent or more of their revenue on advertisement and recruitment" in order to attract more students. A report shows that in 2003 alone the conventional *minban* colleges had to admit all students, while more than a quarter of the students admitted did not show up, and about 10 percent of them eventually dropped out during the course of their studies because they were not satisfied with the *minban* institutions (Lin 2004). Hence, the conventional *minban* institutions are in a relatively disadvantageous position.

With government endorsement and preferential treatments, the rise of the second-tier colleges inevitably raises a question: Is Chinese education developing toward a diversified system? A close scrutiny of what has been developing in China's higher education sector has suggested that the recent launch of second-tier colleges seems to have obstructed the process of diversifying higher education in China. More importantly, the rise of these second-tier colleges may threaten the survival of the conventional *minban* institutions, especially when the state/public sector intervenes in the emerging education market originally started by the conventional *minban* institutions in the mainland. Thus, a "governed market" has evolved with the state directly manipulating the market forces in shaping the demands and needs for its "governed education market" of second-tier colleges.

Discussions and conclusion: politics of educational decentralization

In the analysis of state intervention in education, scholars primarily focus on the presence of externalities of education. In this sense, it is held that the state is obligated to meet the social needs of education. This provides the legitimacy for its intervention in both financing and provision of education (Tomlinson 1986; Levin 1987; Blaug 1991). Similar views are also held in the Chinese context (Yuen and Zhou 2003, pp. 17–23), the Chinese authorities simultaneously advocate the participation of various "social forces" in the provision of education.

This leads to a diversification of school administration. However, it is argued that such a development does not represent the decline of state influence in education.

Under the present regulations, all educational services in China shall be run on a nonprofit making principle. To attract participation from the private sector, private education participators are allowed to get benefit from *minban* educational institutions as the payment for staffing instead of the bonus for investment. In addition, the policy authorizes the *minban* education institution, as an independent legal identity, to own its property. In case, the institution is dissolved in debit, the school operators shall take the responsibilities. Nevertheless, if the institution is in surplus, the operators can only get their initial investment back and the rest shall be submitted to the local government agencies of education. This arrangement is based on an argument that the privilege policies offered by the government are aimed to subsidize the externalities of education instead of the educational institution itself. The profit made by the government policies shall hence return to the government for facilitating education development (Yuen and Zhou 2003).

Despite the fact that *minban* institutions have been granted legal status and they are now given the right to share the profits being generated from running their institutions, the conventional *minban* colleges have never been immune from the government's control. Even after the promulgation of the "Private Education Promotion Law" in 2002, presidents and senior administrators of these *minban* institutions consider that the rise of the second-tier colleges have really created more hurdles for their colleges' future development. Since many of the conventional *minban* colleges do not have the authority to conduct undergraduate degree programs, their "academic status" is under severe question. In addition, these *minban* colleges have to follow the central ministry's guidelines closely, particularly their autonomy is well constrained in developing and launching academic programs, designing curricula, conferment of degrees, or qualifications, etc. Seen in this light, we should be very careful when discussing the education decentralization in the post-Mao China.

Our earlier discussion has demonstrated the fact that even though the education provision has been proliferated in the post-Mao period, it has never meant that the state has withdrawn from controlling the higher education sector. On the one hand, the state has devolved responsibilities to lower levels of governments and individual HEIs (no matter whether they are private or *minban*) with more flexibility in running their institutions. On the other hand, the state has tried to manipulate the market forces to create another "governed education market" to compete with the conventional *minban* education market. The Chinese government has attempted to mobilize various social forces and different social organizations in education financing and provision. At the same time, the state has attempted to strengthen its regulatory framework to maintain control over the *minban* education institutions. As Lin has rightly suggested, "private [*minban*] higher education in China has been a contested terrain with regard to control and autonomy. Private universities are calling for the loosening of government controls. Government officials argue that the private sector requires rigorous supervision and control" (2004, p. 17).

Our earlier discussion has clearly reflected the complicated relationship between the state and the conventional *minban* colleges. The policy of decentralization being adopted in China's higher education sector should not simply be understood as the state's genuine efforts in decentralizing the sector for the sake of diversity. Instead, the proliferation of higher education provision and the diversification of higher education financing could be understood as the state's intended strategies in bringing in more nonstate resources and actors to create additional higher education opportunities for meeting the citizens' heightened expectations and pressing demands for higher education. Nevertheless, such diversification and proliferation processes are not aimed at genuine decentralization in education in terms of delegating authority from the central to lower levels of governments or even empowering individual institutions to determine their own policies and developments. As I (Mok 2005a) argue elsewhere, the proliferation of education providers and the diversification of higher education funding sources could be effective strategies adopted by the state in steering the higher education development in a far more effective and efficient way since the state can excuse itself from being overloaded with providing and financing higher education. At the same time, the state can better manage and govern the sector by strengthening its regulatory role.

The official endorsement of the rise of the second-tier colleges has clearly shown how the Chinese state has manipulated the education market by its political influence. By creating its own "quasi-education market" and "quasi-*minban*" colleges, the state can easily control the "governed" education market. The adoption of such a policy has served two major purposes. On the one hand, the state has skillfully and tactically made use of the conventional *minban* institutions in resolving the state's own problem in fulfilling the national goal in higher education expansion. Thus the Chinese government can easily control and regulate the "education market" by creating an unfair internal competition between its affiliated second-tier colleges and the conventional *minban* institutions; this is like a double-edged sword. By making use of the blurred public and private boundary in higher education, the Chinese state is able to capture both the public and nonpublic education sectors by riding over the complicated nature of public/ *minban*/private education in the mainland.

Putting the earlier stated observations together, we can argue that the decentralization of higher education in China has never been a pure "autonomization" process. Like other university systems in other parts of the world, China's higher education sector is now experiencing processes of "centralized decentralization," the processes of which have become increasingly common especially with the governance model of modern universities being oriented toward new management strategy along the line of managerialism. Modern universities, nowadays, are on the one hand given more "autonomy," but on the other hand are under stringent regulation in the name of quality assurance and accountability (Braun and Merrien 1999; Neave 2001). Therefore, operational decentralization is combined with the centralization of strategic command in university governance, whereby the academic autonomy is a regulated one (Hoggett 1991; Mok and Lee 2000).

Hence, we may find the coexistence of trends that are centralizing, decentralizing, and recentralizing in the governance of education in the same countries since these processes are fluid and change over time (Bray 1999).

In conclusion, our case study of the decentralization of higher education in China has clearly reflected the coexistence of decentralizing and recentralization especially when *minban* institutions are now confronted with "centralized decentralization" as the model adopted by the state in higher education governance, while the conventional *minban* institutions have to continue their quest for genuine autonomy and they have to struggle very hard for getting an equal status as other public universities. The "centralized decentralization" governance model is clearly reflected when we analyze the Chinese experience of educational decentralization in the context of political ideologies, historical legacies, and other social and political factors in the post-Mao period.

6 Hong Kong's response to globalization

Questing for entrepreneurial universities

Introduction

This chapter sets out in the context of globalization to identify, examine, and discuss issues related to structural adjustment and educational restructuring in Hong Kong, with particular reference to how universities in Hong Kong have attempted to promote entrepreneurial spirit and practice. Particular attention will be given to examine how universities have expanded the university mission from teaching and research to entrepreneurial activities. The emergence of the entrepreneurial academic model should not be simply understood as a pure higher education reform but rather a fundamental change in the relationships between the state, the university sector, and the industrial and business fields. The first main section of the chapter focuses on how universities in Hong Kong have begun to shift their missions and paradigms toward academic entrepreneurialism and entrepreneurial university by strengthening their relationships with the government and industrial and business sectors. The second main section of the chapter will reflect upon the role of the Government of the Hong Kong Special Administrative Region (HKSAR hereafter) in promoting entrepreneurialism, especially examining in what way the HKSAR promotes research and development collaborations between the university sector, and the business and industry in commercializing research products. The final main section of the chapter will discuss changing governance strategies that the HKSAR has adopted in higher education and economic policy to cope with globalization challenges.

Globalization, educational restructuring, and entrepreneurial university

Throughout the discussions in Chapter 1 and in Chapters 4 and 5, no one can deny the fact that processes of globalization have increasingly affected developments in many aspects of the contemporary society. The same globalization processes affect education, like other public policy areas. Therefore, globalization's substantial effects on education are hardly disputed any more, indeed a number of authors have pointed this out in recent years (Currie and Newson 1998a; Jones 1998; Burbules and Torres 2000; Crossley 2000; Welch 2000, 2001; Mok 2001a; Mok and Chan 2002; Mok and Welch 2003). In order to make individual nation-states more competitive, schools and universities in different parts of the world have been under tremendous pressures from government and the general public to restructure/ reinvent the way that they are managed in order to adapt to the everchanging socioeconomic and sociopolitical environments. As Martin Carnoy has pointed out, "globalization enters the education sector on an ideological horse, and its effects in education are largely a product of that financially driven, free-market ideology, not a clear conception for improving education" (Carnoy 2000, p. 50). Education reforms, under the context of globalization, could be characterized by a finance-driven reform emphasizing decentralization, privatization, and better performance (Carnoy 2000; Mok and Welch 2003).

With heavy weight being attached to the principle of "efficiency and quality" in education, schools, universities, and other learning institutions now encounter far more challenges, and are being subjected to an unprecedented level of external scrutiny. The growing concern for "value for money" and "public accountability" has also altered people's value expectations. All providers of education today inhabit a more competitive world, where resources are becoming scarcer; but at the same time, providers have to accommodate increasing demands from the local community as well as changing expectations from parents and employers (Currie and Newson 1998a; Mok and Currie 2002). Attaching far more weight to entrepreneurial efficiency and effectiveness, contemporary universities are under immense pressures to transform their roles to adapt to rapid socioeconomic and sociopolitical changes. It is particularly true when modern governments have encountered reduced financial capacity to finance growing demands for higher education.

In response to calls for "cost-effectiveness" and "value for money," and to prepare better for the knowledge economy as characterized by key notions of knowledge and information, communications, value-added, technology-based innovation and creativity, and entrepreneurship, new managerial doctrines have been adopted and management-dominated type of decision-making has become common practice in the university sector. An entrepreneurial competitive culture has emerged and become the new ethos. In order to become more competitive, universities have changed the ways they manage themselves. "Terms of new discourse" have emerged such as mission statements, system outputs, appraisal, audit, strategic plans, cost centres, and public relations (Duke 1992). In addition, the success of higher education reforms is merely measured by the lesser degree of state intervention, while increased management autonomy and market-oriented instruments are playing a far more significant role in such review exercises (World Bank 1994b). Under the strong tide of managerialism, universities have become more managerialist and bureaucratic in nature (Currie 1998). The global tide of managerialism has accelerated the movement of faculty and universities toward the market, which can clearly be reflected by the ideology of "the market knows best," business practices, performance indicators, corporate managerialism and line management, commercialization of research as well as commodification of knowledge (Currie 1998). Observing the fundamental changes in the university sector, Slaughter and Leslie propose that:

> To maintain or expand resources, faculty had to compete increasingly for external dollars that were tied to market-related research, which was referred

to variously as applied, commercial, strategic, and targeted research, whether these moneys were in the form of research grants and contracts, service contracts, partnerships with industry and government, technology transfer, or the recruitment of more and higher fee-paying students. We call institutional and professional market or marketlike efforts to secure external moneys *academic capitalism.*

(1997, p. 8)

Based upon the idea of *"academic capitalism"* proposed by Slaughter and Leslie, I would argue what has been taking place in the university sector both globally and locally in Hong Kong is a process of *"academic capitalization."* By the process of "academic capitalization," I refer to the scenario where professors and academics, like other professionals, have gradually become involved in the market. No matter how and in what ways academic staff and universities are incorporated into the market, we can easily observe that professional and academic work has been patterned in line with a "market-driven" approach (Mok 2001a).

By using academic capitalization as our central concept, we situate our analysis of the impact of marketization and corporatization on Hong Kong's higher education sector in the reality of the nascent environment of public research universities, an environment full of contradictions, in which academic and professional colleagues expand their human capital stock increasingly in competitive situations. Engaging in far more market-oriented activities in the areas of research, teaching, and university governance, academics are becoming more like "state-subsidized entrepreneurs." In order to generate additional revenue to sustain the development of universities, academics nowadays are increasingly involved in applied, commercial, strategic, and targeted research to generate additional resources, proactively engaging in securing research grants and contracts, service contracts, establishing closer partnerships with industry and government, technology transfer, or recruiting more fee-paying students (Slaughter 1998; Apple 2000). "Satellite operations" or offshore campuses have been set up in Southeast Asia or other parts of the world by institutions based in Britain, Australia, and the United States to market their programs not only regionally but also internationally. Academic institutions and university faculties are increasingly involved in business-oriented activities to generate additional resources (Slaughter and Leslie 1997; Clark 1998, 2002; Yang 2003).

The processes of academic capitalization in general and the pursuit of academic entrepreneurship in particular have changed the relationship between the government, the university, the business, and the industry. A new "university-academic-productive sector relations" has emerged (Sutz 1997), while notions such as "corporate academic convergence" (Currie and Newson 1998a), "entrepreneurial universities" (Marginson 2000), "campus inc." (White and Hauck 2000), "capitalization of knowledge," "strong executive control," and "corporate characters" are used to conceptualize current changes in contemporary universities (Etzkowitz and Leydesdorff 1997). It is, therefore, not surprising that "the language of human capital dominates official policy recommendations dealing with growing economic and

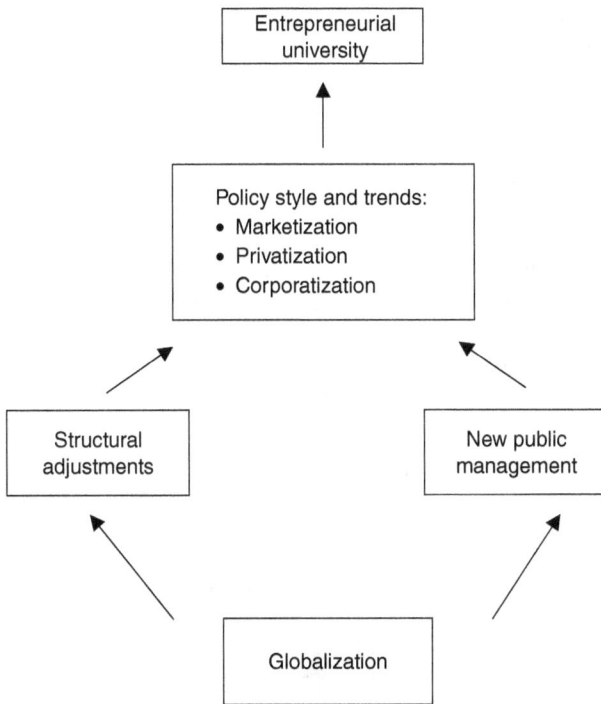

Figure 6.1 Globalization, new policy trends, and the entrepreneurial university.

social problems" (Spring 1998, p. 163). Figure 6.1 shows how globalization accelerates higher education restructuring along the lines of "marketization," "corporatization," and "privatization," universities going the entrepreneurial way is becoming an increasingly popular restructuring strategy for promoting efficiency, effectiveness, economy, and competition in the higher education sector (Mok 2002b; Tai 2002). It is also against such a wider policy context that universities in Hong Kong have begun to shift their paradigms from purely upholding the mission of research and teaching to the third mission of promoting economic and social development. The pursuit of academic entrepreneurship and the transformation toward entrepreneurial university have started in Hong Kong (see Figure 6.1).

Strategies in fostering entrepreneurship

When examining the promotion of entrepreneurship in Hong Kong, we have to identify the triple-helix network system of interactive spirals between the government, the university sector, and the industry and business sector to promote economic development and academic entrepreneurship (Leydsdorff and Etzkowitz 2001). According to Manfield (1991), Lissenburgh and

Harding (2000), the growing role of the university in the new economy is well beyond providing industry and the state apparatuses with trained personnel and engaging in research that provides a knowledge base for industry to draw upon. Instead, modern universities have to engage in the second academic revolution by promoting the third university mission, that is, developing the institution into an entrepreneurial university by promoting economic and social development through the commercialization of research results. Situated into a far more competitive global marketplace, modern universities have to expand their commercial and business arms to reach out to the private sector for private appropriation. As Leydesdroff and Etzkowitz (2001) suggested, the triple-helix network system "opens a window on a universe of discourse that generates a set of coordinates transcending the points of reference of discourses that previously took place within separate institutional spheres" (p. 4). Such a network system creates a "transaction space" for different actors including users, producers, entrepreneurs, and policymakers to explore possibilities for economic and social development. With this triple-helix network system in place, "industry itself" is now increasingly present within academia, potentially co-constitutive of the knowledge production

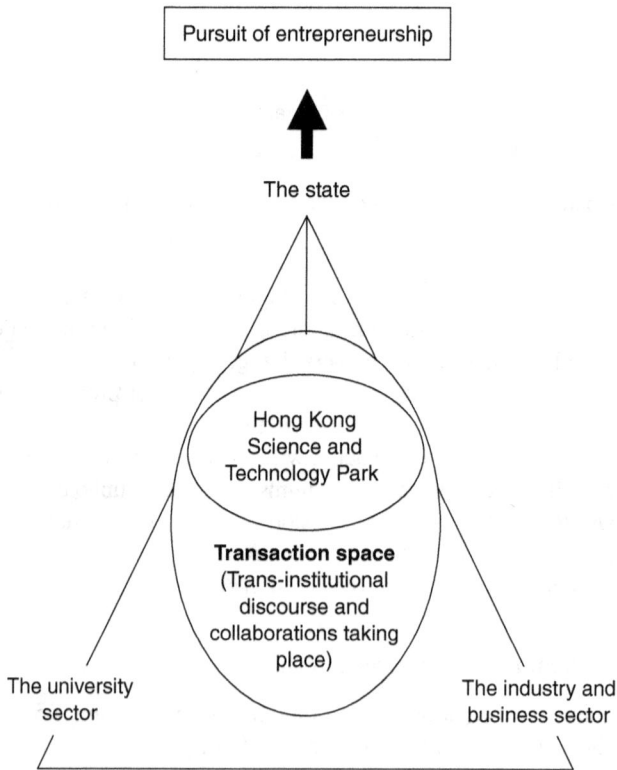

Figure 6.2 Triple-helix government-university-industry/business network system in fostering entrepreneurship.

process...in an asymmetrical way, the university through these institutional innovations is also co-constitutive of its industrial environment' (Leydesdroff and Etzkowitz 2001, p. 7) (see Figure 6.2).

Unlike the old days when the economy was prosperous, the HKSAR could bear the primary responsibility to finance activities in the university sector; the fiscal deficit crisis that the Hong Kong society is now facing has driven the HKSAR to cut back its financial subsidies to the university sector. In order to generate additional financial resources, coupled with the need to work closely with the business and industry to advance technology and promote innovation, the university sector and the business and industry in Hong Kong have engaged in closer collaborations by exploring business opportunities through commercializing research results. Hence, a better understanding of the HKSAR's role in fostering entrepreneurship in the city-state could be obtained by examining the triple-helix of network system of the government, the university, and the business and the industry. Being a part of the network, the government plays the role of coordinator and facilitator to engage the university, and the business and industry in fostering entrepreneurship. By setting up the Hong Kong Science and Technology Park as the "transaction space" between the government, the university, and the business and industry to transfer technology and innovation into commercial opportunities, the triple-helix government-university-industry/business network system can facilitate entrepreneurial activities in the city-state (see Figure 6.2). Having discussed the conceptual framework in analyzing changing government-university-business-industry relations, let us now turn to what strategies that the HKSAR in general and local universities in particular have adopted in promoting entrepreneurial spirit and practise in Hong Kong.

The government role in fostering entrepreneurship

When comparing and contrasting the role of the government or state intervention in the economy of Hong Kong with other Asian societies like Taiwan, South Korea, and Japan, the government of Hong Kong is believed to be the least interventionist in the world (Haggard and Chen 1987; Patrick 1991). Hong Kong's success, in the eyes of a neoclassical economist, is mainly attributed to an "automatic corrective mechanism...alters internal costs and prices to bring [the economy] quickly into line with costs and prices in the rest of the world" (Rabushka 1979, p. 2). During the colonial period, particularly under the regime of Sir Hadde-Cave, the ex-financial secretary in the 1970s, and the key architects of the Hong Kong economic miracle were closely related to the government's philosophy of positive noninterventionism. According to Sir Hadde-Cave, the colonial government had few obligations such as controlling the foreign exchange market and banking system, forming industrial and economic advisory broads, and providing essential services such as social welfare, education, medical services, etc. (Chung 1992). Apart from creating a favorable business environment, the government very much depends upon individual firms' initiatives to promote entrepreneurial activities.

Believing that Hong Kong's entrepreneurs have always, and still are, noted for their considerable business acumen and ability to "strike a good deal," the HKSAR has attempted to protect its entrepreneurial environment and the major role of the government is to create a conducive business environment for fostering entrepreneurial activities. According to Hau (2001), much of the entrepreneurial spirit in Hong Kong comes from Hong Kong's strong belief of the following four "frees," namely, first, free flow of information; second, free movement of people; third, free and efficient flow of funds; and fourth, free port with free flow of goods (p. 5). It is to Hong Kong's credit that its free market philosophy has earned her a reputation of being a world trade and financial center. Openly recognizing that the success of Hong Kong rests very much upon its low and simple tax system, an excellent regulatory framework, and the rule of law upheld by an independent judiciary; an ideal geographical location of where the city-state lies also provides the HKSAR further miles for development (Chua 2003), the HKSAR firmly acknowledges the significant role of small and medium enterprises in its economy. Its numerous initiatives and programs are based on a manifesto of creating:

> A favourable business environment, including a stable macro economy, a simple and clear tax regime with low tax rate, good infrastructure, ample supply of human resources, a culture which encourages application of technologies, as well as a sound legal system to protect individual rights and intellectual properties. With a favourable business environment and minimum necessary regulation, small and medium enterprises will be able to operate freely and realize their full potential.... The aim is to strike a balance between maximum support and minimum intervention.
> (Hong Kong Government 2001, cited in Chua 2003, p. 11)

Honoring the principle of "positive noninterventionism," the government sees its role as that of a facilitator, coordinator, and enabler instead of intervening in the market. Assuming the role as "coordinator" and "facilitator," the HKSAR provides a very efficient public administration to enable people to start up business in Hong Kong in a simple way. Simplified procedures and responsive government administration has been identified by Global Entrepreneurship Monitor (GEM) project (a project that develops an annual measurement of entrepreneurial activity by examining its link with economic growth and the factors that contribute to an entrepreneurial climate) as one of the strengths that promotes entrepreneurship in the city-state (Chua 2003). With the establishment of Invest Hong Kong, a government office responsible for supplying latest information on Hong Kong's business environment; delivering government information on funding and other support, taxation, import/export regulations, employment legislation, and immigration requirements; identifying and matching potential investors with business partners; assisting investors in dealing with government departments on setting up business in the city-state, such initiatives show the HKSAR's attempts to create a favorable environment for entrepreneurial activities (www.investhk.gov.hk).

In addition, the HKSAR takes the lead in providing a physical infrastructure for business and industry development. The strengths of the physical infrastructure in Hong Kong include excellent telecommunications, efficient and international airport, and good transport and road systems, one of the largest containers terminals in the world and free port status. The setting up of the Hong Kong Science and Technology Park in 2001 further provides a "one-stop" infrastructure support services for technology-based companies (www.atip.org). In order to facilitate small and medium enterprises to set up business in Hong Kong, the HKSAR also offers business advisory services such as trade consulting, offering accounting, marketing, management, and legal advisory services through the Hong Kong Applied Science and Technology Research Institute Company, Ltd., the Hong Kong Productivity Council, the Trade Development Council, and the Vocational Training Council (Chua 2003). After discussing some general principles that the HKSAR has adhered to promote entrepreneurial spirit and practice, let us now examine how the HKSAR shapes industry policy, funding policy in technology and innovation advancement, and education policy to make the policy environment more conducive in fostering entrepreneurialism.

Industry policy

Openly acknowledging the importance of developing a value-adding high-tech plank to the economy, Tung made his position clear in his 1998 policy address *From Adversity to Opportunities* that "innovation and technology are important drivers of economic growth. In a technology-based global economy, they are essential in adding value, increasing productivity, and empowering our overall competition" (www.policyaddress.gov.hk.1998). In order to nurture the development of technology and entrepreneurship in Hong Kong, the government set up the Innovation and Technology Commission to advise the government in long-term strategies for technology development and established a science park as a vehicle to foster further technology development in the city-state (www.atip.org.public/atip.reports.98). In the first policy address of his second term as chief executive of the HKSAR in January 2003, Mr Tung highlighted three major measures for revitalizing the local economy, such as promoting economic restructuring, forging closer economic cooperation with the mainland, and eliminating the fiscal deficit. According to Tung, "the knowledge and wisdom of Hong Kong people, their innovative entrepreneurial spirit and agility combine to form a sound foundation for the development of creative industries" (www.policyaddress.gov.hk). Treasuring the entrepreneurial spirit and wisdom of Hong Kong citizens, the HKSAR Government adheres to its long-standing economic philosophy of providing maximum support to industry and minimum intervention in the market. According to the Trade and Industry Bureau of the HKSAR, Hong Kong's success relies very much on its dynamic private sector. Hong Kong firms are renowned for their entrepreneurial dynamism and their international character. With a productive and adaptable workforce, together with the continual investment in higher education turning out high quality and capable graduates, Hong Kong has developed itself as one of the major business centers in Asia. Capitalizing on the robust research culture in its universities and the vibrant and well-developed capital market, the HKSAR has played the role as "promoter" by signaling to industry and the community at large the relevance and importance of innovation and technology to Hong Kong. The Trade and Industry Bureau makes it clear that the government should play the role of a facilitator and supporter in promotion of entrepreneurship by the following strategies like:

- making essential investments in the physical, human, and technological infrastructure;
- creating a business environment conducive to innovation and technology development, commercialization, and use;
- providing policy encouragement and incentives;
- coordinating industrial and business efforts; and
- providing financial support where appropriate.

(www.info.gov.hktib/roles/first/chap4)

Moreover, the Innovation and Technology Commission also recommends that the role of the government in promoting innovation and technology should be as a promoter, facilitator, and supporter in the following areas:

- strengthening technological infrastructure and promoting technological entrepreneurship;
- building up human capital to meet the needs of a fast-changing, knowledge-based economy;
- enhancing technological collaboration with the mainland;
- fostering university and industry partnership; and
- lowering information, financing, and regulatory barriers.

(Innovative and Technology Commission 2004)

Measures in promoting innovation and technology advancement

In addition to the strategies outlined earlier the HKSAR Government has created the following funds to encourage entrepreneurship, such as:

- *Special Finance Scheme for Small and Medium Enterprises (SMEs)*: a fund scheme set up to assist SMEs cope with liquidity crunch problem. Under the Scheme, the government provides guarantees to facilitate SMEs to secure bank financing from participating lending institutions;
- An *Applied Research Fund* was set up to encourage technology ventures that have commercial potential;
- The other fund is *Innovation and Technology Fund* which supports projects that contribute to innovation and technology upgrading in local industry as well as those that contribute to the upgrading and development of the local industry.

(Hau 2001)

The Innovation and Technology Commission has few more programs to foster innovation and technology development in particular and in promoting entrepreneurship in general. For instance, the "Support for Research and Development" program is to promote and support applied research and development activities, which can contribute to innovation and technology upgrading in industry. Another program entitled "University-Industry Collaboration Programme" (UICP) has a principal goal to promote university-industry partnership in R&D projects. It aims to stimulate private sector interest in R&D through leveraging the knowledge and resources of universities. The emphasis is on close collaboration between private companies and universities in Hong Kong. Under this particular program, there are three major schemes. First, "Teaching Company Scheme," a scheme specially designed to support local companies to take on graduate students pursuing a higher degree in local universities to assist in proprietary R&D work. The participating parties of the scheme will each bear half of the fees for the graduate students. Second, "Matching Grant for Joint Research" aims to foster university-industry collaboration in R&D projects. The grant will cover half of the cost incurred by the university in the project including manpower, equipment, and other direct expenditures relating to the project. Last but not the least, "Industrial Research Chair Scheme" is developed to support research efforts of universities and industries in technology fields that are not yet developed in Hong Kong but for which there would be good development potential. If such potential research areas are identified, a distinguished researcher from the university will be invited to be the chair-holder to lead the project for a finite duration (www.itf.gov.hk).

Other funding programs under the Innovation and Technology Fund framework are "Promotion of Technological Entrepreneurship," offering financial support to promote technological entrepreneurship and providing essential support to technology-based entrepreneurial activities. "General Support Program" aims to support projects that contribute to fostering an innovation and technology culture, while "Small Entrepreneur Research Assistance Program" is to help small, technology-based and entrepreneur-driven companies carry out business-oriented research in the preventure capital state. Putting all these financial support schemes or programs together, we may well argue that the HKSAR has performed the role as "facilitator" by offering research grant or financial support to promote technological advancement and entrepreneurial activities in the city-state. With such policies related to innovation and technology development in place, the government intends to create a conducive environment for private firms and the industrial sector to directly engage in the development of technology. Instead of actively intervening in the sector, the HKSAR has chosen the role of a facilitator or an enabler in promoting entrepreneurship.

Education policy

When reflecting upon the role of the HKSAR in higher education, we must examine the policy directions recommended by the University Grants Committee (UGC), a statutory body responsible for advising the government on higher education policy and development. In 1996, the UGC conducted a comprehensive review of the higher education system in Hong Kong, clearly specifying the objectives for research in post-1998 period. The first is to ensure that academics and students in Hong Kong's higher education institutions (HEIs) are participants in the global endeavor to extend human understanding by engaging in pure research. The research findings can be communicated to the international academic communities and be published in internationally recognized journals. The second objective for research, according to UGC, is to "increase the proportion of work which is linked with the interests of the community and to carry out more of it with local partners, both active and passive." With the recent introduction by the HKSAR of funding for applied research and collaborative projects between universities and industry, the UGC strongly encourages all HEIs to develop closer collaborations with the industrial sector and local communities. Believing that the symbiosis between the HEIs and the community should not be confined only to industry and commerce, the UGC advocates that a closer relationship should exist between the government at all levels and social and other services (www.ugc.hk/HERVW/Chapte28, p. 2).

Intending to make its universities more competitive in the global marketplace, the HKSAR appointed an overseas consultant to conduct another comprehensive review of the higher education system and the review report was published in March 2002. Attempting to position Hong Kong's university sector in a higher position in the international academic community, the UGC again urges the HEIs to establish closer links with the local industry and community. Applied research and commercialization of research products are highly encouraged. The UGC believes that it will be in very rare cases that an area of excellence will be externally generated. Instead, an area of excellence will gradually develop and emerge when government or a private sponsor recognizes a teaching or research need of pressing importance to Hong Kong and therefore the UGC keeps on encouraging the HEIs to explore external funding other than the UGC research grants. Strengthening the relationships between the HEIs and the government and local industry will certainly extend the pool of research money (www.ugc.edu.hk/HERVW/Chapte29, p. 2; UGC 2002, p. 36). Hence, the UGC recommends setting up a working group with representatives from the government, the private sector, the HEIs, the UGC, and the Research Grants Council (RGC) to review the existing policies in R&D investment policies in Hong Kong. Throughout his first term of appointment as chief executive, Mr Tung Chee-hwa, repeatedly emphasized the importance being attached to cultivate talents and his administration in the previous years had put education and human resource investment on top of its political agenda. It clearly shows the HKSAR's strong commitment in human resource investment, believing the nurturing of high quality people as fundamental to the future success of Hong Kong.

The role of the university sector in fostering entrepreneurship

Universities engaging in commercialization of research results

In order to adapt to the changing environment as discussed earlier, universities in Hong Kong have begun to reflect upon their roles in the newly emerging knowledge economy. Realizing the changing policy environment and encountering globalization challenges, universities have begun to change the way that they are managed and some of the UGC funded universities in Hong Kong have begun to adopt a proactive approach in promoting entrepreneurial spirit and practice. The Hong Kong University of Science and Technology (HKUST) Faculty Entrepreneurship Program (FEP) was introduced to assist faculty, staff, and students in establishing technology-based start-up companies. The major objective of the FEP is, to fulfill one of the missions of the HKUST, to promote entrepreneurial activities for the benefit of the Hong Kong economy and society. Intending to promote academic entrepreneurship, the HKUST has taken a few measures, including setting a Technology Transfer Center to serve as a bridge between the university and the business community; the foundation of Engineering Industrial Consortium to establish industrial contacts and cooperation, to organize professional development and training programs, to build collaborative research activities and to promote technology diffusion. A few more units were set up by the HKUST to strengthen its research and development (R&D) and to promote commercialization of research results, services, and technology development, including Applied Technology Center and Entrepreneurship Center. Another unit, HKUST R&D Corporation Limited was set up in 1993 as a commercial entity within the university to provide full exploitation of the commercial opportunities arising from research conducted not only at HKUST but worldwide in fields vital to Hong Kong's economic prosperity. The aim of the Corporation is to nurture a true entrepreneurial spirit by forging a partnership between the business and academic communities (HKUST website).

Similarly, City University of Hong Kong (CityU) has set up a Technology Transfer Office (TTO) as the technology-marketing arm of the university to reach out to the industrial and business communities. Intending to transfer the advanced technologies and know-how of CityU into commercial products in order to enhance the competitiveness and development of local industries in Hong Kong, the TTO set up a CityU Business & Industrial Club to strengthen the links between the university and the industrial as well as business sectors in Hong Kong. In addition, CityU also set up its commercial arm CityU Enterprises to commercialize its research results. In recent years, CityU has also successfully developed and marketed the "TeleEye Long Distance Monitoring System," and the trading of TeleEye shares marks a significant milestone in the development of CityU, the first HEI in Hong Kong to successfully nurture a technology company from start-up to public listing. Moreover, commercialization of research results has attracted investors to support BonVision Technology (HK) Limited, e. Energy Technology Limited, and Warren Health Technologies Limited, three subsidiary companies under CityU Enterprises. According to H.Y. Wong, director of CityU's TTO, technology transfer and product development certainly enables academics to convert their research results into commercial products, the transformation of which has brought additional incomes for the university (TTO, City University of Hong Kong website). In order to extend its research and development arm to mainland China, CityU established its applied R&D centers in Shenzhen and Zhuhai, capturing opportunities to transfer its applied research results into business and commercialized products (CityU website).

Like HKUST and CityU, PolyU Technology & Consultancy Company, Limited (PTeC) was also set up by the Hong Kong Polytechnic University (PolyU) to serve as the professional arm of the university to offer fresh ideas and leverage business plans toward higher productivity and competitiveness through rapport of the PolyU and its alliance institutions. Poly U has established an Enterprise Development Center to promote more collaboration with medium and small-sized enterprises in Hong Kong. Through the deployment of a team of over 1,000 dedicated and talented academic staff from its academic departments and research centers, the PTeC offers a large range of services, including consultancy services, contract research, laboratory testing, surveys and studies, system design and improvement, product design and development, technology development and transfer, and commercialization of technologies. To further enhance its capacity to provide a wide range of research, development, and consultancy services, the PolyU also establishes International Strategic Alliance (ISTA) comprising 18 member universities representing major academic and applied research strengths in China, the United Kingdom, and the United States. In 2001/02 fiscal alone, PTeC made a notable growth in its business activities and generated a total of HK$57 million (PolyU website).

Considering that there are three streams of research, namely, "upstream" research refers to curiosity-driven, experimental and theoretical work aimed at advancing the frontiers of human knowledge, "midstream" and "downstream" that refer to research projects linked to further technological development and commercialization purposes, the University of Hong Kong, the oldest university in the territory, is now committed to broadening the scope of its research to encompass applied research and developmental work by working in close partnership with industry to bring about direct benefit to the society of Hong Kong (HKU website). When we put the entrepreneurial activities of these universities into perspective, we may well argue that a culture of academic entrepreneurship is emerging among Hong Kong's universities, indicating that universities in Hong Kong are experiencing a second academic revolution.

Table 6.1 shows the first and second academic revolution in the university sector, indicating that contemporary universities have expanded their mission

Table 6.1 Academic revolutions and changing university missions

Expansion of university mission

Teaching	Research	Entrepreneurial
Preserving and disseminating knowledge	First academic revolution	Second academic revolution
New missions generate conflict of interest controversies	Two missions: teaching and research	Third mission: economic and social development; old missions continued

Source: Adapted from Etzkowitz 2003, p. 110.

from purely research and teaching to the third mission of making universities more entrepreneurial in nature to promote economic and social development. Capitalizing on the opportunities for additional research and development grants offered by the HKSAR, more collaboration has been forged between the local industry, business sector, and the community. Charts 1 and 2 indicate the amount offered by the Innovation and Technology Fund to various parties, showing the triple-helix relationship between the government, the university, and the industry/business sector has become increasingly popular in the promotion of entrepreneurship and academic entrepreneurialism in Hong Kong. In particular, with the formation of the Hong Kong Science and Technology Park, together with the Hong Kong Productivity Council and Hong Kong Technology Transfer Corporatization, such a collaboration relationship has been strengthened particularly when the Hong Kong Science and Technology Park now offers good venues as "transaction space" to foster collaborations and cooperation between the universities and the industry and commercial sector (see Figures 6.3 and 6.4).

Universities reforming curricula in fostering entrepreneurship

In addition to the entrepreneurial activities being conducted in the field of research and commercializing research results into business opportunities,

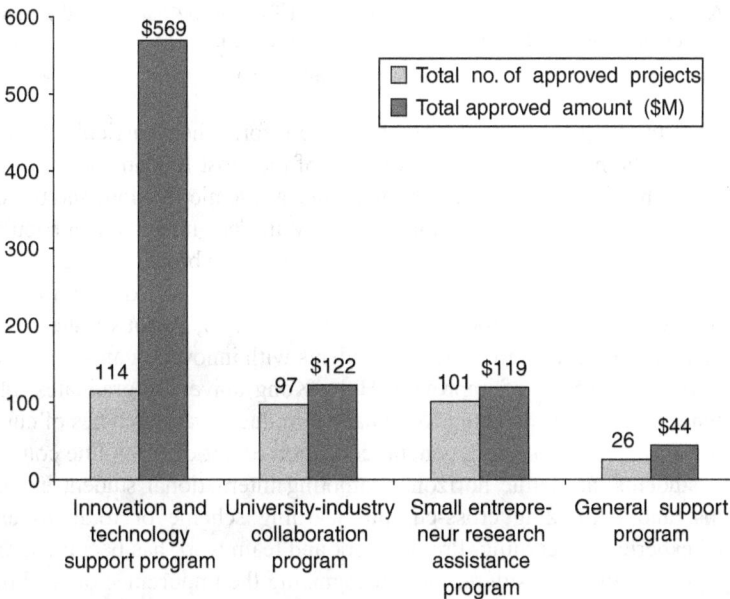

Figure 6.3 Number of approved projects and funding under individual programs (Position as at December 31, 2002).

Source: Adapted from Innovation and Technology Committee 2002, p. 14.

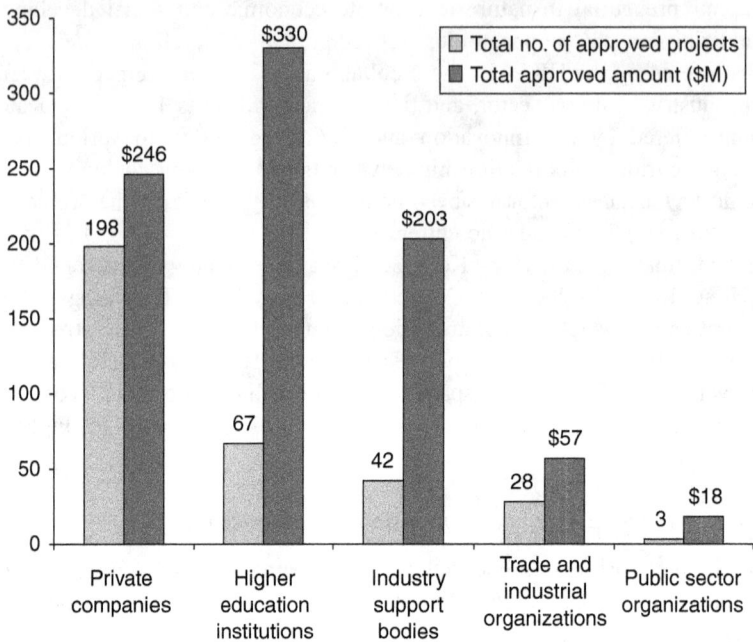

Figure 6.4 Breakdown of the approved projects and funding by nature of the recipient organizations (Position as at December 31, 2002).

Source: Adapted from Innovation and Technology Committee 2002, p. 15.

universities in Hong Kong have also started to reform their curricula design by making students more market sensitive. One of the most fundamental principles that HKSAR has long adhered to is to guarantee academic freedom and therefore universities are given flexibility and autonomy in designing their curricula. In order to create more room for university students to have a broad-based curriculum, the HKSAR is actively considering how to convert the existing three-year university education into a four-year system (*Ming Pao*, various issues in May and June 2003). Believing in nurturing students with innovation and creativity as very important elements of improving Hong Kong university graduates' global competence, universities in Hong Kong have introduced various types of curriculum reforms, including offering general education or out-of-discipline courses to broaden students' academic horizon, promoting international student exchange programs, and organizing cross-cultural learning scheme or tours to enrich students' experiential learning. Project work and team work has become increasingly popular with university teachers recognizing the importance of working in teams and working independently. In recent years, students have been given more choices in courses and they can develop their own study plan by choosing electives, minors, and majors. Double majors programs are made possible in some of the universities such as the University of Hong Kong and the HKUST.[1]

Intending to make Hong Kong students more cosmopolitan and international, the UGC designates additional resources for promoting international student exchange programs between local and overseas university. Bringing students to the real world is also another dimension that universities in Hong Kong have been working on by taking students to professional attachment schemes, summer internship programs, study tours, industrial attachment projects, etc. in order to prepare them for the real world/work environments. Intending to move beyond the "teacher-oriented" to a "learner-oriented" paradigm, some universities in Hong Kong have begun to organize "whole-person development schemes" to fully maximize students' potential and train them as future leaders in the local community.[2] As in Singapore, the UGC has started to review the university admissions systems and new changes have already been introduced in recruiting not only students with high public examination scores but also students of different talents (UGC 2002b). All in all, the teaching and learning strategies discussed earlier have clearly shown that universities in Hong Kong have already taken a proactive approach in coping with the globalization challenges by making their students more sensitive to changes, preparing them for becoming more innovative and creative, and engaging them in fostering entrepreneurship.

Other market-driven activities

Realizing that depending upon the state funding alone can never be sufficient to establish all universities in Hong Kong as world class universities, the UGC has adopted the principles of "selectivity" to identify a few institutions and areas of excellence for providing them with additional funding for further development. Performance-based assessment is becoming increasingly prominent in funding methodology. The UGC makes its position very clear that "all education in all countries is expensive and occupies a substantial part of national budgets. But higher education is particularly costly." The policy of raising fees has been adopted by the UGC whereas the Hong Kong government has set the minimum fee level in subvented universities to recover 18 percent of costs from 1997 onward. In addition to the increase in tuition fees, another noticeable change is the reform in the grants/loans system. Under the new scheme, more loans will be given to students instead of committing a huge amount of government funds on student grants.

In recent years, the UGC has begun to cut back its subsidies to all UGC-funded universities; self-financing programs and courses are launched in Hong Kong. For instance, the UGC has decided to gradually withdraw its funding to nearly all taught master programs, students who are interested in postgraduate taught programs have to pay full fees now. In order to "balance the book," universities in Hong Kong have to venture themselves in the education market by developing sources which can appeal to the public, market forces are certainly shaping the design of curricula and the academic plans in the university sector in Hong Kong. Distance courses, conversion courses corun by local and overseas universities and continuing education programs such as Master of Business Administration and Law courses are being offered by local institutions on a self-financing basis. In addition, continuing education is considered one of the major sources of additional incomes, all universities in Hong Kong have set up their community colleges or continuing education units to offer programs to cater for the market needs (Mok and Tan 2004).

In addition, the Hong Kong government has set up a "matching grant scheme" for rewarding universities who manage to raise additional funds from other nonstate sources. Every dollar that universities raise will be matched with the same amount of funds from the UGC to encourage universities to diversify funding sources. Nowadays, every UGC funded university in Hong Kong has established a "Committee of Donation" to raise funds. Many of the universities' campus facilities are financially supported by the third sector. For instance, the new student hostels in CityU are fully sponsored by the Hong Kong Jockey Club and Hong Kong Shanghai Banking Corporation. For traditional universities in Hong Kong such as the University of Hong Kong, the oldest university and the Chinese University of Hong Kong, the second oldest university in Hong Kong, their networks with the industry, business, and the commercial fields should have enabled them to secure additional funds to attract additional funds from the newly established "matching grants;" while the newly established universities such as City University of Hong Kong and Baptist University of Hong Kong would encounter difficulties in fund raising.

All in all, the strategies and measures adopted by the universities in Hong Kong to strengthen their financial position has indicated how prominent the use of market principles and market strategies are in the administration of higher education. By encouraging universities, to become entrepreneurial universities, and establishing and strengthening their relationships with other nonstate actors, universities in Hong Kong have now become more engaged with the business and industrial sectors. Notions of "public-private partnership," "academic capitalism," and "entrepreneurial universities" are becoming more common in the Hong Kong higher education sector (Mok 2003c).

Hong Kong as "market facilitating state" in fostering entrepreneurship

In the globalization literature, there has been an argument that the state is being killed off during the globalization processes. Considering that social, economic, and political issues are becoming far more complicated that modern states may not have the capacity to tackle it, there has been a phenomenon of state denial and modern states are seen to be declining. State denial hypotheses have evolved, including the "collapse of the welfare state" and the "death of industrial policy" to the "end of national diversity" and the "demise of the nation-state" (Weiss 1998, p. 3). Opposing the view that modern states are weakened in the context of globalization, some scholars argue quite contrarily that modern states may become more proactive and activist states by adopting adjustment strategies and changing governance modes in response to the changing socioeconomic and sociopolitical environments (Rodrik 1997; Hinnfors and Pierre 1998; Weiss 1998; Held 2000; Dale and Robertson 2002; Mok 2003c). In order to maintain the competitiveness of modern states in the new social, economic, and political environment, new forms of governance and new governance philosophies have emerged and fundamental transformations have taken place in public policy instruments and public management (Faulk 2000; Lane and Ersson 2002).

Theories of "new governance" propose that modern governments are adapting to radical changes in their environments by turning to new forms of governance which are "more society-centered" and focus on "co-ordination and self-governance" (Pierre 2000, pp. 2–6). Peters (1995) highlights four governance models as alternatives to the traditional system, namely, the market model, the participatory state model, the flexible government model, and deregulated government model. Central to these governance models is to involve sectors other than the state like the market, the society, and other nonstate sectors in governing the public domain. Networks and partnerships supplant hierarchical command and control (Rhodes 1997, 2000); in the delivery of services, public authority is shared between governments and with nongovernment actors—what Salomon (2002, p. 2) calls "third party government"; services are decentralized and in some cases privatized; and the role of governments in managing the economy is more sharply delineated and circumscribed by new arm's length (from government) market-supporting instruments, in some cases relying on self-regulation (Gamble 2000, pp. 130–31; Jayasurya 2001). Many possible causes have been highlighted: ideological changes such as the discrediting of "statist" models; fiscal and bureaucratic "overload" problems; the growth in supranational bodies that undermine a government's control; and economic globalization eroding state "steering capacities."

In recent years, pressures for broad governance changes have been strong, especially coming to a head during the financial crisis of 1997. A feature of these pressures is the presence of influential international agencies such as the IMF and World Bank. Their preferred models of governance reflect many of the same tendencies noted earlier: a less interventionist and arbitrary state; a strengthening of "juridical" forms of regulation (often associated with fundamental legal reform); more disaggregated and decentralized forms of government, including partnerships and a stronger "co-production" role for civil society groups; and a preference for market-like mechanisms over bureaucratic methods of service delivery. Hence, it is not surprising that strategies, measures, and policy instruments along the line of marketization, corporatization, commodification, and managerialization are becoming popular practices in public policy and public management (Minogue 1998; Lane and Ersson 2002; Mok and Welch 2003).

Analyzing the triple-helix government-university-industry/business network systems discussed earlier in light of the new governance theories, we may find that the role of the government may not necessarily be weakened. Picking up the thread of developmental state theory, a theory that tries to account for the success of the rapid economic growth in East and Southeast Asia by incorporating an important statist component in analysis, we may realize that the role of the state has never been confined to the economic sphere. Taking the case of Hong Kong as an example, the government has long been providing a certain level of social policy or social services in stabilizing the society and creating a favorable

136 *Globalization and national response*

environment for business and entrepreneurial activities. This kind of "managed welfare capitalism" or "productivist welfare capitalism" found in the region is a very important variable accounting for the success of Hong Kong (Holliday 2000; Holliday and Wilding 2003). Moreover, the government in Hong Kong has for long worked closely with the nonstate sectors, including the market and the community to promote entrepreneurship. Judging from what the government has done to create the favorable policy environment for doing business and trade in Hong Kong discussed earlier we may argue that the state does have significant steering capacities in fostering entrepreneurialism in the city-state (Schiffer 1983; Harris 1986; Chung 1992).

Despite the fact that globalization forces have considerably challenged the state in Hong Kong in recent years, our discussion earlier has indicated that the HKSAR has played a significant role in promoting entrepreneurialism by extending its network system and involving nongovernment actors in entrepreneurial activities. By transforming its governance mode through the revitalization of the university, and the business and industry sector in commercializing R&D, the role of HKSAR is becoming increasingly one of coordination and steering rather than command. The process of governance change can be interpreted as part of a state strategy for retaining and enhancing policy control instead of weakening the state role in public policy domain. Enacting the role of a "market facilitating state," the HKSAR has somehow resolved its own fiscal deficit problem by accelerating the market and other social forces to promote entrepreneurial activities. By making use of the market ideas and mechanisms, the HKSAR has engaged the university, the industry, and the business sector to accelerate entrepreneurial spirit and practice. Such a governing through governance process has indeed pulled more resources from different nonstate sectors together not only to develop research and development but also to promote entrepreneurship.

Conclusion

This chapter has discussed how and what strategies that the HKSAR has adopted in fostering entrepreneurship in the city-state. Our earlier discussion has highlighted that the HKSAR has chosen to act as a "coordinator" in terms of providing macro policy framework and a "facilitator" or "enabler" role in offering start-up grants in support of R&D and the promotion of entrepreneurialism. Strengthening the partnerships and coalitions between the university, and the business and industry, the HKSAR can steer the development of innovation and technology advancement in particular and foster entrepreneurship in general from a distance. Governing through governance by involving other nonstate sectors and actors in providing and financing technology and innovation advancement and promoting entrepreneurial activities has certainly enhanced the state to become a more "competition state" in the increasingly competitive global market. The triple-helix government-university-business-industry network system could be interpreted as the state's governing strategy to steer economic development from a distance. Most important of all, our earlier discussion also reaches the conclusion that the coalitional relationship between the government, the university, and the business and industry may have made the state more proactive and activist rather than reducing the state steering capacities. In conclusion, the coalitional or partnership relations between the state, the university, and the industry/business sector, when strengthened and made closer, will certainly promote not only entrepreneurship but also the advancement of research and development in Hong Kong.

7 Singapore's response to globalization

Marketization of higher education

Policy context of Singapore higher education

As in the case of Hong Kong, Singapore's higher education policy and development have been affected by socioeconomic changes generated from external and internal environments. Being a small city-state and an open economy, Singapore has never isolated itself from changes resulting from globalization challenges. The ruling People's Action Party (PAP) has consistently made the whole society well aware of potential challenges and threats in both the regional and global contexts (Quah 1999).

In order to compete with global advanced economies such as Japan, the United Kingdom, and the United States, in June 1997, the Prime Minister Goh Chok Tong announced *Thinking Schools, Learning Nation*, a blueprint for reforming the education system in Singapore. The concept of "thinking schools" entails education institutions developing future citizens who will be capable of engaging in critical and creative thinking. The concept of "learning nation" emphasizes that education is a continuum starting with the early childhood years and continuing throughout one's life. Education reforms require a change in mindset among Singaporeans to bring about a spirit of innovation, learning by doing, and self-improvement in order to achieve the ambition of national excellence (Goh 1997). Realizing that future economic competitiveness depends very much upon creativity and innovation, the Singapore government is attempting to change people's mindsets through the reform of its education system. Therefore, various government initiatives have been developed to promote independent thinking skills and creative expression in recent years (FitzPatrick 2003).

In 1999, the Singapore government published a report entitled Singapore 21: Together, We Make the Difference, highlighting how the island-state might cope with the emergence of the knowledge economy in the twenty-first century. In the borderless knowledge economy, knowledge and information are fast changing. A lot more brain than brawn is required for work, and a lifelong learning is essential for human resources (Singapore Government 1999, pp. 9–10). The Singapore government has identified globalization and information technology revolution as the two driving forces behind the changes in the new century. Besides the increased flows of trade and investment, globalization is also about the flows of people, ideas, and knowledge. Globalization is not a choice but a necessity. It means new markets and increased investments and opportunities. Education plays an important role in preparing citizens to manage the impact of globalization. At the same time, the government envisages the need to prepare workers and the next generation for lifelong learning and employability (Goh 1999). On the other hand, the forces of globalization challenge the powers of government as civic groups and nongovernmental organizations will want to play a bigger role in governance. With the advent of the knowledge economy, skills, creativity, and entrepreneurship will command a premium. Education has to be relevant to the needs of society by bestowing upon the younger generation their culture and heritage in addition to their capacity to understand the complexities and the potential of globalization in order to compete and live in the global village (Goh 2000).

Apart from the globalization impacts and the potential pressures generated from the regional environment, Singapore's higher education developments have been affected by the wider public sector management reforms taking place in the city-state. The Public Service for the 21st Century (PS21) project, a reform package aimed at reinventing the public administration of Singapore, has been started by the government to pursue total organizational excellence in public service, to foster a culture of innovation and enterprise, and to cultivate a spirit of openness, responsiveness, and involvement (PS21 Office 2001). The most recent theme of this project is to cultivate a culture of entrepreneurialism among civil servants by making them aware of the importance of creativity and innovation (PS21 Office 2001). In addition, the Quality Movement has shaped higher education development in Singapore. SPRING Singapore, an institution responsible for promoting high quality services in Singapore, has been adopting market principles and practices to assure a high quality of services offered by both the private and public sectors. Organizations that can reach a certain quality benchmark will have their achievements recognized and certified by SPRING Singapore in the form of Singapore Quality Class awards (Mok 2003a). Hence, the latest higher education reforms and governance changes should be connected to the wider public sector reform and Quality Movement taking place in Singapore.

Most recent higher education reforms

Believing in the quality of its population as fundamental to further success of the city-state, the Singapore government has been aware of the importance of quality higher education. Since the late 1980s, the government has started various comprehensive reviews of its higher education system and different reform strategies have been adopted to strengthen and make higher education competitive in the regional and global contexts. The Singapore government believes universities have a strategic role in the dissemination, creation, and application of knowledge. With the ultimate aim of making the two existing public universities, the National University of Singapore (NUS) and the Nanyang Technological University (NTU), world-class higher education institutions (HEIs) and expand tertiary education opportunities for its citizens, there are two main policies for the future development of higher education in Singapore. One is to expand postgraduate education and research at the universities. Another is to review undergraduate curricula to place more emphasis on cultivating students with creativity and thinking skills. The ultimate goal of reforming university education is to transform Singapore into a hub of education, learning, and information in the Asia Pacific region (*The Straits Times* January 25, 1997). Apart from the restructuring of curricula, more emphasis has been placed on quality assurance and enhancement.

There have been three major stages of higher education reforms in recent years. The first stage was started by setting up an International Academic Advisory Panel (IAAP), comprising prominent scholars from international HEIs or community leaders from big corporations, to help the universities develop into world-class institutions in terms of teaching and research. Taking the recommendations made by the IAAP seriously, the government started to review its university admissions system by adopting a more flexible admissions policy (Ministry of Education 1999a). Moving beyond recruiting students based solely upon their academic scores, both the public universities announced in 1999 that they would henceforth pay attention to students' nonacademic performance and recognize their achievements in cocurricular activities and school-based project work.

In order to prepare and equip students for globalization challenges, the Singapore government has reviewed the curriculum design of university education and emphasis is now placed on a broad-based cross-disciplinary university education (*The Straits Times* August 13, 1999). More innovative ways of teaching and assessment have been introduced with a focus on creative and critical thinking. Meanwhile, the role of universities in knowledge creation has been strengthened through postgraduate and research education in the universities. Universities constitute a significant resource of new ideas and inventions with the potential for commercial applications by enhancing their research capabilities and engaging in more multi-disciplinary research initiatives (Lee and Gopinathan 2001).

The second stage of higher education reforms saw the establishment of Singapore's third university in August 2000. The privately owned Singapore Management University (SMU) was formed in collaboration with the Wharton School of Business at the University of Pennsylvania. The formation of the SMU was a landmark in Singapore's higher education history. By introducing different governance and funding style, the government intends to make its higher education sector more vibrant and dynamic. It also intends to inject a certain degree of "internal competition" into the university sector despite the fact that these three universities have been tasked to develop their own unique characteristics and niches (Lee and Gopinathan 2001).

The third stage of higher education reforms is closely related to the review of university governance and funding. With a very clear vision to make its higher education system comparable to top international universities, the government commissioned a committee to review the governance and funding systems of the two public universities (*The Straits Times* April 4, 1999). The purpose of such a review was to ensure systems and structures in relation to talent management; organizational processes and resource allocation within the universities were properly linked up to their mission and objectives of development in the long run. Overseas study trips to Hong Kong, Canada, the United Kingdom, and the United States were conducted in September 1999 to identify good practices in overseas universities (Ministry of Education 2000a).

The review committee released its recommendations on public university governance and funding in July 2000. In exchange for greater autonomy, the NUS and the NTU were urged to be more responsive in making timely decisions and adjustments in order to achieve excellence. At the same time, the universities had to put in place systems and structures of talent management, organizational processes, and resource allocation to achieve the highest value for money and rates of return from public investment in university education. In short, given further operational autonomy, the universities had to adhere to the principle of greater accountability to ensure an efficient and effective way of spending public funds. Three broad areas of governance principles and structures, funding policies and mechanisms, and staff management and remuneration were covered in the review. In order to foster an entrepreneurial climate and to leave more room for the institutions to manage their funds, the universities were urged to recruit and reward their staff according to their performance in terms of productivity and quality (Ministry of Education 2000b). In 2003, the Trade and Industry Ministry announced it would consider allowing a fourth university to be set up as a branch campus of a foreign university.

As discussed in the previous chapters, the Singapore government has engaged in a "partnership" with a few major world class universities in offering undergraduate education not only for local Singaporeans but also for other nationals in the region. Aspiring to become a regional hub of higher education and professional training, the Singapore government is committed to look for ways to improve its higher education to make the city-state one of the most important higher education centers in the world (Lee 2003b; Mok and Tan 2004).

Changing governance in Singapore higher education

Provision

Higher education enrollments in Singapore have expanded since the 1960s. In 1965, 3 and 2 percent of the relevant age cohort gained admission to local universities and polytechnics respectively. By 1989, 14 percent of the primary one cohort was enrolled in local universities while 17 percent received education in the polytechnics. The 1990s saw a massification process taking place in Singapore's higher education. The university enrollment rate grew at a relatively stable pace and rose to 21 percent in 1999. The polytechnic enrollment rate increased very rapidly by 15 percent within five years to 32 percent in 1993 and then steadily to 38 percent in 1999 (Singapore Department of Statistics 2000, p. 62). Since the mid-1990s, about 60 percent of secondary school graduates have enrolled in both the university and polytechnic sectors. Figures 7.1 and 7.2 show recent university enrollment rates and enrollment figures.

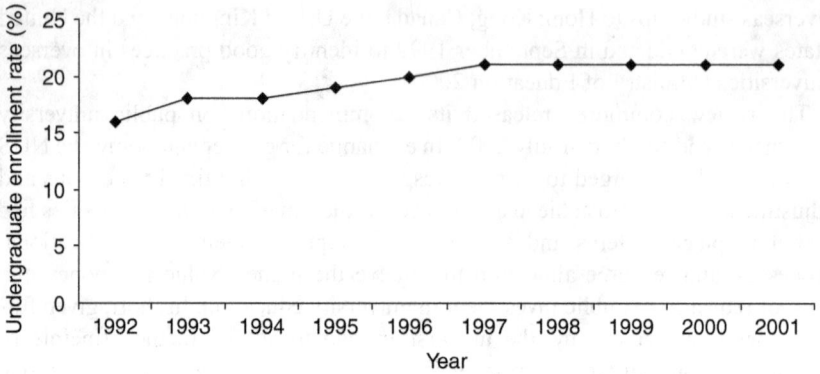

Figure 7.1 Undergraduate education enrollment rates in Singapore.

Source: Lee 2003a, pp. 280–81; Singapore Department of Statistics 1998, 1999, 2000, 2001, 2002.

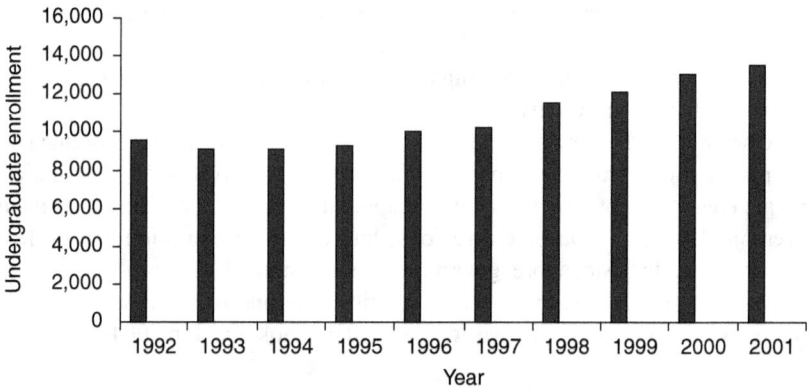

Figure 7.2 Full-time undergraduate education enrollments in Singapore.

Source: Lee 2003a, pp. 280–81; Singapore Department of Statistics 1998, 1999, 2000, 2001, 2002.

Such high participation rates in higher education is comparable with most developed countries such as the United Kingdom, France, the Netherlands, Germany, Italy, New Zealand, and Japan, where gross enrollment ratios range between 40 and 60 percent (World Bank 2000). The Singapore government has decided to raise the cohort participation rate in universities to 25 percent by the year 2010 (Ministry of Education 2003). In other words, the annual intakes into local and overseas full-time first-year first-degree programs will be increased from about 10,000 to 15,000 by 2010 (*The Straits Times Weekly Edition* April 28, 2001). One point that deserves particular attention is the role that the Singapore government has played in higher education provision. Before 2000, the government had basically monopolized higher education provision in Singapore since universities and polytechnics were primarily state funded. As in the case of

Hong Kong, the role of the private sector in higher education provision had been minimal, with only a few offshore campuses being set up by overseas reputable universities in Singapore for training purposes. This picture changed when the SMU was formed in 2000.

In order to encourage competition and avoid wasteful duplication, the three universities have been urged to develop their own unique characteristics and niches. While the NUS and the NTU perform their roles as comprehensive universities, the SMU is supposed to serve the business and service sectors of the local economy. There is supposed to be enough room for individual universities to develop their own areas of excellence, whereas a certain degree of inter-institutional competition can improve the quality of university education as a whole (Teo 2000).

The setting up of a private university aroused discussions and debates on whether the existing public universities ought to be privatized. There has been a considerable degree of autonomy enjoyed by the universities in academic matters. In order to make the universities more innovative and entrepreneurial in nature, the Ministry of Education has continued to set the overall level of funding and spending on development projects while encouraging the NUS and the NTU to have a greater degree of operational autonomy in financial and personnel matters and the internal allocation of resources. However, it has rejected talk of plans to privatize the two universities (Ministry of Education 2000c). The concept of the SMU operating as a "private" university is problematic because the government subsidizes it through providing land, campus buildings, financial resources, and regulating the level of tuition fees to be identical to those charged by the other two universities. Instead of viewing it as a genuinely "private" university, it is perhaps more appropriate to call it a "privately-run, publicly-funded" university (Lee and Gopinathan 2001, p. 82).

We can argue that there is a mixed economy in Singapore's university sector. The emergence of the "private university" suggests a process of diversification of higher education provision in Singapore. It is important to note that the notion "private" should not be understood in a conventional sense. The diversification of higher education actors also shows how the government has now become more of a "consumer" in university services while the universities are to ensure the quality of their products and services within the emerging higher education market.

Finance

Similar to Hong Kong, higher education in Singapore has rapidly expanded in the past decade. This massification has resulted in a sharp increase in public expenditure being allocated to higher education development. Despite the fact that diversification of higher education financing has started in the higher education sector, the government is still the major fund provider of higher education. Similar to Hong Kong, higher education financing is heavily dependent on public expenditure. Recurrent expenditure on universities increased by threefold from S$310 million to S$1,125 million between 1987 and 2001. As for polytechnics,

Table 7.1 Public expenditure on higher education
in Singapore

Year	Amount of recurrent expenditure on universities (S$ million)
1992	442
1993	465
1994	541
1995	561
1996	606
1997	705
1998	596
1999	632
2000	982
2001	1,125

Source: Lee 2003a, pp. 280–81; Singapore Department
of Statistics 1998, 1999, 2000, 2001, 2002.

the same figure increased by sixfold from S$99 million to S$594 million during the same period of time (Singapore Department of Statistics 2001). Table 7.1 shows a steady growth of public expenditure on higher education with the only exception being in 1998.

Despite the fact that Singapore has experienced economic recession in recent years particularly after the 1997/98 financial crises in Asia, the Singapore government has continued to increase the input of public money into the higher education sector. Nevertheless, the incessant increase in government funding for the higher education sector does not mean that there are unlimited resources available for higher education financing, since the government needs to cope with competing demands from other public policy areas such as national defense, health care, and social welfare.

Revenue generation strategies

The adoption of the user-pay principle

Similar to its counterpart in Hong Kong, the Singapore government realizes that solely depending upon state resources can never satisfy pressing demand for higher education. Therefore, the government has begun to diversify higher education financing by involving sectors other than the state to finance higher education and to adopt a user-pay principle to recover partial operation costs through tuition fees in recent years (Tan 2003; Lee 2003a). In concert with the strategies of higher education reform put forward by the World Bank (1994a), public universities are encouraged to depend less on the state sector for financial resources. With the user-pay principle, tuition fees have been levied to recover partial operation costs. The recovery rate of tuition fees to the total operating costs of the two public universities is about 21 percent. About 75 percent of university expenditure is funded by government grants.

Searching for private financial sources

In addition to recovering partial costs from student tuition fees, the government has begun to mobilize greater nonstate or private financial sources for university education. In the early 1990s, the government set up a S$1 billion Universities Endowment Fund (UEF) to encourage the universities to raise money from the nonstate or the private sector, in particular alumni and industrial and commercial corporations. Besides making an initial S$500 million contribution, it also promised dollar-for-dollar donations. The two universities were expected to raise at least S$250 million within five years. The government announced its ultimate goal of having government grants form 60 percent of total operating costs, while raising the contribution of student fees to 25 percent. The remaining 10 percent of the costs would be derived from the endowment fund (*Business Times* May 8, 1991; *The Straits Times* October 14, 1991). The UEF could be seen as the first step toward reduced reliance on government funding and greater involvement of alumni and the community in financing university education. Moreover, the fund formalized the long-established tradition of private and corporate donations to the universities (Gopinathan and Morriss 1997, pp. 152–53).

At the end of 1996, the UEF was dissolved and the government created separate fund-raising programs for the NUS and the NTU. The government promised to give S$2 for every dollar raised by the two universities for their own endowment funds. On top of the previous dollar-for-dollar pledge, the government would now give S$3 for every dollar the NUS and the NTU managed to raise.

Both universities have witnessed an increase in the amount of their endowment funds in recent years. The NUS endowment fund increased from S$699 million to S$721 million between 1998 and 2000 (NUS 2000). As for the NTU, its endowment fund increased from S$359 million to S$451 million between 1997 and 2000 (NTU 1999, 2000). The SMU has also recently set up an endowment fund with a government pledge to give S$3 for every dollar raised. Its endowment fund aims to promote research among faculties of the university and to enhance the international standing of the university in the region and beyond (Teo 2001). The motive for the government encouraging the setting up of endowment funds for the three universities is not to completely shed its responsibility for financing university education. Rather, endowment funds provide the universities means to obtain nongovernmental sources of income, before the problems of financial stringency and resource shortage occur (Lee 2003a, pp. 268–70).

Strengthening university-business-industry partnerships

Seeking partnerships with industry is another means to find alternative sources of funding. Such partnerships may involve the formation of enterprises to conduct researches of high market value and potential to make profits for supporting other research and development projects. Both the NUS and the NTU have set up a number of research and development enterprises in recent years.

Whereas the Singapore government provides funding support for both basic and applied research, the universities have to explore alternative sources for research funding. With the move to a knowledge economy, universities have to serve as engines of innovation and entrepreneurship and thus position themselves for the new economy. The universities have to strengthen the focus on technopreneurship in the restructuring of their curricula. In addition, the two public universities engage in entrepreneurship-related activities such as business plan competitions and enterprises.

Regulation

Before the 1990s, the Singapore Government adopted a "state control model" in regulating the higher education sector, resulting in a "centralized governance model" and "interventionist regulatory" framework in higher education governance. By directly appointing vice chancellors to the universities, the government could easily monitor and direct the developments of higher education (Lee and Tan 1995, p. 135). The first time was in 1968 when Toh Chin Chye, who had been minister for science and technology, was appointed vice chancellor of the University of Singapore. According to Gopinathan (1989), Toh's appointment marked the transformation of a university modeled along classical principles of university autonomy and academic freedom into one in which government influence and control had become the norm (p. 217). Once again, in 1980 when the NUS was established as a result of a merger between the University of Singapore and Nanyang University, the then prime minister Lee Kuan Yew appointed Tony Tan, who was then minister for education, as the first vice chancellor of the NUS in the 1980/81 academic year (Lee and Tan 1995, pp. 187–88). The erosion of autonomy inside the university became even more obvious when the government did not allow the formation of a trade union of academics in the NUS (Gopinathan 1989, pp. 220–21).

The NUS was under the clear influence of the political establishment and was even an agent of government policy. No academic program existed without a sense of serving the nation-state's aims of development. In addition, academic freedom as a basic feature of a Western-style university in which the role of the academic as independent critic diminished considerably (Gopinathan 1989, pp. 222–23). In short, universities were under strict control of the government when the interventionist regulatory framework was in place.

The governance style has begun to change especially as the government has realized that its model is increasingly inappropriate in the globalization context. Therefore, a process of decentralization started in the mid-1990s to allow universities to have more flexibility to run and decide their businesses (Lee and Gopinathan 2001; Mok 2003d). In 2000, a government committee recommended granting the public universities more operational autonomy regarding governance, finance, and personnel matters. This seems to be a departure from the direct control model imposed by the state over the administration of universities. The government intends to adopt a "deregulated model" to govern the running of the public universities. The devolution of managerial powers from the state level to the institutional level is meant to enable the universities to better cope with market demands and also to compete in emerging higher education markets. It accompanies a shift in government forms of regulation to achieve a higher level of accountability with the use of information provision, capacity building, and performance funding (Dill 2001, pp. 29–33).

The Singapore government is determined to introduce more competition among the universities for research grants and funds as part of its adoption of performance funding in the context of public accountability. Instead of imposing "micro control," the government has shifted to a "state supervisory model" in governing universities. The universities have been engaging in quality assurance and management systems in order to ensure that quantitative expansion is not at the expense of quality enhancement. Quality enhancement in higher education has been operationalized and reinforced with four main measures, namely, a stringent tenure policy; rewards for good teaching and research performance; favorable staff-student ratios accompanied by well-equipped teaching and research activities; and the provision of staff training to upgrade skills and performance (Selvaratnam 1994, p. 5).

In the late 1990s, both the NUS and the NTU outlined their approaches and methods to improve the quality of education and institutional management. In the case of the NUS, a more comprehensive quality assurance and management system was put in place to enhance the institution as a center for quality education. The university recognized the need to identify and nurture future academic leaders who are strategic in thinking and effective in policy implementation, and also champions of the academic ethos. While the quality of teaching, research, and other services will be monitored closely and periodically, the staff appraisal and development system will also be reviewed regularly to ensure that it can motivate staff and reward them in accordance with individual performance. In relation to the notion of management of change, decision-making processes in the university have been modified to improve productivity through decentralization, better utilization of information technology, and a well-managed system of empowerment and accountability in response to the new "block grant" system, which induces greater autonomy in fund management (NUS 1998; Mok 2000a; Lee 2003b).

The NTU aims to re-engineer itself as an educational enterprise by instilling a corporate culture of excellence, nurturing capable and committed leaders in academia and administration, and inculcating a consultative and responsive management style with an emphasis on decentralized decision-making and autonomous fund management. Apart from the quality of teaching and research, the notion of quality is extended toward both personnel and institutional management. Besides evaluating the quality of teaching and research regularly, the university has promised to institute an innovative and systemic management and more open appraisal systems in order to motivate staff with the use of commensurable rewards. In addition, it has recognized the need to groom able and committed leaders to ensure the continuity and quality of institutional management (NTU 1998; Lee 2003b). In terms of governance, the Ministry of Education continues to set key policy parameters on higher education but the universities have to operate within a systematic accountability framework on the basis of greater operational autonomy. Such a systematic accountability framework focuses on the universities' achievement of outcomes and processes leading to the outcomes. Even though the universities run their own internal quality reviews, the Ministry of Education will commission an external review once every three years to validate these reviews.

In terms of funding, the universities have to diversify their sources of funding by developing their links with alumni, industry, and local community. The universities are now given a lump-sum grant every three years instead of once a year. Moreover, the institutions can retain surpluses to top up any shortfall in their own funds, provided that appropriate internal resource allocation systems are put in place to support and motivate faculties, departments, and individual academics to prioritize activities and achieve outcomes. The allocation of research funding will increasingly be subject to competition across the universities. In terms of staff management and remuneration, a new remuneration system was introduced in 2000. Such a system consists of a basic component and other variable components reflecting differences in performance, responsibilities, and market relativities. Automatic, time-based increments will be abolished and staff will be paid and given increments based on performance. Based on the merit of each individual, the basic pay of assistant professors has been increased by up to 20 percent in order to retain talent in local universities. In addition, the development of more rigorous appraisal systems is necessary for the universities to set out their criteria for assessing the performance of their staff members. Decisions on rewards, annual merit increments, promotions, and the granting of tenure are based on the information derived from staff performance appraisal mechanisms (Ministry of Education 2000b; *The Straits Times* July 5, 2000; Lee and Gopinathan 2001, pp. 83–84).

Discussion

Marketization of higher education in Singapore

The changes taking place in higher education provision, financing, and regulation are in line with wider marketization, decentralization, and corporatization of ideas and practices. It is clear that higher education in Singapore has been experiencing the process of marketization. It is particularly important to note that the Singapore Government has long been market conscious. From a historical perspective, the process of marketization had started since the independence of Singapore. As Singapore has been a trading port since the Second World War, its government has been very aware of the importance of making the city-state more competitive in both the regional and global marketplaces. Wang Gungwu, director of the East Asian Institute at the NUS, has suggested that Singapore is a "market" in itself and that the government runs the country as a huge enterprise (Interview with Wang Gungwu March 8, 2001). The Singapore government is always keen to manipulate market forces to stimulate competition between local and foreign world class universities. One point, which deserves particular attention here is that the marketization of higher education, is not merely caused by the problem of financial stringency but rather, is driven by the intention to improve managerial efficiency and cost effectiveness in the universities and thus prevent any wastage and shortage of resources in the university sector. The government continues to perform an active role and exerts its influence on public policy through regulation and funding (Low 1998, p. 280).

Openly recognizing the lack of the spirit of inventiveness and risk thinking, and, at the same time, worrying about the lessening of its competitiveness in the globalizing economy, the Singapore government has begun to launch projects in promoting entrepreneurship. Comparing Singapore to Taiwan and Hong Kong, entrepreneurial activity is relatively low since the Singapore government has long been orchestrating the developments of the city-state. Having been too paternalistic, the Singapore government has put the promotion of entrepreneurship top on its political agenda in recent years (Tan and Tan 2002; Tan 2003). According to unofficial estimates, the Singapore government, together with its linked companies, employs more than half a million people in the island-nation (*Asia Times* November 27, 2002). Singapore, being regarded as a "government-made city-state" (Low 2001), the levels of government intervention has been very high across different social, economic, and political aspects. With criticism mounting on the government for over concentration of economic decision-making, control of factors of production (including corporations), and unnecessary influence over pricing and supply of land and savings, the Singapore government has attempted to change its governance strategies by introducing privatization to the Government of Singapore Investment Corporation (GIC) (Institute of Policy Studies 2003).

In addition, the government designates the minister of state to be responsible for promoting a more entrepreneurial Singapore. By setting up PS21 project (PS21 Office), an office directly under the Prime Minister, the government hopes to make the civil servants think more innovatively and creatively. In addition, the Civil Service College of Singapore has been organizing different kinds of exhibitions and symposia in promoting the spirit of entrepreneurship. For instance, I was invited as one of the speakers for the conference of *Fostering Entrepreneurship: The Role of Government* held in Singapore on October 2003; I got the opportunity to share the experience of Hong Kong while the other speakers talked about experiences in Canada and elsewhere. My other visits to the PS21 Office and the ministry of education in Singapore repeatedly confirm how important the promotion of entrepreneurship in Singapore is. On the public administration front, the Singapore government has started reforms in making its administration more efficient and responsive to changing market needs (PS21 of Singapore, website). Believing education significantly determines the creation of entrepreneurial spirit, the Ministry of Education in Singapore has started a new reform movement called "Enterprise and Innovation." Students are encouraged to venture into the commercial sector by developing their own small firms or engaging students in selling and buying activities after school (MOE of Singapore, website).

Acknowledging the potential problems in the Singapore economy and that the sources of innovation have primarily been reliant upon foreign corporations and multinational subsidiaries (Mahmood and Singh 2003), the Singapore government has decided to accelerate the development of local enterprises or small medium enterprises (SMEs). More recently, the government has changed its regulatory framework to facilitate setting up small and medium sized enterprises in the island-state. To refine its legal systems to promote entrepreneurship, the government has made amendments to the immigration regulations, bankruptcy, and regulations for government tenders, etc. (Tan 2003). Like Hong Kong and Taiwan, the Singapore government has attempted to withdraw partially from direct management of economic affairs and R&D by empowering the National Science and Technology Board (NSTB) to oversee and coordinate R&D activities in recent years (Lai 2003).

Realizing the conventional university governance model (i.e., a state directed and centralized model) can never drive state universities in Singapore to become entrepreneurial, the Singapore government has set up an SMU an adopting a entirely new governance model. Intending to make SMU more flexible in governance and more responsive to changing education needs of the business and commercial sectors, the Singapore government deliberately made SMU a publicly funded but privately run university. When SMU was set up, the government provided the set-up fund and an endowment has been established to finance the future development of SMU. According to Prof. Tan Chin Tiong, provost of SMU, the newly established university has been very successful in developing close relationships with the business and commercial sectors not only in Singapore but also overseas. In response to the Singapore government's University Matching Grant Scheme, SMU has been able to match the fund raising targets set by the government. By approaching Dr Lee Ka Shing, a very famous Chinese businessman in Hong Kong, SMU secured a billion for the endowment fund. In addition to fund raising, SMU has maintained a very close relationship with business and commercial sectors (Field Interview, February 2005).

When designing the curricula for its business and management students, SMU has reached out to the relevant fields seeking advice and ideas in developing courses and programs to cater to the educational needs in accordance with the changing business and commercial environments (Field Interview, February 2005). Having reflected upon the changing university governance models and evaluated the recent experiences of SMU, the ministry of education in Singapore has decided to change the governance models of the existing state universities, namely, NUS and NTU by making them independent legal entities through the process of "corporatization" (Field Interview, December 2004). By incorporatizing these state universities, the Singapore government hopes that universities on the island-state would become more entrepreneurial.

Strengthening state control in higher education

The earlier discussion has suggested that globalization may not necessarily bring about "the end of the state." Instead, it has encouraged a spectrum of adjustment strategies chosen by the state to cope with globalization challenges. In the end, the state may become a more activist state, especially when modern states have tried to reconstitute and restructure their institutions or governance models in response to the growing complexity of processes of globalization (Rosenau 1997). The Singapore case study has clearly indicated that the role of the island-state is not necessarily diminished in the context of globalization.

The government possesses important tools for influencing economic, political, social, and technological change in Singapore. In addition, the Singapore government has a tradition of anticipating problems and developing proposals to prevent and deal with them (Bellows 1995). The higher education restructuring reforms are not aimed purely at tackling the problem of financial stringency in universities. Rather it is aimed at enhancing managerial efficiency of the universities so as to prevent the wastage of resources that has been identified as an important factor causing the financial problems facing other places such as Australia, the United Kingdom, and Hong Kong. In addition, packaging education restructuring within a globalization discourse may well give national governments additional political strength to push for local public sector reforms (Yang 2003).

Conclusion

This chapter has discussed the driving forces behind higher education reforms in Singapore. The discussion has suggested that there are many changes in common between Singapore's higher education transformations and those elsewhere, which suggests that Singapore's university system has been affected by similar global trends. Upon close scrutiny, the Singapore government has tactically made use of the globalization discourse to push its own policy agenda. In spite of the growing impact of globalization, the Singapore government has managed to manipulate market forces to make competition a viable means to stimulate better performance and higher quality of services among public sector institutions, including the two public universities and one private university. Seen in this light, globalization does not necessarily mean that the nation-state has inevitably been weakened and has become powerless. Rather, the case of Singapore demonstrates that the state has become even more powerful and is equipped with stronger capacity to "balance and check" such global market forces in shaping local public policy agendas and determining the ongoing process of national development in terms of social and economic progress. In a way, the Singapore government is a selective borrower of foreign practices and experiences to reform the public sectors, including higher education. In conclusion, the Singapore government has successfully maintained control over its public policy domains by tactically using globalization discourse to justify its local policy objectives.

8 Taiwan's response to globalization

Changing governance in higher education

Introduction

The principal goal of this chapter is to examine and reflect upon the effects of globalization on national policy, with particular reference to how the higher education sector in Taiwan has transformed itself under the global tide of marketization and decentralization. More specifically, this chapter examines the most recent reforms and changes in Taiwan's higher education, particularly focusing on changes in educational provision, regulation, and financing. The core of the chapter is to examine in what ways and what strategies the Taiwan government has adopted to reform its higher education systems in response to the changing local socioeconomic and political context and regional and global environments. The chapter concludes by discussing the policy implications for changing higher education governance in Taiwan.

Policy backgrounds

Policy of centralization and Taiwan's higher education

Before the mid-1980s, the Taiwanese lived under a totalitarian regime and higher education was under a rigid government control as well, clearly reflected by suspending people's freedom of speech, assembly and association, and rights to elect their representatives to the legislature. Political parties and mass media speaking against the Kuomintang (KMT) were banned and political dissidents were arrested before the revocation of the martial law in 1987 (Tsai 1996b). In order to preserve the cultural and national identity rooted in mainland China, the Taiwan government had adopted a "centralist" model in governing every aspect of the society (Knowles 1978; Husen and Postlethwaite 1985). With the "centralist" model in place, the government has tightly monitored higher education development (Law 1998b). Needless to say, no significant institutional power was devolved to individual higher education institutions before the political reforms initiated in the late 1980s in Taiwan.

Under this governance model, the Ministry of Education (MOE) controlled the establishment of institutes and departments, the appointment of university executives and academics, the allocation of finance, the design of university curricula, the adoption of textbooks, and the procedure of student admissions and graduation (Law 1996a; Chen 2001). Students were forced to take political ideology courses that transmitted the doctrines and ideas of Sun Yat-sen (founder of the Republic of China in 1911) and his successors. During this period, compulsory courses such as The Thoughts of Dr SunYat-sen, General History of China, the Constitution of the Republic of China, Readings of Classical Chinese for University were imposed on students and male students had to go through military training, etc. in order to preserve the cultural and national identity rooted in mainland China (Lo and Weng 2005). Similarly, university presidents or academics could be easily dismissed without reasonable reasons. Academic publications were assessed and screened by the MOE. Living in such a sociopolitical environment, academic freedom and intellectual autonomy seemed to be a very remote thing to students and academics (Law 1996a; Morris 1996).

Changing sociopolitical context and changing education governance

With the economic growth since the 1970s, coupled with the expansion of the civil society in Taiwan, there have been fundamental changes taking place in the society and politics. Higher education, being one of the major public policies, has never been immune from the challenges and changes resulting from rapid socio-economic and political changes in the island-state. Therefore, a better understanding of recent higher education changes in Taiwan could be obtained by examining how both the domestic and global variables/forces interact in shaping higher education policy formulation and changing governance.

A glance of what has happened to the higher education sector in Taiwan seems to confirm the convergence thesis that Taiwan has experienced similar global processes of "decentralization" and "marketization" in higher education reform. However, a closer scrutiny of what really has happened to Taiwan's higher education sector discovers that these transformations are the concomitant consequences of the changing sociopolitical and socioeconomic contexts on the island-state (Chiu 1993; Law 1998b; Weng 1999a). The changes in Taiwan's sociopolitical context, particularly the transformations resulting from democratization are the most decisive driving force for educational restructuring. In addition, the change in the philosophy of governance and the socioeconomic changes resulting from the earthquake in 1999, and the massification of higher education in Taiwan, are additional local factors accounting for the recent higher education reform and educational restructuring. In this regard, we should not overstate the impact of globalization in shaping education policy and reform of modern states. Domestic factors and local forces can still determine the way education is developed. Let us now discuss the changing social, economic, and political context of Taiwan in which education changes and higher education reforms have been launched and implemented.

Democratization and higher education reform

With the termination of martial law in 1987, the Taiwan government began to establish a more representative government and more democratic political structures have been institutionalized since, as evidenced by open election of legislators to the Legislature and the election of the president by the people (Gold 1986; Soong 1997; Kan 2000; Tsay 2000). The process of democratization in the past decade has led to the most controversial notion of *song-bang*, that is, releasing strings or liberalization in higher education. In a more specific sense, the idea of *song-bang* is similar to deregulation, by which the education sector in Taiwan would be relaxed from the state's strict control (Chu and Yeh 1995). Having experienced the drastic changes before and after the revocation of the martial law, Weng describes the present social and political context of Taiwan society in the following way:

> [After the revocation of the martial law] Both the political climate and the economic market are freer and more open than before. The people are encouraged to express their wishes and opinions. They are more relying on information and technology [sic]. The Taiwanese society is getting democratic and globalize. In addition, the relation between the two sides of Taiwan Strait [the relationship between mainland China and Taiwan] is much closer than before. In fact, Taiwan's society has been more democratic, flexible, informationlized, hi-tech, competitive, and marketized.
>
> (1999a, p. 35)

Realizing that the sociopolitical context has changed since the democratization project started about a decade ago, Prof. Guo Weifan, the former minister of education, in 1993, openly declared that the "democratization" of higher education should go hand in hand with Taiwan's political development. Announcing that the government was prepared to adopt a decentralization policy in the higher education sector, he promised that the state would gradually devolve powers to higher education managements in four major aspects: personnel management, academic freedom, finance, and curriculum (*Gao Fiao Fian Xun* June 10, 1993).

Under this sociopolitical environment, scholars and academics in Taiwan now enjoy far more autonomy and flexibility in running their educational institutions. University academics have successfully formed their own professional associations at both the university and the inter-university level as political platforms to discuss higher education policy. At the inter-university level, the Committee for Promoting University Reform (CPUR) was set up to comment on higher education policies and offer alternative views to the official ones (Law 1996c, 2003). All these transformations are closely related to the political liberalization that resulted from the democratization process in Taiwan (Law 2003).

Changing governance philosophy and higher education reform

Furthermore, the recent higher education reform is also affected by the changing governance philosophy in Taiwan. Since the reformers have adopted a neoclassical approach to public management believing that the state should not intervene too much in the public domain but create a conducive infrastructure for the market economy. Such a belief has affected the educational governance on the island-state (Field Interview, Taipei, December 1999). Within the context of *song-bang*, together with the changing governance philosophy, the most crucial issue in Taiwan's education sector is to redefine the relationship between the state and education sector, especially when the Taiwan government is considering the policy of "privatization" in education (*United News* December 28, 1999). Despite the fact that the role of the state is vital in higher education, it does not mean that the state should monopolize education and prohibit the operation of universities by private individuals and organizations. The revitalization of the private sector and the mobilization of other nonstate sources to run education not only generates more income/revenue but also can reduce the state's pressure to meet the pressing needs for higher education.

More importantly, the adoption of the decentralization policy in Taiwan's higher education is not only related to the liberalization of politics but also to the need to denationalize public services as a result of sociopolitical and socioeconomic changes. The proposed decentralization and marketization project in Taiwan's higher education can be seen as the government's attempts to improve the efficiency and effectiveness of its education system and to solve the financial constraints that the Taiwan government is now facing after the earthquake in 1999.

Rapid expansion and the need for higher education reform

Another local factor accounting for the recent higher education reform is related to the rapid expansion of higher education on the island-state. Only a few generations ago universities were very selective institutions in Taiwan. Before the 1990s, students who applied for matriculation knew that not all of them would be admitted and those who were not admitted would be disappointed, while for those who were selected for admission therefore comprised a somewhat elite group of students. This group of university students shared similar features: they were typically from the middle and upper class strata, primarily boys, and they represented the majority culture (Greene 1995). Since the lifting of martial law in 1987, Taiwan's higher education system has experienced a rapid expansion. Between 1987 and 1997, the number of universities and colleges increased from 28 to 67, and student enrollments rose from less than 200,000 to over 380,000. The most recent statistics further suggest that the number of university students has expanded. In 1999, there were a total of 463,575 university students at both undergraduate and postgraduate levels (MOE of Taiwan 1999a). Similar to the experiences of the higher education systems moving from massification to post-massification in other Western countries as well as in East Asia, the rapid expansion of higher education may lead to the problems of lowering academic standards (William and Fry 1994; Zemsky 1997). Turning from "elite to mass higher education" has made the Taiwan government very much aware of the importance of quality control. The rapid increase of university students, together with the expansion of private colleges and universities in Taiwan, has raised concern. Therefore, the Taiwan government has started to develop systems to ensure quality in higher education (Yung 1999; Field Interview, Taipei, December 1999). Hence, the introduction of quality control in higher education can be seen as the Taiwan government's strategy to assure and maintain quality in higher education.

The impact of globalization and higher education reform

Believing that there will be far more rapid social and economic changes in the twenty-first century, the Taiwan government is concerned about how to maintain Taiwan as competitive as possible in regional and global markets. In addition, the Taiwan government believes that the prominence of information technology would certainly cause changes not only to social and economic fronts but also to the ways that education institutions are managed. Perceiving that with the economy being dominated by semi-conductor and other information-related industries, future education will definitely bear a more important role to support the knowledge-capital-intensive economy in Taiwan. Prof. Lin Ching-chiang, the former minister of education, conceives that the future society should be a "learning society" in the coming century. Holding such a vision, Lin is particularly keen to develop Taiwan as a "lifelong learning society"; and Taiwan people can be educated to be creative and adaptive to changes and challenges ahead (Lin 1998).

Conceptualizing the current social, economic, and political transformation in the light of the post-fordist perspective, Weng argues that the Taiwan society has become a plural, open, competitive, affluent, technological, informational, international, and individualized society; all these features suggest that Taiwan has become a post-fordist society (Weng 1999). In particular, the awareness of the importance of making Taiwan more international has not been only the concern for the Government but also for the academics in the university sector (MOE of Taiwan 1999b; Law 2003). During our field visits and interviews with Taiwan scholars, we have realized that people living on the island-state are generally conscious of the impact of the globalization and they have attempted to respond positively to the tidal wave of globalization (Field Observations, Taipei, July 1998 and December 1999).

As Taiwan has become a more politically liberal and democratic society, university academics are very keen to establish links with the external world, while the state is very keen to make the island-state more international. For this reason, the stress on the importance of international benchmarking and the significance of internationalization can be understood as the strategies to make Taiwan escape from being isolated by the international community. Despite the fact that the recent reform in Taiwan's higher education sector seems to have been considerably affected by global forces, our earlier discussion has suggested that the Taiwan government has attempted to make use of the globalization discourse to justify its recent reform in the higher education systems. The call to make Taiwan society more cosmopolitan in general and the academic community more international in particular can be understood as the need generated from the local environment to internationalize Taiwan instead of the result of the global impact.

Having discussed earlier the contextual analysis of higher education reforms, we may argue that Taiwan's higher education changes and recent reforms are to address not only the globalization challenges but also the domestic forces and local needs. Let's now turn to some major reform strategies that the Taiwan government has adopted in making its higher education system more globally competitive.

Recent reforms and changing governance in higher education

Upholding the ideal of equal opportunity for education, the Taiwan government has implemented various program/policies since the late 1980s to promote equality in education. These reform measures include (1) the Program of Open Admissions to Upper Secondary Schools in 1990; (2) the Program of Ten-Year National Compulsory Education Based Upon Vocational Education in 1993; (3) the Education White Paper of the Republic of China in 1995; and (4) the Consultation Paper of Educational Reform for the Executive Yuan in 1994–96. Central to these reform programs are other such reforms which look to improve the quality of Taiwan citizens by the expansion of more educational opportunities for senior high schools; to develop the citizens' potentials in terms of their mental, personal, physical activities in the full; to balance the development between the urban and rural schools, as well as between the private and public schools; and to foster further higher education development (Huang 1992; Weng 1999a).

In addition, the Executive Yuan officially established the Council on Education Reform (CER) in the early 1990s, headed by Prof. Lee Yuen-tseh, nobel laureate and president of academia sinica. Engaging in an intensive research for two years, a Blueprint for Education Reform was published in 1994 (Weng 1999a). After a comprehensive review of Taiwan's educational system, The Council on Education Reform published a five-volume Consultation Papers (CER 1995). Central to the Reform Blueprint are:

- deregulation of the system—lifting unnecessary bans, promoting education in all possible ways, and emphasizing autonomy and self-discipline;
- attending to individual needs—developing students' potential by means of curriculum revision, small class teaching, school autonomy, remedial measures, career counseling, and reinforcing special education for aborigines and physically and mentally handicapped, as well as sex equality and preschool education;
- alternative routes for continuous education—establishing specialty and comprehensive high schools, diversified admission system;
- raising education quality—improving teachers' professional training, reinforcing education research assessment, and using resources effectively, and developing diversified and specified technology education; and
- establishing a lifelong learning society—promoting the concepts and system of lifelong learning with the help of school reform, recurrent education, and administrative measures.

(CER 1995; MOE of Taiwan 1997a; Chung 1999; Weng 1999b)

To realize the goals set out in the Reform Blueprint, the MOE published a white paper on Education in 1995, outlining the principles for education reform. A close scrutiny of the white paper reveals that the Taiwan government is very much concerned about the equality of opportunity for educating its citizens. To reinforce the idea of equality of educational opportunities (EEO), the white paper has proposed various strategies to promote education equality in Taiwan. These strategies include: (1) to develop appropriate programs to improve vocational education in rural areas; (2) to encourage the best teachers to teach in rural and/or off-shore areas in order to raise teaching standard in these areas; (3) to establish special schools to meet the special needs students; (4) to offer financial subsidy to private schools; (5) to identify areas for educational development; and (6) to implement educational vouchers. Through these means the MOE hopes that Taiwan can be developed into a more pluralistic and democratic society (MOE of Taiwan 1995, p. 26).

Believing that there will be far more rapid social and economic changes in the twenty-first century, the Taiwan government is conscious about how to maintain Taiwan as competitive as possible in regional and global markets. In addition, the Taiwan government believes that the prominence of information technology would certainly cause changes not only on social and economic fronts but also the ways in which educational institutions are managed. In order to enhance Taiwan's competitiveness in the global market, the Taiwan government has begun to expand its higher education in the past decade and allow private universities to flourish. More recently, the Taiwan government has put even more emphasis on education and openly declared that "the higher the quality of human resource is, the stronger the state is" (Weng 1999b, p. 46). Eight major strategies are introduced to promote education and training. They are:

- developing a pluralistic and flexible mode of education;
- further expansion in junior high schools and higher education;
- renovation of curricula and teaching materials and the strengthening of information technology;
- rationalization of the distribution of educational resources and the encouragement for developing private education;
- establishment of adult education and the promotion of lifelong learning;
- setting up competency-based training, pre-employment and on-the-job training, and second-skill training, as well as more proper training to the business sector;
- improvement of employment information services and the promotion of a system of skill certification by both foreign and domestic authorities;
- fostering community culture development.

(MOE of Taiwan 1997b, 1998b; Weng 1999b)

Despite the fact that there is no chapter specifically written about the reform of higher education in the *Blueprint* or in other documents discussed earlier, the overall guideline for reforming Taiwan's higher education system is closely related to the policy of decentralization and deregulation. In general, the CER is of the view that the government should relax its restrictions on colleges and universities and allow students to develop their individual potentials to full capacity (CER 1996; Hawthorne 1996). One official document that is particularly effective to reflect the spirit of "decentralization" in governing the higher education systems in Taiwan is the revised University Law in Taiwan.

Adopting the "centralist" model for many years, the Executive Yuan revised the University Law. During the period between 1990 and 1994, more than five versions of bills to revise the University Law were sent to the Legislative Yuan, Taiwan's highest legislative body, and received enormous attention from the public. A revised University Law was eventually passed in 1994 (MOE of Taiwan 1994). According to the revised University Law, the goal of university education has changed from "studying for advanced knowledge and training specialists" to "studying for advanced knowledge and developing both wisdom and moral uprightness in specialists able to enhance national development." Meanwhile, the role of the MOE would become that of an administrator, instead of an inspector of individual universities' affairs (MOE of Taiwan 1993). After the revisions, some major areas affecting university governance are as follows:

- The MOE has to consult with faculty members before hiring the presidents of national universities.
- Deans of colleges, graduate schools, and departments engaged from among professors, according to the regulations of each university.
- The title of "student guidance department" changed to "student assistance department."
- The rank of assistant professor created to stand between that of associate professor and lecturer.
- Student representatives attend school administrative meetings related to their academic work, daily life, merits, and demerits.
- Faculty members are required to set up a committee to screen employment, promotions, and dismissals of their colleagues, according to the regulations of each university.
- A university may set up a branch campus after obtaining approval from the MOE.

In addition to the revision of the University Law, the Taiwan government also revised *Teacher Law* and *Private Education Law* to initiate a fundamental change of the relationship between the MOE and other key players in higher education such as university administrators and academics. Undoubtedly, the revised laws governing the higher education sector has granted tertiary institutions more autonomy over finance, personnel, and curriculum, and teachers, individuals, and the community are empowered to control higher education affairs (MOE of Taiwan 1993).

Besides the enactment of the revised University Law, the Taiwan government promulgated a new policy document entitled Education Reform Action Plan in 1998. This action plan sets out the directions of education reform in Taiwan, advocating education liberation (*song-bang*), attaching importance to cultivating and educating good students, diversifying channels for higher education studies, improving the quality of education and establishing a lifelong learning society (MOE of Taiwan 1998a). This action plan can be regarded as Taiwan's response to the everchanging socioeconomic environment. By implementing the action plan, the MOE intends to make its graduates more globally competent; thereby they could be equipped with knowledge and skills appropriate to cope with ever-changing local and international needs.

In 2002, the MOE published another policy paper entitled Integration Plan of Research-Type Universities in order to develop its universities into world class universities by adopting strategies of university merging and university collaborations. For example, the National Tsing Hua University, National Central University, National Chiao Tung University, and National Yang-Ming University have formed an alliance to establish a University System of Taiwan to increase their competitiveness, whereby credits transfer, shared resources, and other cooperations could be done among students and faculty members of the participating institutions (Lo and Weng 2005).

Having discussed the institutional origins for Taiwan's higher education reforms, let us now turn to the major changes in Taiwan's higher education after the reforms. The following discussion will focus on how three major aspects; namely, the processes of decentralization and marketization have affected provision, financing, and regulation.

Provision: a mixed economy in higher education

As socioeconomic and sociopolitical contexts have changed in the past decade, private colleges and universities have come to flourish on the island-state. Despite the fact that the MOE has a supervisory power over all private schools, colleges, and universities, private education institutions nowadays have far more autonomy and they are officially recognized as part of the education system in Taiwan. In the Constitution of the Republic of China (ROC), three articles are particularly effective to show the state's attitude toward the role of private education.

Article 11

This article pertains to freedom to discourse on academic subjects (jiangxue ziyou). Although there are different interpretations, the majority interprets this as 1. The freedom to establish schools to discourse on academic subjects; 2. The freedom to choose topics of research; and 3. Freedom to publish research findings. Thus it guarantees the freedom to establish schools to discourse on academic subjects.

Article 162

This article stipulates all public and private educational and cultural bodies in the nation are subject to government supervision by law. The drafters of the constitution deliberately made the distinction between public and private educational bodies here to validate the role of private education, stipulating that the government can, therefore, according to law, exercise the right of supervision overall all public and private educational or cultural bodies in the nation.

Article 167

This article stipulates that the government encourages or subsidizes the undertakings of individuals. Privately operated educational institutions in the country are partially financed by government grants.

Knowing that the state alone can never satisfy the pressing demand for higher education, the Taiwan government has revised its education ordinances to create room for the expansion of private higher education. In order to prepare all Taiwan citizens for the knowledge economy in the new century and to strengthen the competitiveness of Taiwan in the global market, the MOE has diversified higher education opportunities by allowing different actors/sectors and even the market to engage in creating more opportunities for higher learning (MOE of Taiwan 1999b). For this reason, more and more private higher educational institutions have been formed in Taiwan.

Until 1998, the number of universities and independent colleges jumped to 84 and more than half of them were universities (MOE of Taiwan 1998a) (Table 8.1). With the growth of higher education in Taiwan, about 61.6 percent of students who took the Joint University Entrance Examination were admitted

Table 8.1 Profile of the higher education in Taiwan in 1976–2003

School year	Number of institutions	Number of students			Educational expenditure (NT$ 1,000)
		Total	Day	Evening	
1976	25	145,358	103,526	41,832	4,026,867
1977	26	148,077	105,917	42,160	4,641,948
1978	26	150,653	108,797	41,856	5,046,661
1979	26	154,980	112,590	42,390	7,189,916
1980	27	159,394	116,931	42,463	9,753,150
1981	27	165,536	122,378	43,158	13,233,316
1982	28	171,974	128,259	43,715	16,446,165
1983	28	178,988	133,806	5,182	14,901,770
1984	28	184,889	139,792	45,097	16,585,393
1985	28	191,752	145,974	45,778	18,727,605
1986	28	198,166	151,855	46,311	23,638,140
1987	39	208,054	160,682	47,372	31,471,197
1988	39	224,820	171,630	48,129	32,877,730
1989	41	241,860	184,097	47,968	40,064,663
1990	46	261,454	198,945	48,749	51,018,405
1991	50	280,249	217,866	49,177	59,457,368
1992	50	304,359	237,429	50,132	64,393,016
1993	51	321,812	257,361	48,616	66,831,084
1994	58	341,320	273,695	52,636	70,081,817
1995	60	356,596	287,683	56,042	71,856,340
1996	67	382,710	306,798	64,537	88,398,565
1997	78	422,321	346,920	65,916	89,635,584
1998	84	463,575	386,206	69,495	96,260,602
1999	105	537,263	450,347	80,770	98,550,029
2000	127	647,920	537,146	106,462	167,354,236
2001	135	780,384	671,411	150,185	184,856,770
2002	139	893,165	740,831	150,281	176,608,715
2003	143	981,169	786,488	193,546	195,438,986

Source: MOE of Taiwan 2003, pp. 18–19; 2004.

by either universities or colleges in 1997, showing a growth of 11.2 percent of successful applicants to university education (MOE of Taiwan 1998a). It is noted that the expansion of higher education is closely related to the formal status being granted to private higher education in Taiwan. By the end of 2003, there were 38 private universities in Taiwan, indicating that a significant proportion of university students are with privately run higher education institutions and implying that there is an important role of private universities in Taiwan (MOE of Taiwan 2003).

Financing: multiple channels of higher education financing

In accordance with the revised University Law, the MOE has attempted to devolve the responsibility and power to individual higher education institutions, including autonomy for educational financing. In order to reduce the state's financial pressure to support higher education, the MOE has adopted a new policy to finance all national higher education institutions in Taiwan by providing only 80 percent of the total budget, while leaving the remaining to individual universities to search for their own financial resources. According to Tsai (1996b), the new policy is a great surprise to most of the university/college leaders/ administrators because very few of them have any experience in fund raising. In order to secure adequate funds to sustain their universities,

> different fund-raising approaches were adopted, such as raising money through alumni associations, convincing faculty members and college administrators to donate part of their salaries to their colleges, and offering extension courses to generate extra tuition revenue. It is likely that under the pressures of financial autonomy, Taiwanese higher education institutions will become more market oriented ever before
>
> (Tsai 1996b, p. 2)

Table 8.2 shows the educational expenditure in Taiwan from 1951 to 2003. It is obvious that the educational expenditure had a steady growth from 9.93 percent of the total public expenditure to 19.5 percent in 1996. Nonetheless, the government expenditure on higher education seemed to have undergone a slight decline to 18.9 and 18.5 percent in 1997 and 1998 respectively. Figure 8.1 further suggests that the government expenditure on education in terms of GNP has declined in recent years, a drop from 5.6 percent in 1992 to 5.1 percent in 1998 (MOE of Taiwan 1999a). In a recent meeting, Xiao Renzhang, the premier of the Executive Yuan repeatedly emphasized the importance of education to the future development of Taiwan. Nevertheless, he openly admitted the fact that the government encountered financial constraints since government revenue was limited (*China Times* December 28,

Table 8.2 Educational expenditure in Taiwan in 1951–2003

Year	Public and private educational expenditure					Government's educational expenditure		
	Amount (NT$1,000)	Per student (NT$)	% of GNP Total	Public	Private	Amount (NT$1,000)	Per capita (NT$1,000)	% of Government expenditure
1951	213,082	175	1.73	1.73	NA	213,082	28	9.93
1956	844,838	503	2.27	2.27	NA	844,838	90	12.74
1961	1,671,962	704	2.52	2.22	0.30	1,470,169	136	13.32
1966	3,959,628	1,270	3.38	2.76	0.62	3,234,989	255	14.58
1971	11,236,766	2,815	4.57	3.69	0.88	9,065,121	614	16.51
1973	25,377,015	5,704	3.95	3.26	0.69	20,952,991	1,292	15.12
1981	74,112,578	16,119	4.54	3.69	0.85	60,262,157	3,373	14.71
1982	94,673,666	20,395	5.15	4.23	0.92	77,809,670	4,277	15.14
1983	110,942,492	23,480	5.58	4.62	0.96	91,864,372	4,961	16.51
1984	111,121,047	23,151	4.95	3.97	0.98	89,206,666	4,747	16.28
1985	123,915,028	25,440	5.06	4.10	0.96	100,352,921	5,263	16.57
1986	137,899,432	27,902	5.14	4.21	0.93	112,979,397	5,848	16.45
1987	148,047,536	29,341	4.72	3.80	0.93	119,030,192	6,101	16.54
1988	168,382,593	32,863	4.89	3.92	0.94	135,940,263	6,893	17.27
1989	200,549,624	38,589	5.28	4.29	0.99	163,094,485	8,173	17.39
1990	245,279,765	47,056	5.80	4.79	1.02	202,364,654	10,040	17.47
1991	300,965,051	57,002	6.49	5.34	1.15	247,488,080	12,131	17.77
1992	351,140,259	66,324	6.75	5.58	1.18	290,019,588	17,075	17.86
1993	401,130,100	75,695	6.98	5.79	1.20	332,463,417	15,982	18.43
1994	428,109,963	80,943	6.80	5.56	1.24	350,053,223	16,672	18.58
1995	449,691,445	85,788	6.57	5.36	1.21	366,902,255	17,325	19.36
1996	500,863,136	96,424	6.72	5.47	1.25	407,595,911	19,085	19.50
1997	533,672,566	103,480	6.61	5.21	1.40	420,905,497	19,554	18.91
1998	550,309,889	106,736	6.29	4.92	1.37	430,675,819	19,808	18.54
1999	581,536,145	112,432	6.31	4.92	1.39	435,089,741	20,662	18.80
2000	534,289,235	101,932	5.45	4.10	1.35	401,537,000	18,175	19.18
2001	570,795,923	104,194	5.89	4.22	1.67	409,307,000	18,527	18.02
2002	608,629,450	110,142	6.08	4.39	1.71	438,074,000	19,829	19.76
2003	598,255,972	NA	5.87	4.15	1.75	423,266,000	18,724	20.76

Source: MOE of Taiwan 2003, pp. 48, 62.

Note
Since FY 2002, the education expenditure excludes scientific and cultural expenditure.

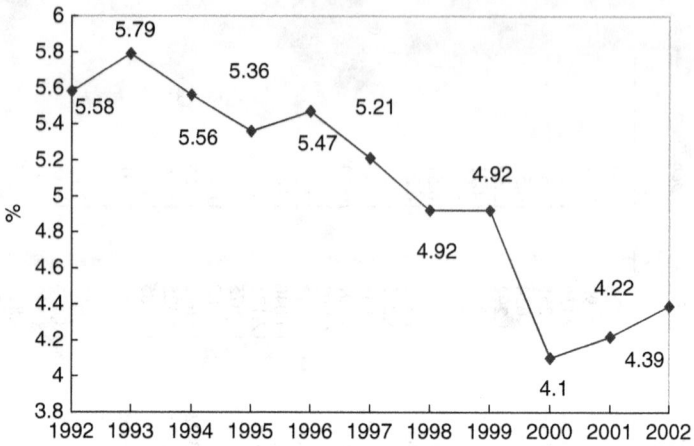

Figure 8.1 Ratio of public educational expenditure to GNP.

Source: Data adapted from MOE of Taiwan (2003).

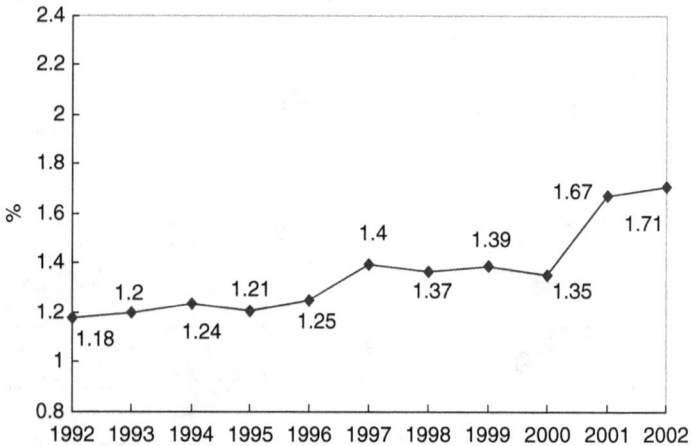

Figure 8.2 Ratio of private educational expenditure to GNP.

Source: Data adapted from MOE of Taiwan (2003).

1999). Like other countries, the Taiwan government encourages the user-charge principle and urges individual universities to search for alternative channels to finance and run their universities. In face of the reduction of government's financial support, the proportion of nonstate sources (Figure 8.2) has increased especially with the Taiwan government deciding to change the status of all national universities to independent legal bodies, that is, the national universities have to search for their financial resources since the government appropriation to higher education will gradually recede (*United News* December 28, 1999).

Table 8.3 Source of funding in selected universities in Taiwan in 1996–98

	National Ching Hua University	National Taiwan University	National Cheng Kung University	National Chiao Tung University
Tuition fee				
1996	168,262	647,451	463,293	221,535
1997	173,030	697,405	460,440	222,141
1998	206,100	772,410	490,671	256,197
Co-operation with other sectors				
1996	470,579	1,106,252	663,150	322,723
1997	662,434	1,909,121	950,872	570,098
1998	777,409	2,125,089	1,165,279	737,843
Education promotion				
1996	6,977	70,962	6,881	27,377
1997	13,640	55,316	105,843	45,772
1998	129,606	70,544	129,606	57,243
Interest				
1996	8,422	14,671	23,848	29,856
1997	29,204	52,317	85,460	59,514
1998	57,769	144,904	157,172	79,232
Donation				
1996	713	3,431	1,600	2,485
1997	587	57,924	3,000	2,502
1998	22,654	46,238	7,900	10,330

Source: MOE of Taiwan 2004, [Internet] Available from: http://www.high.edu.tw

In order to lessen the financial burden of the government, the MOE has encouraged all public universities to establish a "Fund for Administrative Affairs" (Fund, hereafter). According to the Law of Fund stipulated on February 3, 1999, the state is responsible for 80 percent of the total budget of national universities; while all national universities should search for their own means to get the remaining 20 percent funding. In accordance with Article 6 of the Law, the sources of fund include government sponsorship, tuition fees, education promotion fees, incomes from cooperation with other sectors, income from managing the facilities of the university, donation, interests from bank saving, and other incomes. Such a newly established fund is used to support the operation and development of all national universities. Table 8.3 shows the sources of funding in some of the key universities in Taiwan, indicating that the sources of higher education financing have been greatly diversified (see Figures 8.1 and 8.2).

In addition, the MOE has initiated a "Pursuing Academic Excellence Development of Universities Project" to enhance the academic standards in order to foster individual universities in developing their own characteristics. The proposed project deals with not only national universities but also private higher education institutions. In order to reward institutions of outstanding performance, the MOE has decided to allocate additional financial resources to support the development of private higher education institutions, estimating an increase of subsidiary budget up to 20 percent of the regular income of private institutions. Meanwhile, another development grant is established for improving the teaching and research environment of private institutions. Additional awards and sponsorships will be granted to private universities if they could prove themselves to be outstanding in performance.

In addition, the Taiwan government has repeatedly called for the increase of tuition fees since the government no longer treats higher education as free service to its citizens. On various occasions, government officials have repeatedly announced that the state is going to increase students' tuition fees. Prof. Yang Kuo-chih, vice-minister of the MOE and Huang Kuo-tuan, minister of higher education, openly expressed the view that "higher education is not free education so user-charges of the higher educational institutions would be adopted" (*China Times* September 1, 1999, December 28, 1999). It is projected that the tuition fees of both national universities and private universities will increase by not more than 5 and 5.5 percent respectively every year (MOE of Taiwan 1999a). Table 8.4 shows the charging standard of both national and private universities in Taiwan. As the table suggests, the tuition fees for both types of universities has increased by 5 and 3.5 percent respectively in a year's time.

Since 2000, the Taiwan government has implemented a policy to assist private universities to get additional funding. According to the regulations of Private School Education Promotion Fund, there is an increase of tax exemptions for those providing donation to private universities. For example, donations to private universities will have 50 percent personal tax allowance and a 25 percent profit tax allowance. Such a measure aims to diversify the funding channels of private universities for making sure that their education quality would not drop because of insufficient funding sources. With additional state subsidies, it is hoped that private universities can further improve their quality so that they can be able to compete with national universities for recruiting students.

More recently, the Taiwan government has given serious thought to turning all public universities into "independent legal persons" (i.e., making all national universities independent organizations). Such a proposed status change will result in the decline of state subsidy and, hence, individual universities have to search for alternative channels for financing (*China Times* December 28, 1999; *United News* December 28, 1999). Realizing that the public expenditure is severely limited, the Taiwan government has taken the advice of consultants from the United States that "denationalization" of national universities can really resolve the fiscal crisis of the government. In the midst of stringent financial situations, coupled with other pressing social demands for the post-earthquake restoration works, the Taiwan government is seriously thinking about a new funding methodology by making national universities as independent legal entities.

Becoming independent legal entities, universities can have far more flexibility and autonomy to decide their operational matters, including management, financing, and other matters. The Executive Yuan has set up a special committee to conduct a feasibility study of the proposed scheme and the final decision will

Table 8.4 Tuition fees of selected national and private universities in Taiwan in 1998–99 (Unit: in New Taiwan Dollars)

	Medical		Engineering		Faculty of Science/ Agriculture		Business		Tuition increased by (%)
	1998	*1999*	*1998*	*1999*	*1998*	*1999*	*1998*	*1999*	
Public University									
National Taiwan University	29,310	30,770	21,870	22,950	21,700	22,770	18,990	19,930	5
National Normal University	NA	NA	21,870	22,950	21,700	22,770	NA	NA	5
National Cheng Kung University	29,330	30,790	19,000	22,960	21,700	22,770	19,000	19,940	5
National Ching Hwa University	NA	NA	NA	22,900	21,700	22,900	19,000	NA	5
Private University									
Tung Ng University	NA	NA	NA	49,150	NA	48,740	41,250	42,690	3.5
Tung Hoi University	NA	NA	47,320	49,380	47,720	48,960	41,440	42,880	3.5
Fu Yan University	NA	NA	46,980	48,810	47,380	48,400	41,150	48,810	3
Yuan-ze University	NA	NA	NA	49,860	47,490	NA	41,250	43,310	5

Source: MOE of Taiwan 2004, [Internet] Available from: http://www.high.edu.tw/05/05.htm

be made in six months' time. During our interview with Prof. Yang Kuo-chih, vice-minister of the MOE, we got to know that the government is keen to adopt this new funding model. Under the proposed new model, the state will finance about one-third of national universities' total expenditure, while the other two-thirds will be financed by tuition fees and other incomes generated by universities (Field Interview, Taipei, December 28, 1999). Most important of all, the Taiwan government has tried to "package" and "justify" the proposed change in the funding methodology in higher education by drawing the reference to the global trend of "privatization" and "decentralization." It is noteworthy that the introduction of user-pays principle and the reduction of state subsidy is not the unique feature in higher education but has already been popular in the welfare sector, especially with the ideas and practices of commodification, privatization, and decentralization that have been adopted in the welfare sector to run social and welfare services (Ku 2000).

Regulation: autonomization of academics and empowerment of higher education institutions

There are various drastic changes with regards to regulation in higher education in Taiwan after the revocation of the martial law in 1987. As discussed earlier, the revised University Law has actually empowered academics and scholars to have far more autonomy to run universities. The following section highlights several reforms that show academics nowadays enjoy far more autonomy and they are held responsible for university governance.

Election of university presidents in higher education institutions

In the previous decades, matters regarding selection, appointment, and dismissal of university presidents in tertiary institutions were tightly controlled by the MOE. The revised University Law stipulates that colleges/universities are allowed to set up searching committees to look for qualified candidates for the post of presidents. Through such committees, academics can recommend two to three shortlisted candidates for the MOE's final approval (in the case of public institutions) or to the trustees (in the case of private colleges). The MOE (or the trustees) must then form a committee to take a final decision (Tsai 1996b). The changes in the selection and appointment of college and university presidents have clearly demonstrated the process of deregulation in tertiary education. Under this new arrangement, more than 10 colleges and universities have engaged in this new process of selecting presidents. The approaches that these institutions have taken can be classified into two categories: the search committee model and the universal (campus-wide) election model. The MOE finally approved the former but disapproved of the latter, expressing the opinion that "outsiders" should never be elected because then the faculty members would be motivated to take sides. However, college faculty members have expressed their preference for the universal election process because of its opportunity for wider participation (Chen 1995). Although the ultimate model has not yet been finalized, the process of negotiation between the MOE and academics has suggested that academics and scholars are really empowered in university/college governance.

University governed by scholars

One of the mechanisms introduced to diversify the control of higher education is related to the enhancement of faculty power at various levels. At the institutional level, faculty members in public and private tertiary institutions are allowed to elect two or three candidates for university president and for deanships and to refer these names for final selection and appointment to the MOE and university presidents respectively. Despite the fact that final control over appointments still lies with the highest authorities, the election exercise has broadened the legitimacy of university leadership (MOE 1995).

In order to be elected, the would-be candidates for university president and deanships are required to campaign on the basis of their vision and performance, and to answer questions raised by faculty and students. Moreover, the government has granted faculty members the power to negotiate as a body with university authorities. In accordance with the new University Law, tertiary institutions can establish their own university faculty councils to deal with the recruitment, promotion, and dismissal of teachers. Such provisions again suggest that academics and scholars now enjoy more autonomy in Taiwan (MOE of Taiwan 1997a,b).

Self-accreditation for academic programs and courses

The self-accreditation system for universities and colleges was introduced as the second type of mechanism to protect institutional autonomy in the 1990s. Previously, the MOE held absolute power to assess faculty qualifications and publications in matters of recruitment and promotion. The old system could also be seen as a screening process to reject academics and censor research or publications deemed inappropriate by the leadership of the ruling party. From 1991, the MOE has gradually devolved the power of self-accreditation to universities and colleges. By 1996–97, 15 universities were granted such a power. At the moment of writing, 23 universities have already got the self-accreditation status while another 16 universities have applied for the same status (MOE of Taiwan 1997a,b).

In order to gain full self-accreditation status, tertiary institutions must pass through three stages. In the preparation stage, tertiary institutions must satisfy the minimum levels set by the ministry for research publications and outputs in the preceding four years (70 percent for institutions with over 50 teachers who have submitted their publications for evaluation, and 90 percent for those with fewer than 20 teachers submitting publications). In the second stage, the MOE sends inspection teams to review the self-assessment processes of those universities that meet the minimum criteria. In particular, the teams check to see whether university faculty councils have been set up and are functioning properly. If institutions pass the on-site inspections, they proceed to the third stage—a three-year confirmation period, during which they are temporarily granted the power of self-assessment. At the end of this period, they are again reviewed. If they pass, full self-accreditation status is granted. Nevertheless, qualified universities and colleges are still required to send the results of their self-assessments to the ministry for filing, while the others are required to continue submitting their publications for assessment (Law 1996a, 2003).

Putting the recent transformations and changes in Taiwan's higher education sector together, it is worth noting that the forms of "marketization" in higher education now seen in Taiwan are not at all new to East Asia. Japan and Korea have had an abundance of state-regulated private universities for 30 years (Morris and Sweeting 1995), while private and *minban* (people-run or nonstate run) higher education has become more popular in mainland China (Mok 2000d). Our earlier discussion has suggested that what higher education in Taiwan is now experiencing is a move from the centralized governance model to a decentralized one, particularly characterized by the process of "denationalization" of higher education. A close scrutiny of the "marketization" and "decentralization" project in Taiwan's higher education is closely related to the sociopolitical liberalization on the island-state. The strategies that the Taiwan government have adopted in reforming its higher education system is to make use of nonstate actors and even market forces to engage in education provision to meet the pressing needs of higher education. The boom in private higher education and the increase in self-financed students suggest that a quasi-market is evolving. The search for multiple channels for financing higher education, coupled with the more autonomy given to individual higher education institutions, have already suggested that a trend of decentralization is taking place in Taiwan's higher education. All these changes are closely related to social and political liberalization started from the late 1980s instead of purely a response to recent trends in globalization.

Internationalization of higher education

Openly recognizing the importance to maintain its links and establish networks with the external world for the fear of gradually being "marginalized" internationally by the People's Republic of China, together with the growing impact of globalization, the Taiwan government has made serious attempts in recent year to internationalize its higher education. According to the MOE, internationalization of higher education means reinforcing the relationship between Taiwan's institutions and overseas higher education institutions. After accession to the World Trade Organization in 2002, the Taiwan government has become very proactive to make its universities more internationalized. A few major strategies have been adopted, since then, including stressing the importance of foreign language learning. To improve the foreign language level of university staff and students, the MOE has made learning English as part of the Program for Enhancement of the Competitiveness of Taiwan's Universities (MOE of Taiwan 2001, 2002, 2003). In order to encourage higher education institutions to engage students in English learning, the MOE rewards those institutions conducting their teaching and learning activities in English. For example, the National Chengchi University is now allowed to offer three English taught master's programs with additional funding offered by the MOE, while two research institutes of National Taiwan University have participated in an English strengthening program. The participating institutes also receive additional subsidy from the MOE. In order to encourage faculty members to teach in English, some universities in Taiwan, such as National Cheng Kung University reward the teachers conducting their classes in English with less teaching contact hours in recognizing their extra efforts (Lo and Weng 2005).

The second measure in promoting foreign language learning is that all students should pass the English tests upon university admission and graduation. For instance, National Taiwan Normal University, Chung Yuan Christian University, National Sun Yat-sen University, National Chiayi University, and Da-yeh University have required their students to reach high-intermediate levels in the General English Proficiency Test (GEPT) organized by the Language Training and Testing Center (LTTC). The third measure in promoting foreign languages in universities is to create an English-speaking environment. Some national universities in Taiwan have taken a lead in using English as the medium of instruction in administration. For instance, National Chung Cheng University has made efforts to turn all official documents in a bilingual form. Additionally, universities in Taiwan are now keen to establish international students exchange programs with overseas institutions in order to recruit both international exchange students and overseas students to study in their campuses.

In addition to the promotion of foreign language learning, the Taiwan government has realized the importance to benchmark its universities with the international standards. One of the measures is to introduce "internal competition" among the universities in Taiwan to make them perform better. Now, all universities in Taiwan have to go through a role differentiation exercise, through which the MOE hopes to have the universities in the island-state assume different missions and functions. Some of the universities will be classified as comprehensive universities, while the others are tasked with the missions as research universities, teaching and professional training, or even vocational in orientation. According to the Executive Yuan, the Taiwan government is very keen to make at least one of its universities become the top 100 in the world within the next decade (Lu 2004).

In addition, the Taiwan government is committed to develop at least 15 key departments or cross-university research centers as the top centers in the selected disciplines in Asia in the next five years (Lu 2004). University merging and deep collaborations are also strongly encouraged by the MOE in fostering a collaborative research culture in Taiwan. The MOE believes that only when the universities pool their common resources and put the critical mass of talented researchers together can Taiwan be developed as one of the leading centers of higher education research and development in the region. University restructuring has been discussed and implemented in recent years despite the disagreement and strong resistance from the academic circles (Lo and Tai 2003).

Discussion and conclusion

The fundamental changes in Taiwan's higher education sector since processes of denationalization, decentralization, and autonomization and marketization can conceptualize the late 1980s. By "denationalization," I mean that the state has begun to forsake its monopoly on higher education, hence allowing the nonstate sector and even the market to engage in higher education provision. By "decentralization," I refer to the shift from the "state control model" to "state supervision model," whereby educational governance is decentralized from educational bureaucracies to create in their place devolved systems of schooling or universities, entailing significant degrees of institutional autonomy and a variety of forms of school-based/university-based management and administration. As for "autonomization," I mean that university academics now have more academic autonomy and they are empowered to do research projects of any kinds and they have far more discretion to manage and operate their institutions. Similar to the global practices of "marketization" and "decentralization," Taiwan's higher education has experienced transformations along the lines of "decentralization" and "marketization." With a far more sociopolitically liberated environment, the Taiwan government has allowed higher education institutions more autonomy to run their institutions. In order to reduce the state's increasing burden, different market-related strategies are adopted such as the increase of student tuition fees, reduction in state's budget in higher education, strengthening the relationship between the university sector and the industrial and business sectors, and encouraging universities and academics to engage in business and market-like activities to generate more revenues and incomes.

Recent comparative education policy studies reveal that even though there seems to be similar patterns/trends in higher education reforms in the selected East Asian societies, they really have diverse agendas (Mok 2000c). Such observations lead us to conclude that the common contextual factors, particularly the increasingly popular global trend of decentralization and marketization, seem to have considerably shaped education policy throughout the world. But before we jump to the conclusion that the formulation of local policies is merely the result of globalization, maybe we should also bear in mind that an alternative hypothesis like local factors are crucial and determining factors for changes.

More specifically, the considerable convergence on the policy rhetoric and general policy objectives may not satisfactorily explain the complicated processes of changes and the dynamic interactions between global-regional-local forces that shape education policymaking in individual countries. This case study of the transformations and reforms in Taiwan's higher education has revealed that even though Taiwan seems to follow similar global trends of marketization and decentralization, still the nation-state has skillfully shaped its political agendas under the policy framework of globalization. The practices of "decentralization" and "marketization" in Taiwan's higher education seem to be global in nature, our contextual analysis in terms of how local factors contribute to recent reforms has suggested that policy formation is driven by local forces instead of the reactions to external/global pressures (see, for example, Dale 1999; Green 1999; Mok 2000c).

Seen in this light, we should not discard state autonomy in policymaking and policy shaping. More importantly, our earlier discussion has confirmed what the skeptics and transformationalists have argued all along, that nation-states still remain as the major actors in local policy decision and formulation. The present case study has vividly revealed that Taiwan government is able to shape the local, political, and policy agenda by the globalization package. Therefore, I believe what really causes the current changes in Taiwan's higher education is far more significantly affected by local forces/factors instead of the global ones.

Putting all the observations discussed earlier into perspective, I would argue that the decentralization and marketization practices are the consequences of the "denationalization project" started by the Taiwan government. Instead of a single response to the impact of globalization, the national government in Taiwan has actually orchestrated the fundamental reform in its higher education sector. Perhaps, what Taiwan is now experiencing is a power negotiation between the state and the education institutions. Undoubtedly, the implementation of the policy of decentralization and the approach to privatization has inevitably led to the restructuring/redefinition of the relationship between the state and education sector. (Hanson 1999). During such processes one may easily observe tension and dynamism, and thus the reach of the state and the extent of civil society have not yet been settled. In this regard, it is too early to argue that the policy of decentralization adopted in Taiwan's education sector has led to deregulation and a genuine delegation of power from the state to educational institutions. Whether educational practitioners can really enjoy more autonomy would very much depend on the bargaining/negotiation processes between the state and educational institutions/ professionals (Hawthorne 1996; Law 1998b). But what is more obvious and certain is that the proposed change will inevitably restructure the relationship between the state and higher education in Taiwan (*United News* December 28, 1999).

Thus, while there are clear globalization trends, especially in the economy and technology, the nation-state is still a powerful actor in shaping the nation's development and in resolving global-national tensions. As Gopinathan suggested, "even as educational paradigms and ideas take on a global character, the factors that determine educational policies are essentially national in character" (Gopinathan 1996, p. 84). This study points to the fact that not all nations have responded to globalization in the same way because of the specificities of national history, politics, culture, and economy. Therefore, the so-called global tide of market competition, nonstate provision of public services, corporate governance, and system-wide and institutional performance management should not be treated as an undifferentiated universal trend. These different elements undoubtedly reinforce each other, though they are not equivalent or interchangeable everywhere. Instead, they may take different configurations, which remain national specific as well as global. Therefore, we must not analyze "globalization practices" in higher education in terms of a one-dimensional movement from "the state" (understood as nonmarket and bureaucratic) to "the market" (understood as nonstate and corporate). Rather, we must contextually analyze the interaction between a range of critical shaping factors in the local context and the impetus for change driven by global trends (Mok 1999, 2000c).

9 South Korea's response to globalization

Questing for internationalization and life long learning

Introduction

As in other Asian economies, South Korea has started a series of higher education reforms in order to improve its global competence. Realizing that the old education governance model is inappropriate in the global policy context, the government of South Korea (the government, hereafter) has started to review its education systems and the comprehensive reform strategies that have been adopted since 1993 to make its education systems more responsive to changing social and economic environments. Believing that the newly emerging knowledge economy attaches great importance to people's qualities like creativity, innovation, and adaptability to changing environments, the government has decided to build an Ed-utopia (the promotion of an "Education Welfare State," where educational opportunities would be available to every citizen at his or her convenience to fully realize individual potential). Based on four reform proposals, 120 tasks were adopted in the 1990s to nurture creative and talented citizens who would live in a highly competitive knowledge-based global village (Moon 1997).

Despite the fact that South Korea has experienced changes after the changeover of presidency after the general election in the past few years, the general direction of education reform has been consistent throughout the years since the mid-1990s. The central features of higher education reform in South Korea can be characterized by the introduction of policies that can promote diversification and specialization in higher education. All the reform measures adopted by the government are aimed at making South Korean higher education more responsive and adaptive to external changes. Creativity, innovation, and critical thinking are frequently stressed. Most important of all, education reforms being launched in South Korea have touched upon not only the design of curricula but also management and governance of universities. The principal goal of this chapter is to examine how South Korea has responded to the impacts of globalization by transforming its higher educations. Particular attention will be given to the most recent changes in higher education, especially the governance changes taking place in higher education provision, financing, and regulation.

Centralized model for governing higher education in the pre-reform period

South Korea is widely known as a strong state, and the state has played a significant role in charting directions for social and economic developments in this Asian Tiger (Koo 1993). Education policy and development, under such a strong state model, has long been significantly shaped by the state through its executive arm, the Ministry of Education (MOE). Before the government's initiatives to reform the higher education systems in the mid-1990s, the higher education sector in South Korea had been strictly regulated and governed by the MOE. The highly centralized governance model in education is clearly revealed by a review report published by OECD. After a comprehensive review of South Korea's education systems, OECD concludes:

> Korea has a unique education system characterized by much larger private sector representation and investment, and a relatively small publicly financed sector compared to other industrialized nations. In the past three decades, the government has, through its *highly regulated* and *centralized* governing system, attained remarkable educational achievements.
>
> (2000, p. 57, italics added by the author)

Before education reforms were initiated by the government in the mid-1990s, the relationship between the government and individual schools could be conceptualized in the following way:

> education policy in Korea, for the most part, had been based on the premise that the individual interests of parents, students, and educators should be subordinated to broader public policy objectives. Priority had long been given to the interests of the government and administrators who support and provide services, rather than to the interests of those who teach and learn in the classroom. Centralized administration, far from playing a service role, dominates the main sectors of education—teachers, students and parents. The school has been in a subservient position, serving its master, the administrators.
>
> (Y.H. Kim 2000, p. 89)

Having for long been organized and operated with rigid restrictions and uniform control, there is no denying the point that education systems in South Korea have not been able to respond to the changing socioeconomic and sociopolitical contexts. With power being centralized in the hand of the MOE, local initiatives and autonomy have been deprived, while individual institutions have lacked the enthusiasm for a creative and rational approach to their operation. Their span of self-control is so limited that administrative authorities must direct individual institutions. As passivity prevails in these institutions, their students cannot be offered with diversified education programs. Under strict orders and directives, teachers have little autonomy while participation of parents in school education is limited. Similarly, students have little opportunities to develop own interests, talents, or creativity (Y.H. Kim 2000, p. 89).

Seeing education as a means to serve the general good of society, Article 7 of the Education Law stipulates that all schools (including also colleges and universities) are the public instruments of the state and must be established in accordance with the standards provided by the relevant statutes. Working under such a legal framework, it is beyond doubt that institutional freedom is limited (J. Kim 2000, p. 68). In fact, the MOE controlled a variety of university governance matters before the reform started in the mid-1990s, including granting approval to the establishment of higher education, stipulating detailed regulations governing program design and curriculum design, appointment of personnel, student admission policy, financing, budgeting and facilities, as well as setting academic standards.

Another area of control is related to reporting and audits. All institutions of higher education are required to submit periodically, on government request, various reports covering nearly all aspects of their operations, including financing, staff personnel, and students. Government authorities also make audits on every institution, annually and as needed, on all aspects of the institutional operations (quoted and modified from J. Kim 2000, pp. 70–71). Putting such observations together, we may well argue that the government had adopted a centralized model in governing higher education institutions in South Korea.

Nonetheless, the socioeconomic and sociopolitical changes resulting from the financial crisis in East Asia, together with the growing impact of globalization, have driven the government to realize that Korean higher education system is too rigid and less responsive to the changing socioeconomic and sociopolitical contexts. Hence, the government has begun comprehensive reviews of its higher education, and reforms have been started in the 1990s to make the Korean higher education system more creative, innovative, and adaptive to pressures and challenges generated by the globalization processes.

The policy context on Korean higher education reform

In spite of remarkable achievements in education and the quality of its basic education internationally recognized, the government has recognized that depending upon the existing higher education system alone can never meet the challenges, intense pressures, and challenges generated by processes of globalization. Acknowledging the fact that the existing system was developed to serve the needs of the organization of production in an industrial society, now there is a strong need to reform the higher education system to cope with challenges of the growing knowledge economy. Since the new knowledge economy requires a different type of organization of production, whereby the relationships between worker to work, worker to worker, and worker to consumer have changed, an education system in the new context needs to promote and facilitate people to engage in lifelong learning. The call for "continual learning" leads to a fundamental paradigm shift in education from providing people basic skills to developing core skills, encouraging creative and critical thinking for problem solving and developing specialized skills for specific professional careers and tasks. In addition to the external/global drive for reform, South Korea was hit severely by the East Asian financial crisis and thus the poor work habit and lack of problem-solving ability of the Korean elites were clearly revealed in the postcrisis period (Kwak 2001, pp. 8–9).

Having identified the core problems, the government openly admits that the existing education system has failed to equip the society with autonomous capacity to solve the problems by itself (Kwak 2001, p. 12). In his 8.15 Liberation Day address, Kim Dae Jung, the ex-president of South Korea, specified the necessity of the national task of nurturing autonomous capacity in the Declaration for the Second National Building (Kwak 2001, p. 3). He pinpointed that the key of the Second Nation-Building is to nurture individual citizens civic character and capacity that are creative and responsible (Kwak 2001, p. 4). He followed the basic structure for higher education reform established by the President Commission on Education Reform (PCER) in 1995 and deepened structural reforms in Korean's education systems (Park 2000a, p. 149). The principles of the recently initiated education policies have brought changes to the education scene by shifting educational emphasis from:

- subject knowledge to nurturing moral character;
- standardization to autonomy, diversification, and specialization;
- provider to consumer;
- closed education occurring within the boundary of classrooms to open and lifelong education;
- academic sectarianism to individual capability; and
- quantitative growth to qualitative improvement.

(Yoon 2000)

In order to facilitate the nation-wide effort to implement the reform objectives, the Presidential Commission for the New Education Community (PCNEC) was established in June 1998. It has been promoting education reform by providing professional consultation, linking citizens and education officials, and encouraging active participation of the public (MOE 2000c). Major functions of the PCNEC include reviewing and evaluating progress made by education reform; launching campaigns and training activities as necessitated by the education reform movement; motivating local citizens movements for education reform; directing national awareness campaigns for the new education community; reviewing key issues in education reform as requested by the president. With the establishment of PCNEC, the government has shown its determination to reform its education systems. The reform procedures have focused on:

- a bottom-up process encompassing all of the stakeholders including teachers, parents, and community figures;
- classrooms and schools where education takes place;
- a civil movement stimulating the participation of citizens across various social strata;
- accountability and effectiveness, via evaluating the outcomes of education.

A better understanding of higher education reform in South Korea should be contextualized in the light of the earlier stated wider changing education policy context. With the general goals to train people for the changing needs of social and economic development (see Figure 9.1), higher education enrollment has been expanding and a process of massification has taken place in South Korea in the past decade or so. By the end of the 1990s, the enrollment rate of high school graduates to higher education reached about 85 percent. In order to assure high quality in tertiary education, coupled with the need to provide training for its citizens in coping with new social and economic challenges, the government has started reforms in the higher education sector. Realizing the importance to make its higher education graduates more creative and innovative in thinking, responsive and adaptive to rapid changes, and to internationalize its higher education systems, the government has adopted the following strategies to reform its higher education systems.

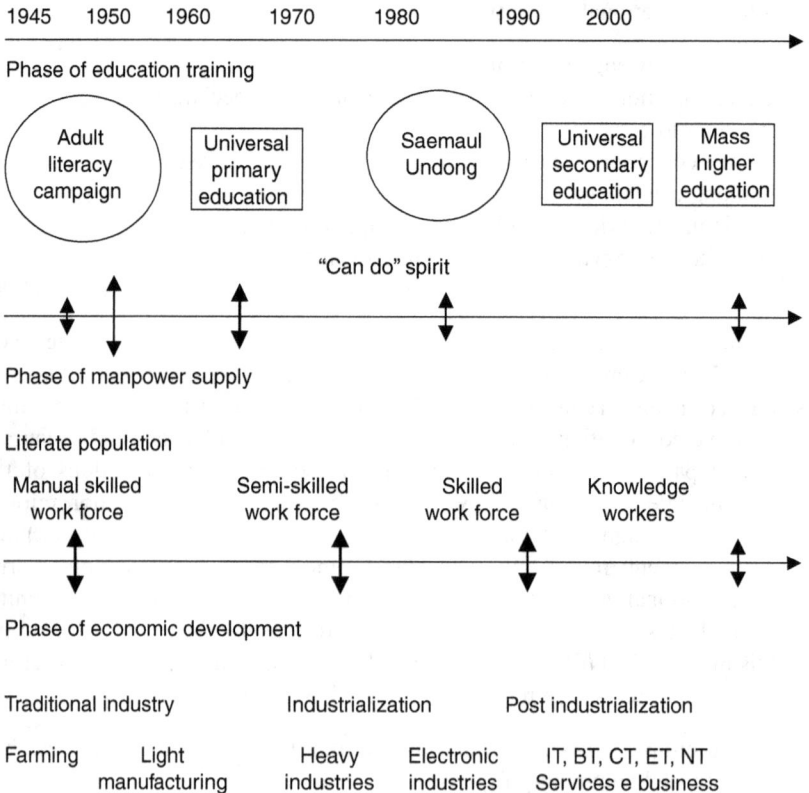

| 1945 | 1950 | 1960 | 1970 | 1980 | 1990 | 2000 |

Phase of education training

Adult literacy campaign | Universal primary education | Saemaul Undong | Universal secondary education | Mass higher education

"Can do" spirit

Phase of manpower supply

Literate population

Manual skilled work force | Semi-skilled work force | Skilled work force | Knowledge workers

Phase of economic development

Traditional industry   Industrialization   Post industrialization

Farming   Light manufacturing   Heavy industries   Electronic industries   IT, BT, CT, ET, NT Services e business

Figure 9.1 Progress of education and economic developments during 1945–2000 in South Korea.

Source: Adapted from Kwak 2002, p. 24.

Higher education reform in South Korea: most recent developments

In March 1985, the establishment of the PCER, under the direct supervision of the president, began the reform processes in higher education. In mid-1990s, the government had a new vision for the country's future development. With the intention to build South Korea into the "New Korea," the PCER presented a review report entitled "Directions and tasks of Educational Reform for the Creation of New Korea" to the President in 1994, emphasizing the importance on strengthening international competitiveness and improving college entrance examination system in South Korea.

In 1995, the First Educational Reform Plan was released, proposing 48 specific tasks and setting out a new framework for education development in South Korea. Central to the specific tasks were related to:

- establishment of an open Edu-topia (education-utopia) society;
- diversification and specialization of universities;
- creation of a democratic and autonomous school community;
- emphasis on humanity and creativity in curricula;
- innovation of a university entrance examination;
- development of diverse education programs;
- establishment of a new form of evaluation system;
- remodeling of teacher training programs; and
- increasing education budget up to 5 percent on the GNP.

In the subsequent years, three reports related to education reform were released. As for higher education, the second reform plan published in 1996 made recommendations to construct a new vocational education system, introducing a professional graduate school system and to reform education related laws. The third reform report released in the following year further supported the move toward empowerment of colleges and universities by giving them more autonomy, while accountability was emphasized at the same time. The government also encouraged using information and technology in higher education. To increase learning opportunities in higher education, diversified access and participation channels were supported. The fourth reform plan announced in 1997 touched upon university governance and management issues.

Most recently, the government has endorsed the general directions of higher education reforms. Synthesizing various higher education proposals adopted in the past decade or so in South Korea, the government is keen to make its higher education systems more diversified and specialized, allowing more autonomy for both higher education institutions and students to have more choices and creativity, and innovation has been stressed. Moving beyond a teacher-oriented approach, recent higher education reforms emphasize the importance of learner-centered education. To cope with globalization challenges, South Korea has made attempts to internationalize its higher education by strengthening foreign language training and expanding its international student exchange programs (MOE 1999; Lee 2000).

From		Toward
Passive receiving education model		Knowledge-Creation Education Model

⟹

A Country of recurring crises	The	A country equipped with the competence to cope with changing situation

⟹

Schools are exam-preparatory institutions	School	Exercising autonomy, creativity, and diversity

⟹

Passive transmitters of knowledge	Teacher	Word class educational professionals

⟹

Rote memory of "correct" answers	student	Raising citizens' capacity and creativity

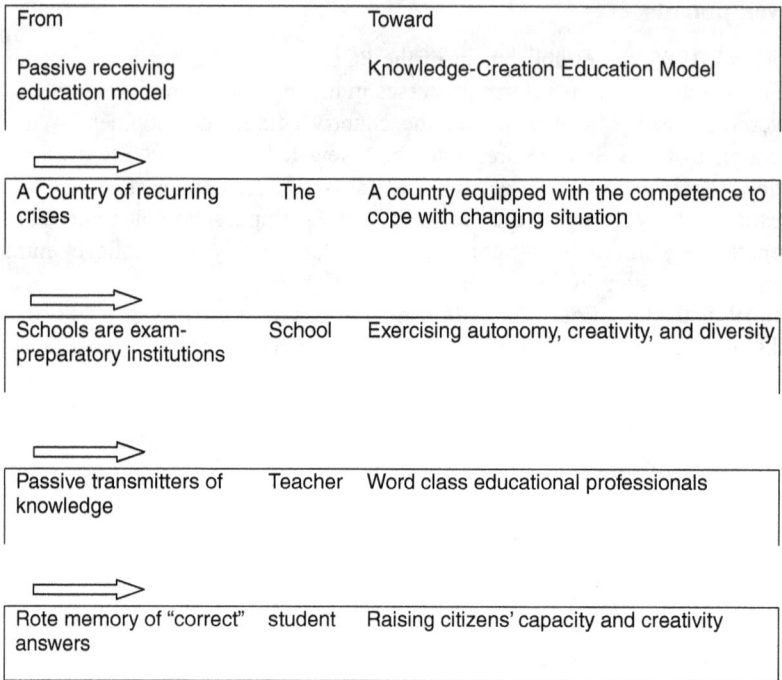

Figure 9.2 Paradigm shift of education in South Korea.

Source: Modified and adapted from Kwak 2002, p. 33.

Figure 9.2 summarizes the paradigm shift in education policy in South Korea, indicating that the government is keen to move beyond receiving education in a passive way to quest for a new way of knowledge creation education. Having discussed the general directions of higher education reforms, let's now turn to specific changes taking place in higher education provision, financing, and regulation.

Changing governance in South Korea's higher education

Provision

At present, up to 80 percent of higher education institutions in Korea are private schools (MOE 2000, p. 48). In 2002, there were 137 private institutions out of a total of 163 higher education institutions in South Korea (MOE 2003, p. 31). However, the high proportion of the private sector in higher education provision shows that the South Korean government has not allocated sufficient resources to promote higher education development and parents have been heavily burdened with tuition fees (see Table 9.1; OECD 2000, p. 62). Acknowledging the

Table 9.1 Types of higher education institutions in Korea by foundation

Classification	Total	National	Public	Private
1990	107	23	1	83
1995	131	24	2	105
1997	150	24	2	124
1998	156	24	2	130
1999	158	24	2	132
2000	162	24	2	136
2002	163	24	2	137

Source: KEDI 2000, p. 188; MOE 2003, p. 31.

important role of higher education in the increasingly globalized economy and the significance to make its higher education system more creative and adaptive to rapid socioeconomic changes, the government has decided to allocate more public fund to finance higher education in recent years.

Despite the high proportion of private universities in South Korea, the private universities have closely followed the national model particularly copying the curricula and structure of the top-ranking university (i.e., Seoul National University). Under the Education Law, all higher education institutions, no matter whether they are public or private in nature, come under the direction supervision of the MOE (MOE 2000, p. 67). In this regard, individual institutions therefore lack autonomy in their management and academic affairs, including student quotas, qualification of teaching staff, curriculum, degree requirement, and other related academic and administrative matters. As a consequence, many universities simply copy each other, hence making Korean universities and colleges fairly uniform (Park 2000a, p. 160).

Brain Korea 21 project

Realizing that its higher education is too uniform and rigid to respond to the external, social, and economic changes, the government has made different attempts to diversify the Korean higher education, and made its higher education more specialized in the past decade. One of the reform strategies is the launch of Brain Korea 21 (hereafter, BK21), which aims to find the creative and advanced knowledge base necessary for the twenty-first century by improving the quality of graduate programs and encouraging research activities. More specifically, major objectives of BK21 are:

- fostering world class research universities which will serve as infrastructure to produce ideas and technology that are creative and original;
- strengthening the competitiveness of local universities; and
- introducing professional graduate schools to train professionals in the field, creating an environment where universities compete with each other not

based on name value, but based on the quality of research outcomes and students' performance.

(Quoted from MOE 2001)

In addition, BK21 project is also committed to develop the following areas:

- expanding graduate schools in universities and strengthening research and development in Korea, setting targets for producing 1,300 high quality people annually;
- raising the quality and quantity of research papers to be published in SCI-level journals from 10,000 in 1998 (world ranking 17) to 20,000 in 2005 (ranking 10);
- questing for becoming top 10 world ranking graduate schools by 2005 and take innovative steps to boost research capabilities;
- investing an addition of 200 billion won annually from 1999 to 2005, or a total of 1.4 trillion won during seven-year period into the project to promote graduate studies in universities;
- investing 11–48.5 billion won between 1999 and 2003, or 170.5 billion won in total during the five-year period to boost research capabilities of graduate schools in Korean universities.

(Chae 2003a)

Four subject areas are covered in the BK21 project, namely Applied Science, Art and Social Science, Korean Indigenous Science, and Newly Emerging Industries. A total budget of US$ 1.2 billion is expected to be invested in the project between 1999 and 2005 (MOE 2000, p. 174). By enhancing the research capabilities of graduate schools in various research areas, domestic institutions are able to achieve diversification in selected academic disciplines. In addition, providing intensive support for graduate schools, professors and graduate students can concentrate on research activities without an overload of additional work (MOE 2001). This enables those graduate schools to focus on particular research areas in order to make their professions more specialized.

Furthermore, the direction of financial support system has been changed from research project assistance to student-centered personnel expenses and scholarships. After implementing the proposed change, a major part of the fund (i.e., 70 percent of 668.5 billion won) has been allocated to 21,994 graduate students studying in master or doctorate programs and 1,982 post-doctorate students and contract professors since 1999. After the launch of the project, research capacities and international cooperation between Korean universities and other international universities have been enhanced and strengthened. In the past few years, 5,306 papers have been published in international journals, a 37 percent of excess of the target (i.e., 3,875), and 5,821 researchers participated in international conferences in the past three years. Meanwhile 9,000 graduate students and professors took part in international conferences and short-term visits and research programs abroad (Chae 2003a). All these figures show how Korean academics in general and universities in particular have become far more internationalized.

Credit bank system

In response to the call for "lifelong learning," another measure adopted by the government is to diversify the provision of higher education by introducing a credit bank system in vocational education. This system enables people who are unable to attend regular universities to obtain tertiary education by accumulating credit points acquired at different higher education institutions. Flexibility provided in this system guarantees people right to access learning, through a diversification of ways of learning (Lee *et al.* 2000).

Since 1998, students who seek for credits or academic degrees need to take the programs posted in the "Standard Education Process" set by the MOE (73 programs for bachelor's degree and 83 junior college programs). At the same time, institutions need to get recognition from the Korean Educational Development Institute by following the "Teaching Outline" (which currently covers 1,932 courses, 312 introductory, and 1,620 major courses). In 2002, 370 accredited institutions offered 8,680 courses under the credit bank system. Among them, 151 institutes with 3,753 courses were run as the lifelong education institutes of universities and junior colleges; 101 institutes with 1,486 courses were run by the private sector; 69 institutes with 2,259 courses were offered as vocational training centers. The rest of courses were in forms of indepth major courses, technical colleges, technical high schools, and specialized schools. Table 9.2 shows the increase in number of students engaging in lifelong learning through the credit bank system. In 2002 alone, it was reported that around 43,275 students enrolling for courses and the accumulative number of graduates reached 6,793 (Chae 2003b).

Provision of distance teaching is also an area being diversified. Before the reform started in the mid-1990s, the previous Higher Education Law prohibited the private sector and conventional universities establishing single-mode or dedicated virtual universities, although offering virtual courses is permitted (Jung and Rha 2001, p. 34). In order to make the Korean higher education more outward looking and comparable to the universities in other parts of the globe, the government initiated a Virtual University Trial Project in February 1998, aiming to develop and implement web-based courses or other types of distance education course. It encourages partnership among universities and the private sector, and the sharing of existing resources in order to create a cost-effective virtual education system without diminishing quality (Jung and Rha 2001, p. 34). Fifteen

Table 9.2 Development of the credit bank system (Unit: in person)

Conferment date	August 1999	February 2000	August 2000	February 2001	August 2001	February 2002	Total
Bachelor's	25	111	143	267	396	718	1,660
Junior college	9	539	227	1,462	334	2,562	5,133
Total	34	650	370	1,729	730	3,280	6,793

Source: Chae 2003b.

virtual entities, including 7 consortia (formed by 65 universities and 5 companies) and 8 conventional universities, have participated in the project. In short, the introduction of the Virtual University Trial Project has diversified the provision of distance learning, which previously was monopolized by the Korea National Open University (KNOU).

Financing

The funding for higher education in Korea comes from tuition fees, government aid, grant and research contracts, endowments, and other sources. Among these sources, Korean universities and colleges rely heavily on student tuition fees for financing university education. Tuition fees account for about 80 percent of the budgets of private colleges and universities and about 45 percent of the public conventional institutions' budgets. Corresponding figures for the MOE supports are 20 and 55 percent, respectively (OECD 1998, p. 52; Park 2000a, p. 170). This situation is not expected to change in the near future especially when market principles are now introduced into the higher education system in South Korea (Jung and Rha 2001, p. 32). To effectively use all the education resources, the government has attempted to deregulate the Korean education market by encouraging a healthy competition.

Since the 1990s, the government has introduced competition in higher education finance by requiring all colleges and universities to compete for substantial portion of government funds based upon their performance. And the distribution of the funds is in accordance with college/university evaluation results. To accompany the granting of autonomy, universities, and colleges are pushed to increase their responsiveness to the needs of the market. It means that the quality of their own education becomes an essence for the higher education institutions surviving in the highly competitive world (OECD 1998, p. 50). In other words, these deregulation efforts had helped to develop the higher education market with an atmosphere of competition among various universities, faculty, and departments.

To diversify university education, students are encouraged to choose universities regardless of their high tuition fees. The government has then provided direct financial aid to private institutions since 1990. By 1994 government aid reached 2.4 percent of the university budget, although the 10 percent goal had not been reached (Park 2000b, p. 109). In 1995, government aid to private universities amounted to 166 billion won or about 1.3 percent of the national education budget (Park 2000c, p. 139). Besides, the government also provides private institutions with aid in the form of grant for specific programs and purposes (e.g., expansion of science laboratories and libraries). Since 1990, private universities and colleges have been awarded categorical grant as well as funds to improve facilities. Both of them are expected to improve the quality of facilities that can be shared by more than one institution (Park 2000b, p. 117). Currently, private universities are cooperating vigorously to create the University Development Fund as a means to solve their financial problems. In addition, they are demanding that the government give them permission to start a donation-based admission policy (OECD 1998, p. 52).

Such new financial arrangements for private higher education institutions reduce the financial burden of students attending private institutions. It maintains equity of students' choice in order to achieve diversification in university enrollment.

Regulation

Over-regulation has been a problem of the tertiary education in Korea over the years. As mentioned earlier, both private and public higher education institutions lack autonomy in their management and academic affairs, with government regulations constraining them in the recruitment and payment of staff, student enrollments and admissions, fee levels, and so on (OECD 2000, p. 62). As a result, deregulation has been a focus of Korean education reform. To increase the autonomy of universities and colleges, the government has revised the Education Act and related regulations to allow individual institutes to choose their own development plans (OECD 1998, p. 51).

Providing managerial autonomy in admission

The university entrance examination system was criticized for causing the entire education system to become too examination driven and memorization oriented (OECD 2000, p. 62; Park 2000a, p. 166). Thus autonomy of individual institutions has been enhanced by deregulation in university admission. In 1998, the government introduced performance-based evaluation, which allows universities to develop their own admission criteria and to apply a performance-based student selection system rather than a pure test scores-based one (OECD 2000, p. 62).

Under the new system, public universities use the Student Complex Achievement Records (SCAR) as the main source of data on which to determine admission. The SAT (a scholastic aptitude test modeled after the one used in the United States) score, writing, interview, and other sources of evidence now become optional. The SCAR changes the student evaluation system from a relative evaluation to an absolute one, as it shows achievement level and class standing in each subject instead of a total score. Besides, the SCAR provides a comprehensive evaluation by including academic transcripts and class standings by subject, aptitude, and special abilities in subjects, attendance, extracurricular activities, social service activities, certification, and participation in contests, wards, personality, and demeanor from grade one to twelve. To protect institutional autonomy, individual institutions can choose their assessment items that they consider appropriate and decide on the value of each subject and item (Park 2000a, p. 167). In addition, institutions are allowed to determine admissions by using different sources of evidence such as student records, essay tests, indepth interviews, certifications, recommendation letters, personal essays, academic proposals, awards, volunteer work, and special activity records, in the selection process (Chae 2003a).

On the basis of three principles, private institutions have also been authorized to determine their own admissions policy. First, to prevent elementary and secondary schools being preparatory institutions for the university entrance examination, admission policy should be geared to the standard curriculum of Korean elementary and secondary schools. Second, the burden for parent expenditure on private tutoring should be reduced under the new admissions system. Third, public announcement is required when a school applies its new admission policy to ensure that students and parents have enough time to prepare (Park 2000a, p. 168). These principles mean that admissions policy of private institutions would not be drastically different from public ones.

Furthermore, higher education institutions (HEIs) are able to admit students at any time of the year. In the past, universities and colleges could make their admission only at certain periods permitted by the government. This policy limited students' choice, as many schools have their admission interview or examination on the same day (Park 2000a, p. 168). The new policy increases the flexibility of university admissions schedules, so colleges/universities and students have more options. This helps to achieve diversification in university admission system.

In addition, universities now apply a dual selection process, including special selection process and regular selection process.

> The special selection process may take place as early as the first semester, allowing universities to flexibly select students throughout the year. The process also grants more leeway in the administrative handling of the process and enables the implementation of a more diverse selection process. The special selection takes place at the end of either semester. To ensure the viability of the special selection process, students admitted through this process are not allowed to apply during the regular selection process.
>
> (Chae 2003)

These changes in admissions system have a great impact on the funding of higher education. Many universities and colleges in Korea rely heavily on student tuition fees, the total number of students being admitted hence affects their revenue accordingly. Since the reform gives individual institutions the flexibility to determine their enrollment, they can increase their income by raising their own enrollment (Park 2000c, pp. 136–37). This represents an empowerment of individual institutions in both university admission and finance.

Evaluation and accreditation system

The current system for university evaluation and accreditation in Korea has been implemented since 1992 (Park 2000a, p. 168). An independent nongovernmental legal entity, the Korean Council for University Education (KCUE), is responsible for accreditation of all four-year colleges and universities. The MOE would provide financial aid to those institutions with positive evaluation result. To encourage specialization in selected fields and also curriculum diversification, assessments are carried out at both departmental and institutional levels. Then government financial aid would be given to each department or school instead of university or college (OECD 1998, p. 50; Park 2000c, p. 137).

More specifically, the East Asian financial crisis that occurred in the late 1990s has fundamentally changed the assessment system of Korean university system from focusing on the hardware to the quality of education, paying far more attention to review the quality of the curriculum, research, teaching, and university management and governance. When assessing the performance of universities in Korea, three major areas, namely, University Financial Assessment, Comprehensive University Assessment, and Academic Assessment Project are introduced. For *Comprehensive University Assessment*, there are four objectives in the assessment exercise, including:

1   to enhance the efficiency of instruction, the sense of responsibility, independence, and cooperation of college education through the creation of a favorable teaching environment;
2   to help universities provide education that meets the social needs of the twenty-first century;
3   to encourage universities to develop strategies to make them stand out from others; and
4   to raise the level of education to that of advanced universities around the world.

Table 9.3 Comprehensive university assessment performances (Unit: University)

Year	Assessment classification				Number of universities
	Undergraduate + Graduate	Undergraduate	Graduate	Branch campus	
1994	National: 6 Private: 1 (Total: 7)	—	—	—	7 (7)
1995	National: 3 Private: 11 (Total: 14)	National: 1 Private: 3 (Total: 4)	—	Private: 5 (Total: 5)	23 (18)
1996	National: 2 Private: 7 (Total: 9)	Private: 2 (Total: 2)	—	—	11 (11)
1997	National: 2 Private: 6 (Total: 8)	National: 15: Private: 1 (Total: 16)	—	Private: 2 (Total: 2)	26 (24)
1998	National: 5 Private: 28 (Total: 33)	Private: 19 (Total: 19)	National: 2 Private: 1 (Total: 3)	Private: 1 (Total: 1)	56 (52)
1999	National: 2 Private: 11 (Total: 13)	National: 9 Private: 5 (Total: 14)	National: 3 Private: 16 (Total: 19)	Private: 2 (Total: 2)	48 (27)
2000	National: 1 Private: 2 (Total: 3)	Private: 21 (Total: 21)	Private: 1 (Total: 1)	—	25 (24)
Total	87	76	23	10	196 (163)

Source: Chae 2003a.

The first round of assessment was conducted from 1994 to 2000. Out of 193 universities, 163 went through with the assessment exercise, while the second assessment has started since 2001 and will be completed by 2006. Table 9.3 shows the comprehensive university assessment performance from 1994 to 2000, suggesting quite a number of universities in Korea went through the assessment exercise in the past few years.

Academic assessment project

In addition to the comprehensive university assessment, universities in Korea have also gone through academic assessment project and financial assessment exercises. The academic assessment project started in 1999 with the principal goal to raise the overall quality of education and competitiveness as well as stimulating diversification among universities, which will ultimately lead to the development of the nation's competitive edge. The academic assessment project consists of a systematic assessment of teaching and research environment in each university and the results will be accessible to the general public. From 1999 to 2001, seven rounds of field visits were conducted and 583 universities have been assessed (Chae 2003a).

Discussion

Changing state and higher education relations

In order to allow HEIs more autonomy and flexibility in governing and managing their own businesses, there have been changes taking place in the legal and administrative systems in South Korea. In March 1998, the government established a new legal framework "Framework Act on Education" prescribing the rights and duties of the citizens and the obligations of the state and local governments on education issues. In line with the new legal framework on education, the Higher Education Act was issued in the same year, with an emphasis on enlarging of educational opportunities, improving education quality, and harmonizing between autonomy and accountability. With this new legal framework in place, individual universities or HEIs have been empowered to decide on issues related to curriculum design, recruitment of students, and deployment of personnel.

It is note-worthy that after the new higher education legal framework was introduced in the late 1990s, the state and higher education relations have begun to change. Attempting to move beyond the "centralized" governance model, the government has started to reform its education administrative arrangements by making the MOE the primary "driver" for education reform in 1999. In addition, the government also set up a Higher Education Support Bureau to replace the former Academic Research Policy Bureau (Lee 2000).

Under the new administrative framework of Higher Education Support Bureau, four divisions, namely, Graduate School Support, Admissions Support, College Academic Affairs, and Higher Education Finance, were formed to promote research and development, managing and improving university admissions systems, establishing education policies, and systems and supporting finance, and improving the coordination and management of the higher education sector. Unlike the old days when the state controlled every aspect of higher education governance, the recent reforms in the legal and administrative structure in higher education have tried to devolve responsibilities to institutions in governing their businesses and therefore they can become more responsive to rapid social and economic changes (Lee 2000).

With individual HEIs given more autonomy and flexibility, the state-higher education relations have changed from a primarily state dominance model to a more deregulated governance model. HEIs, governed under this new model, are now becoming more responsive to rapid social and economic changes whereas the principle of "accountability" has been stressed in the change process.

Globalization discourse justifying local political agendas

Like other Asian societies discussed earlier, the South Korean government has found that the challenges of globalization and the new knowledge-based economy have rendered the old higher education governance model inappropriate. Our earlier discussions and observations have clearly indicated that higher education in South Korea has experienced similar trends of massification, decentralization, and marketization in higher education like what happened in Taiwan, Singapore, Hong Kong, and mainland China. There are a lot of changes in common between the higher education sector in South Korea and that of elsewhere, hence suggesting that similar trends of globalization have shaped higher education developments in these societies. But the earlier discussion has offered an alternative conclusion that educational development is primarily national in character since local factors are crucial and determining factors for changes. More importantly, the nation-states/local governments still enjoy autonomy and they exercise authority to direct higher education reforms in their countries.

The continual questioning of the state capacity in the context of globalization has inevitably drawn people to believe that the state is reduced to the role of the "night-watchman state" of classical liberalism, hence only taking care of law and order, protecting the sanctity of contract, and maintaining the minimum level of welfare to protect those really poor and vulnerable, and facilitating the free operation of the market. Moreover, the reformulation of modern states has led some scholars to believe that modern states have to play the roles as "facilitator," "enabler," "regulator," and "builder of market" (Ma 1999; Sbragia 2000) and new public management is characterized by "governance without government" (Rosenau 1992). In this connection, it seems that the capacity and the role of nation-states have changed in the sense that they become less autonomous and have less exclusive control over the economic, social, and cultural processes and distinctiveness of their territories (Giddens 1998).

Nonetheless, our earlier discussion has indicated that even though we may observe similar strategies are adopted by the government in reforming its higher education systems, a close scrutiny of the domestic forces of reform has revealed that the recent higher education reforms are a result of the social, economic, and political changes in South Korea in recent years. Our discussions have suggested that the impact of globalization may have accelerated the need for reform but we should not think that the recent higher education in South Korea is simply directed or orchestrated by global forces alone. As Hallak (2000) rightly suggested, modern states may tactically make use of the globalization discourse to justify their own political agendas or legitimize their own inaction. Analyzing the current higher education developments in South Korea from a public policy perspective, we may find that the Korean higher education reforms are pursued within the context of managing state-building (or government-capacity) and economic growth in a state-directed (or government-directed) paradigm of governance rather than to de-power the state/government. In addition, the Korean higher education reforms can be interpreted as the strategies adopted by the government to cope with problems of political and bureaucratic governance instead of purely problems of severe economic and social difficulties.

Of course, we cannot rule out the fact that what South Korea is currently facing is the growing impact of globalization, nonetheless we must not ignore the important local factors that reforms are really needed since the system has been too centralized and rigid for facilitating Korea's further development in the changing socioeconomic and sociopolitical contexts. Even when we argue that the recent reforms initiated by South Korea are the consequence of the globalization processes, the earlier discussion has suggested that the presence of diverse national and local agendas have given different meanings to common management jargons and statements. If we accept diversities in domestic administrative agenda as the norm rather than the exception in global public management and governance, then we may have a better reflection of the impacts of globalization. Perhaps, the usefulness of the globalization claim lies more in its rhetoric, such a globalization discourse is adopted to push for local political/policy agendas (Pratt and Poole 1999, pp. 540–43; Cheung 2000).

Conclusion

In conclusion, our earlier discussions have discovered that even though there seems to be similar patterns/trends in higher education reforms in South Korea as that of elsewhere, the recently initiated higher education reforms in South Korea have really had diverse agenda. Such observations lead us to conclude that the common contextual factors, particularly the increasingly popular global trend of decentralization and marketization, seem to have considerably shaped education policy throughout the world including South Korea. But before we jump to this conclusion, maybe we should also bear in mind the alternative hypothesis that local factors are crucial and determining factors for change. Therefore, the considerable convergence at the policy rhetoric and general policy objectives may not satisfactorily explain the complicated processes of changes and the dynamic interactions between global-regional-local forces that shape education policymaking in individual countries (Dale 1999; Green 1999). Instead, a close scrutiny of the transformations and reforms in higher education of these East Asian societies has revealed similar trends but diverse political agenda of individual nation-states/places.

Hence, while there are clear globalization trends, especially in the economy and technology, the nation-state is still a powerful actor in shaping the nation's development and in resolving global and national tensions. This case study points out that not all nations have responded to globalization in the same way because of the specificities of national history, politics, culture, and economy. Therefore, the so-called global tide of market competition, nonstate provision of public services, corporate governance, and system-wide and institutional performance management should not be treated as an undifferentiated universal trend. These different elements undoubtedly reinforce each other, though they are not equivalent or inter-changeable everywhere. Instead, they may take different configurations, which remain national-specific as well as global. According to Gopinathan, "even as educational paradigms and ideas take on a global character, the factors that determine educational policies are essentially national in character" (Gopinathan 1996, p. 18). Instead of simply a process of globalization, the formulation of national policies is the results of the complicated and dynamic processes of glocalization (Mok and Lee 2001; Mok 2000b). Therefore, we must not analyze "globalization practices" in higher education in terms of a one-dimensional movement from "the state" (understood as nonmarket and bureaucratic) to "the market" (understood as nonstate and corporate). Rather, we must contextually analyze the interaction between a range of critical shaping factors in the local context and the impetus for change driven by global trends.

10 Japan's response to globalization

Corporatization and changing university governance

Introduction

As in other East Asian societies, higher education in Japan has been experiencing intense pressure for change in the past decade. Notions and reform strategies along the lines of "marketization," "privatization," "corporatization," and "internationalization" have been adopted and implemented in Japanese higher education with the intention of making the system more responsive and flexible to cope with intensified globalization challenges. Despite the reform efforts, Japanese society is somehow stuck at a crossroads. The Japanese government is very keen to internationalize and incorporate its higher education system in order to enhance its global competitiveness. On the other hand, Japanese society is very much concerned about whether its rich tradition and culture will be damaged, especially when the proposed reforms might lead Japan in far more Westernized directions. What makes the change processes difficult is that people are reluctant to accept and implement changes. This chapter critically examines recent changes and reforms of Japan's higher education, with particular reference to why and how the Japanese government has incorporated its national universities. The primary attention of the chapter will be on how three major educational governance aspects—namely, educational financing, provision, and regulation—have changed, especially after the implementation of "corporatization" strategies among state universities. The chapter begins with a brief introduction to the historical background of higher education, followed by a discussion of the policy context of higher education reform in Japan. The core of the chapter focuses on the most recent higher education reforms and changing higher education governance in Japan.

Historical background of higher education in Japan

The existing educational system of Japan is the product of its unique historical background. During the Edo period, Japan's education was characterized by a dual system under the rule of Tokugawa Ieyasu. There were *hanko* or fief schools for the samurai, while *terakoya* or single teachers ran small private schools for commoners. The values of education in Japan were highly influenced by Confucianism and Buddhism, whereby education was a means to acquire knowledge and skills. In addition, education was adopted as a tool for cultivating students' spiritual or moral values, such as diligence and harmony. For the *hanko* or fief schools, Confucianism was the main philosophy, and while the curriculum, by the end of the Edo period, included not only Japanese and Chinese studies but also Western studies, particularly incorporating Western medicine. During Japan's modernization and 1868 restoration periods, graduates of the *hanko* or fief schools became the pillars of Japanese society. For *terakoya*, the main focus of their studies were the fundamentals of reading, writing, and arithmetic. Although the students were commoners, the demand for schooling grew as their productivity increased from the middle of the Edo period onward.

In 1868, Japan entered the Meiji period, after the fall of Tokugawa Shogunate. The main thrust in education was to modernize the education system based on the Western model. In order to achieve this, the Japanese government abolished the two-tier education system that distinguished the samurai and the commoners. In 1871, the government set up the Ministry of Education (MOE) as the centralized administration for education. Since then, Japanese have enjoyed far more education opportunities and systematic education systems have been institutionalized. At the tertiary level, there were higher schools (*kotogakko*, but this kind of higher school was different from those in the present system), universities, technical colleges, normal schools, and other institutions. Although the enrollment rate of the eligible age group into tertiary education was less than 5 percent in 1940, ideas of egalitarianism were commonly shared among the people. Considering education a chance for upward mobility, Japanese generally believe graduates of elementary education with talents and abilities will get a high position regardless of class and gender. Therefore, the belief in egalitarianism further fostered the national passion toward education.

Nonetheless, militarism and ultranationalism became very popular in the 1930s and educational development was not immune from such ideological influences. After Japan was defeated in the Second World War, major reconstruction work was completed during the Allied Occupation. One of the reconstruction works, education, was greatly influenced by the US model. Subsequently, the education system established at that time has had far-reaching impacts on the modern Japanese education system. Under the influence of the US model, the Japanese education system put emphasis on culture and peace, stressing the importance of developing individuality and individual characters, and equal educational opportunity was consistently promoted. In terms of the higher education system, the higher school in the old system was incorporated into four years of university study. A system of 6–3–3–4 has been established, and access to upper-level institutions has been significantly increased.

In the 1960s, Japan experienced strong economic growth. Flush with abundant national wealth, the Japanese government decided to invest in education to improve its human resources to keep pace with the rapid social and economic growth. It has been the conventional wisdom in Japan that graduates from good schools can get good jobs in big corporations or enterprises and that they can look forward to a brighter future after graduation. Given such a cultural belief, students were eager to study very hard to enter the top universities. As a result of this, the entrance examination has become the most crucial examination for higher school graduates, and competition has increasingly intensified. Despite that fact that the Japanese government has attempted to alleviate the public examination pressures for students, Japanese still generally consider that Japan should be a highly competitive society and good performance in public examinations is still crucial in determining their futures (Arimoto 2002).

Driving forces for national university restructuring in Japan

In analyzing the reasons for higher education reform in recent years, it is impor-tant to understand the unique policy context in which Japanese higher education reforms have been introduced and launched. More important, we must pay particular attention not only to the influences of external forces but also to domes-tic factors, especially when we intend to make better sense of the most current education reforms and policy changes in Japan.

Global forces

In an increasingly globalizing environment, modern states are influenced by globalization forces, and Japan is no exception. As a responsive government, the Japanese government is responsible for initiating and adopting policies appropri-ate to making the country in general and the education system in particular respond proactively to the ever-changing social, economic, and political environ-ments. Acknowledging the importance of human resources in the knowledge-based economy, the Japanese government is keen to further strengthen the intellectual capacity of its citizens through a series of higher education reforms. According to the report "A Vision of Universities in the 21st Century and Reform Measures" published by the Ministry of Education, Culture, Sports, Science, and Technology (MEXT) in 1998, institutions of higher studies in Japan are encour-aged to take an active role in restructuring to differentiate themselves in an increasingly competitive environment. For example, the report makes it explicit that "each individual institution is expected to continuously make efforts to main-tain and/or improve the quality of education and research, improve themselves with friendly rivalry and develop its distinctive features" (MEXT 1998). This statement clearly demonstrates that the Japanese government is very keen to inject "internal competition" to run the higher education system. In addition, this report also shows MEXT's approving attitude toward self-evaluation and moni-toring of university activities and governance procedures. In response to the recommendation of the report, the National Organization for University Evaluation was set up to put the ideas of third-party evaluation into practice. In April 2000, the National Institution for Academic Degrees and University Evaluation (NIAD-UE) was established to coordinate activities relating to uni-versity evaluation, research on university evaluation and quality assessment, and analysis of the data regarding university evaluation (Yonezawa 2002a). In light of the most recent reform measures adopted by the Japanese government in assuring university quality, I believe that globalization forces have accelerated higher education reforms in Japan, particularly when the government has introduced different reform measures to strengthen its higher education system by making it more international and globally competitive (Poole 2003a).

Acknowledging the challenges of the knowledge-based economy, which requires people to be innovative, creative, and flexible in responding to rapid changes, the Japanese government recognized that the conventional education system of the 1980s might not enhance students to the extent of acquiring the abilities and skills just outlined. It has long been the tradition that Japanese students are trained to be very disciplined and spirited from their kindergarten education onward. Going through such a schooling system, students in Japan have become used to following the instructions of teachers rather than thinking independently and critically.

On the other hand, there is a criticism that students are not intellectually mature enough to adapt to university education, especially when university education is wholly concerned with independent and critical thinking and individual abilities in terms of problem solving (Brady *et al.* 2003). The difficulties of Japanese students in adapting to the new learning styles of being creative and innovative are sometimes argued to be related to Japanese culture (Hendry 2003).

However, how to develop creativity through education reform is not very clear. In the past two decades, the Japanese government has tried to reduce the volume of curriculum contents that have to be memorized, and there are various channels to enter higher learning without going through standardized testing. However, there is a strong criticism that this policy merely lowered the basic academic achievement of university freshers, even in the top universities. In addition, Japan has had a strong sense of national superiority, even during the period of isolation, because it was a self-sufficient country for a long time. After Japan's defeat in the Second World War, its economic success and advanced technology are a real cause for national pride, which again reinforces the self-confidence and self-identity of the Japanese (Hendry 2003). In Japanese bureaus and companies, it is said that local people who are proficient in foreign languages sometimes do not enjoy high social status. Instead, mastering good English may attract discrimination in the workplace and could be disadvantageous for career promotion because of the social belief that fluency in foreign languages represents a pass only in specialist examinations, not in higher-level examinations. Therefore, ordinary Japanese are less willing to learn English because many of them think it is not necessary to learn English to communicate with the Westerners because they already have very good translation systems in Japan. Table 10.1 shows the mean Test of English for International Communication (TOEIC) scores across native Asian countries. By comparing Japan with other Asian countries, it can be noticed that the scores of Japanese in the TOEIC are lower than those other Asian nationals (cited in Reesor 2003).

Nonetheless, the growing impacts of globalization have forced Japan to rethink the strategies of communicating with the external world. Believing that the

Table 10.1 Mean TOEIC scores across Asian countries

Country	Number of test-takers	Percentage of test-takers	Listening mean	Reading mean	Total Score mean
China	3,529	0.3	256	246	502
Japan	862,509	62.7	246	206	451
Korea	405,822	29.5	250	230	480
Malaysia	1,079	0.1	363	305	668
Taiwan	11,462	0.8	257	218	475
Thailand	27,330	2.0	272	215	487

Source: Extracted from Educational Testing Service (2000) [Internet]; available from http://ftp.ets.org/pub/toefl/TOEICreporttesttakers.pdf

increasingly globalizing economy requires proficiency in English for communication, business, and trade purposes, the Japanese government has adopted new strategies to internationalize its higher education. Recognizing the importance of opening Japan to the global market, the Japanese government has tried different reform strategies to make its education system more responsive and adaptive to external pressures and changes, in particular, devising methods to make its citizens more innovative and creative in their thinking (Poole 2003a,b).

Local variables

In addition to the forces of globalization, which may be part of the reason for the recent reforms and changes in Japan's higher education, we should not underestimate the influence of internal variables. A better understanding of policy change in education can be obtained through a contextual analysis by looking into how changes in education are proposed to address local issues and domestic needs. In particular, the formulation of education policy has never been conducted without meeting local challenges and domestic needs. A close scrutiny of education reform and policy change in contemporary Japan reveals that education reform agendas have been significantly shaped by the unresolved issues resulting from the massification of education, the changes in its demographic structure, and the changing values of Japanese society (Ogawa 1999).

Addressing issues of the universal access and competition in education

Higher education has seen wider participation in the past decade, and the quality of higher education has consequently deteriorated. There is a keen and severe competition for entrance to top universities every year. In contrast, there is an oversupply of less prestigious universities. Some university graduates have even been criticized for their low academic standard even when they have completed their university education. Hence, the universal access to higher education in Japan has raised social concern and the general public has asked the government to reform higher education to assure the quality of education for university graduates.

The education system of Japan has been described as "diploma disease" by Dore, and parents have been asking for a relaxation of "examination hell." In Yoshimoto's study, approximately 95 percent of the students started seeking a job at least one year before graduation. This implies that to enterprises the ability of students at the time of entrance matters more than what they have achieved at the end of their study in university. In terms of the vigor of the university entrance examination, it can be explained by the strong tendency for the vital criteria on which employers hire employees to depend on which university a student has graduated from. It is believed that if a student has graduated from a top, prestigous university, he/she must be able to secure a good job in a Japanese corporation or enterprise. As the choice of university is so important that it may determine one's career development and opportunity for social mobility, most students are competing with others to enter the top universities, leading to extremely severe competition in university entrance examinations. Clearly, Japanese students who desire to study in a top university are under great pressure, and this sheds light on why parents in Japan have kept on seeking to release their children from "examination hell." The education reforms started in the 1980s have to address these issues.

Addressing changing demographic structure and manpower training needs

Population restructuring and the crisis of an ageing population have drawn the attention of the Japanese government to education, since manpower planning and human resource development are is crucial to the future development of Japan. According to the National Institute of Population and Social Security Research, the trend toward fewer children and an ageing population will become a risk for Japan as there will be a dramatic change in demographic structure. According to the report *Population Projection for Japan 2000–2005*, the child population (aged under 15) has decreased from 18,505,000 (14.6 percent) in 2000 to 16,197,000 (12.8 percent) in 2005. This declining trend will continue and it is estimated that the number of children will fall below to 13,233,000 (11.3 percent) in 2030 and further to 10,842,000 (10.8 percent) in 2050. In addition, the working age population (aged 16–64) is also expected to decline. It is suggested that the working age population will decrease from 86,380,000 (68.1 percent) in 2000 to 77,296,000 (61.2 percent) in 2015. And it will further drop to 69,576,000 (59.2 percent) and 53,889,000 (53.6 percent) in 2030 and 2050, respectively.

In contrast to the declining trend of the child population and working age population, the number and proportion of aged population (aged 65 and above) will keep on increasing. There were 22,041,000 aged people (17.4 percent) in 2000. In 2015, the size of the aged population is expected to rise to 33,772,000 (26.0 percent) and further increase to 34,770,000 (29.6 percent) in 2030. In 2050, it is anticipated that this age group will constitute about 35.7 percent of the whole population in Japan. In short, while the birth rate keeps decreasing and the size of the aged population keeps growing, Japan will experience a demographic change and a decrease in the labor force population. With such demographic changes, the Japanese government has already been made well aware of the potential negative consequences (National Institute of Population and Social Security Research 2002). Therefore, the Japanese government is very keen to develop proper policies to tackle the problems that will be caused by the demographic changes by proposing and implementing policy changes in education and human resource development in order to maintain a stable, highly educated workforce for Japan's future development.

Addressing changing environments and changing university governance

In addition to the government's urge for reforms, higher education institutions in Japan also find the need for improvement and reform. This is particularly true of the private universities since their main sources of revenue are students' tuition fees. Driven by "market forces," private universities are very sensitive to the renewed expectations of students, and they have continued to improve their education delivery in order to maintain their attractiveness to students and secure enough enrollments. The competition over student numbers is further intensified owing to the diminishing of number prospective applicants who are aged 18. As shown, the population of teenagers has declined since 1992, and this declining trend is expected to continue. Therefore, private universities in Japan must be adaptive to changes in order to survive.

For national universities, although the sources of funding are more stable than those of the private ones, academics in public universities are well aware of the crisis over losing competitiveness in research conducted by the national universities. Some professors in the fields of science and engineering who have studied in Western countries complain of the continual decline of research quality in Japan. And they share the concern that Japan's scientific research may fall behind international research in science and technology if no further action is taken for improvement. Given the unforeseeable future of the quality of research in Japan, coupled with the intention to keep pace with the rapid changes in the rest of the world, the Japanese government has decided to devise new strategies to reform research in higher education (Amano and Poole 2004).

The changing structure of the industrial sector has led to higher expectations of university graduates. In the past, the education system was only expected to train graduates with general, basic knowledge and discipline. Firms in the 1980s had their own in-house job training and development centers for staff training and professional development, while Japanese firms were inclined to invest money in overseas universities (particularly in the United States) for research and development purposes. With the collapse of the bubble economy, Japanese firms have found it difficult to maintain huge investments in research in overseas universities. Since then, Japanese firms have begun to rely much more on local universities for research and development, and therefore they now have higher expectations of local universities (Asonuma 2002). Confronting the growing impact of globalization, there is a threat to Japan's industry from other Southeast Asian economies since they have become more industrialized and their production costs are far lower than those of Japan. Thus, the industrial sector in Japan yearns for a fundamental curriculum change in the education system, with additional weight being attached to creativity, innovation, and the employability of university graduates (Hirota 2003, p. 4). Moreover, many multinational industries have established manufacturing plants in mainland China and Vietnam, and English has become an important medium of instruction for communication (Yonezawa 2003a). In order to compete with neighboring countries, Japan has strong need to improve the standard of English of graduates and to internationalize its higher education system. Having discussed the policy context of higher education reform, let us now turn to the most recent reform initiatives in Japan's higher education.

Major higher education restructuring strategies

Liberalizing the "centralized" governance system

To launch education reforms, a National Council on Educational Reform (NCER) was set up in 1984. After a comprehensive review of the education system in Japan, a final report was submitted by the council in 1987 to the government and has become the blueprint for recent higher education reforms in Japan. In response to the report's recommendations, the University Council (Daigaku Shingikai) was set up in September 1987. In 1988, the University Council published a report entitled "Making Graduate Studies More Flexible." One of the major reform recommendations was "the relaxation of the university establishment standards in 1991 which has induced widespread deregulation and accountability" (Tsuruta 2003a, p. 3). In order to make the Japanese higher education system more responsive and flexible to external changes, autonomy was allowed to individual institutions to change their curricula design. Since then, "interdisciplinary" and "international" notions have been stressed. The 1988 report highlighted a few major principles governing the higher education reforms in Japan, including

- developing a more flexible credit transfer and accreditation system in order to encourage more student mobility;
- setting up more independent and central management of national universities;
- institutionalizing more rigorous and plural evaluation;
- facilitating more varied and flexible access to higher education;
- encouraging more liberal arts education; and
- developing more diverse and independent graduate schools and curricula.

(Tsuruta 2003a, p. 3)

Before the reform, all universities had to comply with the general requirements for graduation of 36 units of "general education" subjects. Being granted more autonomy in designing their curricula, nearly 80 percent of universities have reviewed their own curricula and redesigned them appropriate to their own distinctiveness. In addition, the institutional arrangements for graduate studies have become more diverse and flexible now than before. Since the late 1980s, a federation-type graduate school has been adopted that enables several universities to jointly supervise graduate students; moreover, students with high abilities enter directly to masters programs without completing four-year undergraduate study (Okano and Tsuchiya, pp. 214–15). On January 25, 2001, MEXT published a report, "Education Reform Plan for the 21st Century," which is based on the final report of the NCER in 2000, to highlight "Seven Priority Strategies" in higher education:

- improving students' basic scholastic proficiency in "easy-to-understand classes";
- fostering open and warm-hearted Japanese through participation in community and various programs;
- improving the learning environment to one which is enjoyable and free of worries;
- promoting the creation of schools trusted by parents and communities;
- training teachers as "education professionals";
- promoting the establishment of world-class universities; and
- establishing a new educational vision for the new century to improve the foundations of education.

(Cited in MEXT 2004a)

This new framework of "Seven Priority Strategies" is intended to encourage more diversification and respect for individuality in higher education, in the hope that through the adoption and implementation of such strategies the quality of universities can be improved so that they become world-class universities.

Incorporating national universities

MEXT launched another reform in 2001 entitled "Toyama Plan" (renamed the Center of Excellence Program for the 21st Century later), which was part of Prime Minister Koizumi's structural reform introduced in the new century (Tsuruta 2003b). This reform has taken on a more economic and industrial orientation. It aims to respond to the emergence of the "knowledge-based economy" by establishing a more competitive environment for higher education and developing excellent human resources and professionals for the future development of Japan. With the aim of strengthening the universities in Japan to become more academically rigorous and internationally competitive, three major strategies have been adopted: the reorganization and merging of national universities, starting the process of "incorporation" of national universities, and introducing "internal competition" to make all universities perform and achieve higher standards by institutionalizing performance evaluation by independent external bodies (Tsurata 2003b; Yonezawa 2003b; MEXT 2004a).

In order to further develop and facilitate universities to achieve the highest international standards, the National University Corporation Law, together with five other related laws were implemented from July to October 2003. Now, all national universities have become *kokuritsu daigaku hojin* (national university corporations) and they have been independent of the government since April 2004 (Oba 2003a; MEXT 2004a). According to MEXT, the incorporation of national universities is one of the most dramatic higher education reforms since the Meiji era in Japan. More specifically, there are six key directions of the "incorporation" project whereby all national universities are turned into a new institutional form:

- incorporation of all national universities;
- introducing management techniques based on "private-sector concepts";
- involving people from outside the university in managing national universities;
- improving the process of selection of the president of national universities;
- assigning non-civil servant status to personnel; and
- making information public and performance evaluation transparent.

(MEXT 2003a)

According to the OECD IMHE-HEFCE project report entitled *"Financial Management and Governance in HEIS: Japan,"* central to the transformation of the existing national universities into national university corporations are three major reform aspects:

- increased competitiveness in research and education;
- enhanced accountability together with the introduction of competition; and
- strategic and functional management of universities.

(HEFCE, OECD 2004, p. 15)

National universities have nowadays become incorporated and they can enjoy more autonomy; nonetheless, they are held accountable to the public and the government. After incorporation, university presidents are expected to play a more significant role in university governance and each is now both the head of the university and the head of the corporation. Exercising more autonomy, university presidents now can decide the recruitment and promotion of clerical personnel and participate in formulating medium-term goals and medium-term plans. In the meantime, they are responsible for leading the university to achieve higher academic and scholarly standards and, of course, they are also responsible for the overall performance of the universities (RIHE 2003).

With the introduction of a new governance structure and management, all national universities are subject to a performance assessment by the Evaluation Committee for National University Corporations (Evaluation Committee), a special committee set up within MEXT. Flexible personnel systems are being deployed such as flexible forms of recruitment, salary structure, and working hours, which are strongly advocated by MEXT to reward high achievers and good performance in order to solve the problem of overrigidity in the old personnel management system. Meanwhile, all national universities have to submit medium-term goals and medium-term plans to the minister of education. The medium-term goals and medium-term plans will be used as a yardstick for the Evaluation Committee to assess the performance of the university. The government's financial allocation depends on the performance of the university. Therefore, all national universities in Japan are now subject to more external scrutiny and they are caught between autonomy and accountability. As Yamamoto (2004) and Tsuruta (2003a) have suggested, the incorporation of national universities initiated and implemented by the Japanese government is the most radical reform introduced in the higher education sector since the Meiji era. After the corporatization project was started, higher education in Japan experienced significant changes not only in terms of reform measures resulting from the introduction and implementation of education reform but also in the three major governance aspects, namely, provision, financing, and regulation. Let us move on discussing the changing governance of higher education in Japan.

Restructuring impacts and changing university governance

Provision

After the Second World War, the philosophy underlying the Japanese education system was equal opportunity. The strong belief in equal opportunity has resulted in a mass education system; hence all Japanese citizens are provided with education. Following the same philosophical line, the enrollment rate for higher education has been increasing in the past few decades. In 1954, the enrollment rate for university and junior college was 10.1 percent and it had increased to 49.0 percent in 2003 (MEXT 2004b). Despite the fact that the higher education enrollment rate is relatively high in Japan, the major higher education provider is not the government but the private sector (see Table 10.2).

In 2003, there were a total of 702 (100 national, 76 local/public, 526 private) universities in Japan, among which private universities constitute the largest proportion (around 74.9 percent). Even though a majority of the students studying in national institutions are at the master and the doctorate levels, the main provision is still the private sector (68.6 and 67.3 percent, respectively). Comparing the

Table 10.2 Number of higher education institutions in Japan by control (2003)

	Total	National (%)	Local/Public (%)	Private (%)
Universities and junior colleges	702	100 (14.2)	76 (10.8)	526 (74.9)
Universities providing masters courses	507	99 (19.5)	60 (11.8)	348 (68.6)
Universities providing doctoral courses	392	86 (21.9)	42 (10.7)	264 (67.3)

Source: MEXT 2004c [Internet]; available from http://www.mext.go.jp/english/statist/gif/078.gif

provider role of the private sector with the public one, it is apparent that the proportion of public funding to tertiary education is relatively small. Following a strong suggestion by the government, the merger of national institutions was implemented in parallel with incorporation. Actually, the number of national universities was reduced from 100 in 2003 to 87 in 2004. According to MEXT (2004d), the purpose of reorganizing and merging national universities is not to reduce the number of universities. Rather, the proposed merging strategies have to do with the enhancement of education quality and scholarly research in order to make the universities of Japan more "distinctive" in the competitive environment. Moreover, the Japanese government believes resources can be utilized wisely through "scrap and build" procedures to consolidate existing institutions and departments. In a press release dated January 24, 2002, MEXT announced a plan to merge at least 24 national universities and a discussion on mergers has been started among 12 institutions. In coping with the growing socioeconomic challenges, coupled with the intention to maintain their competitiveness in the globalizing world, a number of universities have begun to set up linkages with other institutions; measures including consortia, credit transfer systems, joint programs, joint graduate schools, and distance learning have been adopted for survival purposes. For example, the Tokyo Institute of Technology, Hitotsubashi University, and the Tokyo Medical and Dental University have signed a corporate agreement in designing a new course that is available for students in these three institutions. Similarly, Tokyo Gakugei University and other local universities have also reached a corporate agreement to establish a joint graduate school (cited in Ogawa 2002). Responding to the calls from MEXT to cooperate more with industry and business with the intention of turning Japan into a country based on creativity in science and technology, universities in Japan are now exploring different ways and alternatives to work and collaborate with the industrial and business sectors (Tsuruta 2003b, p. 132).

Financing

According to the official statistics (2004), the proportion of public expenditure on education, science, sports, and culture decreased from 1955 to 2000, especially when measuring the expenditure relative to total public expenditure and gross domestic product in the same survey period. Table 10.3 shows that the proportion of public expenditure on education constituted around 19.7 percent of total public expenditure in 1980. Yet, this proportion reduced gradually during the following two decades. In 1990, the proportion was 16.5 percent and it further declined to 15.9 percent in 2000. Meanwhile, although the proportion of public expenditure on education relative to gross domestic product showed a slight increase to 4.7 percent in 2000 from 4.5 percent in 1990, this ratio had in fact dropped by 1 percent when comparing the figures for 2000 (4.7 percent) with those 1980 (5.7 percent). All these data suggest that although the Japanese government is very keen to improve the quality of higher education, it has not allocated additional resources to the field. Nevertheless, institutions of higher studies are

Table 10.3 Total expenditure and public expenditure on education, science, sports, and culture, relative to total public expenditure and gross domestic product

Year	Relative to the total public expenditure	Relative to gross domestic product
1980	19.7	5.7
1990	16.5	4.5
2000	15.9	4.7

Source: MEXT 2004e [Internet]; available from http://www.mext. go.jp/english/statist/gif/172.gif

expected to achieve more and perform well; all of them have to "do more with less," and they are bound to manage and govern their institutions in a more efficient and effective way (MEXT 2004e).

In order to diversify financial resources to support higher education development in Japan, the Japanese government strongly promotes a partnership between national universities and industry. Some of the examples are joint research and commissioned research. For joint research, researchers from private corporations and professors from national universities can conduct research together, and the private corporations are responsible for the research costs and for paying fees to university. For commissioned research, private corporations offer capital as investment to national universities for conducting the designated research. In return, universities have to submit research results and research reports to private corporations. Official statistics show that both forms of "partnership" and "commissioned research" are increasing significantly (MEXT 2003b). National universities engaging in these research activities could create more channels to generate additional funding from the nonpublic sector/private sector to finance higher education.

In addition, the government has introduced a competitive funding method among universities. In 2003, 4.3 percent of the total MEXT budget was allocated to competitive funding. For this competitive funding, additional funding would be granted to some scientific research/strategic and creative research promotion, programs, coordination of science and technology promotion and industry-academia-government cooperation to create innovation (MEXT 2004a). It is obvious that the government yearns to introduce a more competitive environment to drive the national institutions to achieve excellence in research, particularly in the fields of science and technology. Likewise, the government will foster the top 30 universities in Japan and these top universities will get additional funding other than the grant-in-aids. Moreover, the government also has created additional aid grants to private universities to cover current expenses since the 1970s, and the share of project funds to the private sector has increased substantially since the 1990s (Yonezawa 2003a). The method of allocating funding to higher education has become more diversified and more competitive.

After the legislation of the National University Corporation Law, the funding allocation to national universities depends more on the performance of individual universities. Nowadays, universities have to submit medium-term goals and medium-term plans to the Minister of Education and the specified goals of the universities must be achieved within a certain period. The medium-term plans are proposals to illustrate how the goals are to be achieved and these plans act as the basis of budget requests for operational grants. Thereafter, how much funding a national university can get will largely depend on the performance evaluation by the Evaluation Committee.

Regulation

In its quest for world-class universities, the Japanese government insists on the importance of continual improvement and performance of universities. The "Centre of Excellence Plan for the 21st Century" (COE21) was introduced in 2002 as a special grant to foster world-class research units through the national peer selection system. In 2004, NIAD-UE also started performance assessment for national institutions after three years of a pilot evaluation scheme.

Evaluation of university performance in Japan dates back to 1947, when the Japan University Accreditation Association (JUAA) was set up as an accreditation body to assess university education. In 1956, the Japanese government set out another quality standard for universities. However, these quality assurance exercises only set minimum requirement for university education and just assured education quality at the time of establishment. In 1991, the University Council required universities to have self-monitoring and self-evaluation in order to maintain and improve the quality of university education, along with the relaxation of curricula design in national universities. Although self-evaluation and self-monitoring exercises have become increasingly popular among national universities in Japan, the University Council considers such exercises insufficient in enhancing the universities' performance to meet the required level set out in the university reform (Yonezawa 2003a). Therefore, MEXT has introduced a third-party evaluation, establishing an independent body, NIAD-UE, to conduct university evaluations in 2000.

The evaluation results published by the third party will be reported not only to the university concerned but also to the public as well. In this regard, the evaluation results are not simply a kind of internal assessment but are now made open to the public for reference. By conducting the evaluation exercise, MEXT hopes to acheive an upgradation of universities to world-class academic level and transformation to a university of marked individuality or outstanding characteristics. The funding allocation of universities is closely linked with the universities' academic and research performance and it is a matter of public image and prestige for the universities (Yonezawa 2002b).

For implementing the performance assessment of national university corporations, the Evaluation Committee has been set up under MEXT. The Evaluation Committee is responsible for (1) evaluating the performance of activities of national university corporations and (2) evaluating other items in relation to the competence attributed to the evaluation committee by the National University

Corporation Law. For more specialized education and research conducted by universities, the evaluation will be carried out by the National Institution for Academic Degrees and University Evaluation and the report on the results of evaluation will be submitted to the Commission on Policy Evaluation and Evaluation of Independent Administrative Institutions in the Ministry of Public Management and Home Affairs. Opinions or recommendations can be submitted to the Evaluation Committee if necessary (Oba 2003). By introducing the

(1) Present scheme

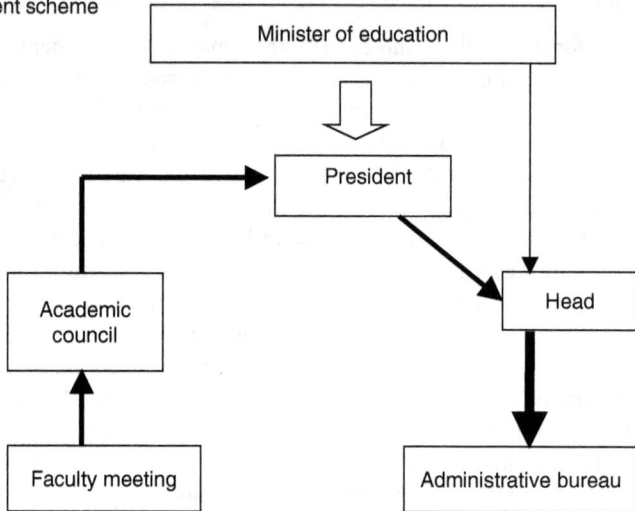

(2) New scheme

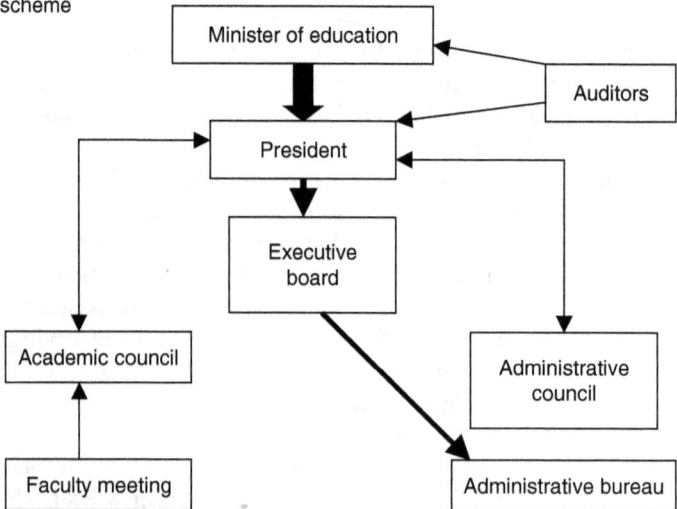

Figure 10.1 Governance of national universities.

Source: Adapted from OECD 2004, p. 11.

medium-term goals and medium-term plans, national universities have to set out their goals with distinctiveness in relation to the following aspects, as stated:

- duration of medium-term goals;
- basic goals for the university as a whole;
- goals relating to the improvement of quality in the university's education and research;
- goals relating to the improvement and efficiency of the administration of operations;
- goals concerning improvements to finances;
- goals concerning accountability to society; and
- other important goals.

(MEXT 2002)

After the legislation of the National University Corporation Law, universities have to develop their own medium-term goals and medium-term plans, which have to conform to the these aspects. If universities fail to achieve the goals within a given period of time, their funding from the government will be directly affected. Figure 10.1 shows the differences in the accountability framework before and after the corporatization of national universities in Japan. By means of these evaluation strategies, the Japanese government has certainly tightened its control over universities and national universities, are now held accountable to the government and the public.

Discussion

Changing state roles in university governance

By launching a series of higher education reforms the Japanese government has attempted to benchmark its universities with international standards and encouraged them to strive to become world-class universities. Although the government has reduced its role in providing and financing higher education, it does not necessarily mean that the state has withdrawn from the higher education domain entirely. In contrast, the Japanese government has indeed strengthened its role by reforming the regulatory framework of higher education to assure high quality. As discussed earlier, the Japanese government further encourages the participation of private and nonstate actors in financing and providing higher education. By encouraging cooperation between universities and private corporations, the government believes additional funding and resources will be generated for the university sector. In terms of financing, the Japanese government has created a keen competetive environment to push institutions of higher studies to search for additional resources. The criteria for getting additional funding are primarily performance driven and evidence based. The rationale behind this move by the government is to improve the quality of higher education in Japan rather than simply respond to the forces of globalization.

Table 10.4 Changing roles of coordinating institutions in education
governance

Coordinating institutions	Provision	Financing	Regulation
State	+ −	+ −	+ + +
Market	+ +	+ +	+ +
Community/civil society	+ +	+ + +	+ + +

Notes
+ −   Important but reduced in importance.
+ +   More active role and becoming more important.
+ + + Anticipated to become more important.

In addition, the legislation of the National University Corporation Law is clearly a step forward by the government in granting more autonomy to universities to develop their own distinctiveness and uniqueness. At the same time, universities enjoying far more autonomy have to perform, thus suggesting that universities in Japan are now caught between autonomy and accountability. In this regard, the "liberalization" process taking place in Japan's higher education should not be understood simply as a genuine decentralization of power from the state to individual universities. Instead, universities are under pressure today to perform and show their achievements in order to secure additional income and resources for running their institutions. In addition, through the introduction of third-party evaluation, university monitoring and performance evaluation is now open to the community and universities are now subject to public scrutiny.

Table 10.4 demonstrates the changing roles between state, market, and community/civil society with regard to provision, financing, and regulation. It suggests that the role of the market, the community, and civil society is expected to grow, while the role of the state is declining in terms of education provision and financing. Hence, the relationship between the state and the nonstate sectors (including the market, the community, and civil society) will eventually alter. With the greater involvement and the growing investment of the market and the community/civil society in education financing and provision, it is not surprising that these nonstate actors will become more prominent and would try to influence the education policymaking process in general and the education regulatory framework in particular. Therefore, the power relationship between the state and the nonstate actors will change, especially when the latter assume an increasingly role in education financing and provision for state universities.

Universities encountering the autonomy and accountability dilemma

The changes in university governance has made the relationship between the state and the nonstate sectors problematic. This occurs when the state is reluctant to reduce its control over education regulation in the fear of lowering academic standards and because of the requirement for quality assurance. Analyzing the case study of Japan in the light of this particular framework, I anticipate that Japanese universities will be caught between autonomy and accountability. On the one hand, they are empowered and given more autonomy to determine their own development goals and strategies. On the other hand, they are under immense pressure to perform, especially now they are subject to the public scrutiny and they are also accountable to the government and the public. Similar to higher education systems in Australia, Hong Kong, Singapore, and Britain, universities in Japan have to cope with "autonomy" and "accountability," particularly when university performance is measured in terms of "productivity gains," "research output," and "success in entrepreneurial activities."

Like higher education in other parts of the globe, national universities in Japan have to address two competing demands. First, they are made far more autonomous and entrusted with additional responsibilities. Second, they have to prove their performance with reduced state budgets. Provoking university corporatization really "has a dual meaning, enhancing autonomy as university reform and downsizing as public sector reform" (Yamamoto 2004, p. 178). The recent higher education governance change, therefore, is better interpreted as part of the higher education sector's response to the larger public sector restructuring/reengineering project in Japan. Seen in this light, higher education reforms in general and changing higher education governance in particular should not be understood as a global-regional-domestic response. Instead, such changes are the consequences of a more complicated reform process, which involves global, regional and domestic variables. A deeper reflection on higher education governance changes from a global perspective reveals that the recent changes and reform initiatives adopted by the Japanese government are more related to local forces and domestic variables. This is particularly true when the national university system is part of the larger public sector reforms and economic restructuring processes. Being a huge public/state structure (particularly given its traditional and stubborn nature), there is a strong need for the Japanese higher education system to change and reform in keeping pace with rapid changes generated by both internal and external forces. In this regard, we should not underestimate the local forces and domestic factors shaping and influencing higher education reform agendas in Japan.

Conclusion: unfinished university governance reforms

In this chapter, we have discussed how Japan has experienced a series of higher education reforms. Some scholars argue that the series of education reforms undertaken by the Japanese government is due to globalization forces. Nevertheless, as discussed earlier in this chapter, local factors have played a more prominent role in shaping higher education reforms and policy change in Japan since the government treats education reform as part of the structural reform initiated by the present government. Seen in this light, globalization acts only as an accelerating force. Although the main provider of higher education is the private sector rather than the government, the government has not withdrawn its control over the universities. On the contrary, the government makes use of different evaluation systems to monitor the performance of universities. Financially, the government adopts a "carrot and stick" approach to induce universities to do better before they can get additional funding or they may face the risk of a budget cut for their poor performance. The introduction of new public management into the government system in general, and national universities in particular, is highly related to the "Anglo-Saxonization" or globalization of public administration. Seen in this light, national university reform should be understood as a transformation from German-style university governance to the Anglo-Saxon styles. Therefore, universities in Japan are now confronted with a dilemma, bridging autonomy and accountability, while the Japanese government is at a crossroads, choosing between globalization and localization.

Discussions and conclusions
Globalization and education

Introduction

When reflecting upon education reforms in contemporary societies, different scholars and policy analysts may have different interpretations of the impacts of globalization on education policy change and education governance. No matter how we assess the impact of globalization, it is undeniable that contemporary societies are not immune from prominent global forces on the economic, social, political, and cultural fronts (Sklair 1995; Rodrik 1997; Giddens 1999; Held *et al.* 1999; Hirst and Thompson 1999; Mittleman 2000). Believing that market values and practices can promote efficiency, effectiveness, and economy not only in the economic sphere but also in the social and public domains, modern states have made serious attempts to demolish the old Keynesian national welfare state and to establish a "competitive state" in response to challenges generated by "global capitalism" (Held 2000; So 2003). The same processes of globalization occurring in other countries affect the selected East Asian societies discussed in this book.

Despite differences in terms of historical, socioeconomic, and political developments among the selected cases, our discussions have shown that similar trends and patterns in terms of education governance changes and reform strategies have emerged in these East Asian societies. The principal goal of this concluding chapter is to discuss to what extent the education governance and policy formulation of the selected Asian societies have been affected by the growing impact of globalization. More specifically, this concluding chapter focuses on the analysis of the observations generated from the case studies that I have presented in Part II in the light of the theoretical framework outlined at the beginning of this book.

Globalization and education

With capitalists more directly confronting other capitalists, the keener competition at the global scale has led some scholars to argue that we are living in a world of "hypercompetition," a situation that could be conceptualized as "a concerted effort to increase market instability and to establish the uncertainty of operations" (Mittleman 2000, p. 16). It is in such a socioeconomic context that the psychology of market participants and business strategies have necessarily changed (D'Aveni 1994). On the political front, this climate has led to fundamental changes forcing modern states to become "competition states" by playing the roles of enablers or facilitators and trying hard to prevent market failure (Cerny 1990). With strengthening the state's competitiveness, coupled with the fear of declining state capacity, as its justification, there has been a growing trend whereby modern states adopt corporate logic and a market-oriented approach, "embracing variants of neoliberal ideology to justify the socially disruptive and polarizing consequences of [their] policies and subjecting [their] own agencies to cost-cutting measures" (Mittleman 2000, p. 17). Reform measures and new governance strategies along the lines of marketization, privatization, corporatization, and commercialization have become increasingly dominant in public policy formulation and public sector management and governance. To realize the material gain from globalization, modern states increasingly facilitate the acceleration of structural change (Cox 1987; Palan and Abbott 1996).

In an increasingly competitive global context, schools and universities in different parts of the world have been under tremendous pressure from government and the general public to restructure or reinvent the way that they are managed in order to adapt to the ever-changing socioeconomic and sociopolitical environment and to maintain individual nation-states' global competitiveness. As Martin Carnoy has pointed out, "globalization enters the education sector on an ideological horse, and its effects in education are largely a product of that financially driven, free-market ideology, not a clear conception for improving education" (Carnoy 2000, p. 50). Education reforms, in the context of globalization, can be characterized as finance driven, emphasizing decentralization, privatization, and better performance (Carnoy 2000; Mok and Welch 2003).

With heavy weight being attached to the principle of "efficiency and quality" in education, schools, universities, and other learning institutions now encounter far more challenges and are being subjected to an unprecedented level of external scrutiny. The growing concern for "value for money" and "public accountability" has also altered people's value expectations. All providers of education today inhabit a more competitive world, where resources are becoming scarcer; at the same time, providers have to accommodate increasing demands from the local community as well as changing expectations from parents and employers (Currie and Newson 1998a; Mok and Currie 2002). Attaching far more weight to entrepreneurial efficiency and effectiveness, contemporary universities are under immense pressure to transform their roles in order to adapt to the rapid socioeconomic and sociopolitical changes. This is particularly true with modern governments going through a financial crunch and finding it hard to continue financing the growing demands of higher education.

It is against the socioeconomic context discussed in this book that the processes of academic capitalization in general and the pursuit of academic entrepreneurship in particular have become increasingly popular in terms of shaping the relationship between government, university, business, and industry. Therefore, new "university-academic-productive sector relations" have emerged (Sutz 1997); notions such as "corporate academic convergence" (Currie and Newson 1998a), "entrepreneurial universities" (Marginson 2000), "campus inc."

(White and Hauck 2000), "capitalization of knowledge," "strong executive control," and "corporate characters" are used to conceptualize current changes in contemporary universities (Etzkowitz and Leydesdorff 1997). In the context of reduced financial support from the state, higher education systems across different parts of the world have attempted to generate incomes through entrepreneurial activities (see, for example, Marginson and Considine 2000; Mok 2003c; De Zilwa 2004). It is, therefore, not surprising that "the language of human capital dominates official policy recommendations dealing with growing economic and social problems" (Spring 1998, p. 163).

The discussions in this book have consistently reported similar trends of marketization, corporatization, privatization, and commercialization along with the ideas and practices of neoliberalism. These trends have become increasingly prominent in shaping education policy and governance in East Asia. But before we come to the conclusion, let us examine three major issues related to globalization and education, namely, globalization and governance changes, globalization and the withering of the state, and globalization and the East Asian developmental state. The chapter is ended by a few concluding remarks based upon the earlier chapters.

Globalization and governance change

The growing impact of globalization has caused a number of modern states to rethink their governance strategies in coping with rapid social and economic changes. When examining the capacity of modern states in the context of globalization, both skeptics and transformationalists believe nation-states still retain the ultimate claim of legal legitimacy within their territories even though they have to respond to external pressures generated by international laws and authorities. Contrary to strong globalists' arguments, the institutionalized state-society linkages (i.e., the mobilization of nonstate sources and actors to engage in social/public policy provision and financing) may not necessarily diminish the state's capacity. Instead, globalization could be a conductive process for reconfiguring modern states, creating forces to drive modern states to restructure their governance models and reform the ways that they manage the public sector (Pierre 2000). As discussed at the beginning of this volume, these changes could also be seen as productive forces for modern states to shift from "positive coordination" to "negative coordination," thereby allowing the state to choose to perform the role of regulator, enabler, and facilitator instead of heavily engaging in the role of provider and funder (Scharpf 1994; Jayasurya 2001).

Realizing that depending only on state financial resources can never satisfy growing education needs, the East Asian governments discussed in this volume have begun to search for additional sources of finance (Mok *et al.* 2000; Yang 2000). Nongovernment resources, market initiatives, individual payments, family contributions, and social donations have become increasingly popular. For instance, the Hong Kong Special Administration Region (HKSAR) plans to double the number of higher education graduates in 10 years by utilizing these resources (Tung 2001). Similarly, governments in these East Asian societies have encouraged the market/private sector to take a larger role in higher education. In South Korea and Taiwan, for instance, the majority of higher education students are now enrolled in private universities, while the Singapore and Hong Kong governments have attempted to recover recurrent costs from student tuition fees and additional income generated by individual universities (Bray 2000; Tai 2000b; Mok 2001a; Law 2003). Similar strategies are employed in Japan and mainland China to diversify channels to finance education. The involvement of the market and private sector, the revitalization of local communities and social forces, and the increase in tuition fees are clear indicators showing the declining role of the state as the primary source of education financing. Table C.1 shows different nonstate sectors that have begun to assume increasingly important roles in education provision and financing.

Analyzing the changes in education finance in the light of the theoretical framework outlined in Chapter 1, it is obvious that these East Asian societies are experiencing a fundamental change in their approach to education governance, shifting to an *interactionist* model (government as a partnership with society), a stronger "coproduction" role for civil society groups, and a preference for market-type mechanisms over bureaucratic modes of service delivery.

In addition, our earlier discussions in Part II regarding individual East Asian societies' responses to the intensifying globalization pressures have illustrated how globalization has accelerated changes and restructuring processes in contemporary East Asian societies, thus causing fundamental changes to education policy and governance. Having offloaded social policy/social welfare responsibilities to other nonstate actors, these East Asian states now take up the roles of facilitator, enabler, policy coordinator, and regulator. By performing such roles, they can retain control over education policy without overburdening themselves for resolving problems of provision and financing. Governing through "new governance," these East Asian states have successfully made use of globalization pressures to push local political changes and public sector reforms. Our earlier discussions have clearly demonstrated how tactical and skillful these Asian

Table C.1 Changing roles of state and nonstate sectors in education provision and financing in East Asia

	Hong Kong	Singapore	Taiwan	South Korea	Japan	China
State	++	++	+−	+−	+−	+−
Market	+	+	+++	+++	+++	+++
Civil society	↑	↑	↑↑	↑↑	↑↑	↑↑

Notes
+++   very important role.
++   important.
+   increasingly important.
+−   reducing in importance.
↑   emerging.
↑↑   growing in influence.

"developmental" states are, especially when they can adapt themselves to the rapidly changing socioeconomic and sociopolitical environments by choosing "policy instruments" to cope with intensified global challenges.

At the same time, these governments can streamline their bureaucracies and make their public administration frameworks much more responsive and appropriate to the changing global market economy by implementing reforms with a managerialist and neoliberal orientation. Seen in this light, the education reform strategies that these East Asian states have adopted in transforming their education policy could be analyzed as strategies adopted to tackle the problems generated from the "centralized" governance model, an approach that had long been implemented in running the education sector. Despite educational decentralization, these East Asian states are still the major players in education. What really changes the education sector in these societies is the different roles that the states play and have played. During the reform and restructuring processes, these Asian governments have chosen the role of regulator, enabler, and facilitator instead of being heavily engaged in the role of provider and funder. Such findings, when put together, suggest "not only have changes in the nature of the state influenced the reform of education, but the reforms in education are themselves beginning to change the way we think about the role of the state and what we expect of it" (Whitty 1997, p. 302).

Most important of all, the above analysis has suggested that although the nature of the state/government does change in a very broad sense, the real transformation is the state's move from carrying out most of the work of education itself to determining where the work will be done, by whom, and on what terms. Hence, globalization could be conducive to reconfiguring modern states, driving modern governments to restructure their governance models and reform the ways they manage the public sector (Pierre 2000; Pierre and Peters 2000). In order to cope with such challenges, individual states have been prompted to change their roles and reform their institutions in order to accommodate, and not just adapt to, the demands and pressures generated from the external environment (Giddens 1999; Waters 2001).

Globalization and the withering of the state

Another major concern of globalization discourse is related to whether the capacity of modern states will be weakened under intensified globalization pressures. Marginson and Rhodes (2002) clearly describe the challenges posed by globalization to modern states, stating that the role and functioning of the state in the context of globalization are skewed toward the competitive state (see also Cerny 1996), which prioritizes the economic dimensions of its activities above all others. Therefore, maximizing welfare to promote enterprise, innovation, and profitability in the private and public spheres is becoming popular. It is in such a context that Dale argues that the world is in the process of becoming wholly commodified, both through the recommodification of those elements of public provision that the welfare state decommodified and much more by the extension of the commodity form into all those areas of the world that were previously concealed from it (Dale 2000, p. 95). Only when we place the restructuring experiences discussed in this volume in their unique political and cultural contexts and the broader policy environment of decentralization in both political and economic realms, will we be able to have a better grasp on the tensions and dilemmas that these East Asian societies are now facing.

On the one hand, these Asian developmental states are well aware of the importance of education in strengthening their "global competence" and "competition" in the global economy; therefore these governments are keen to make use of the energies and potential unleashed from the nonstate sources, including the market, local communities, and other nonstate sectors in providing and financing education. On the other hand, these Asian governments are worried about the decline in the quality of education once education providers have proliferated and education services have diversified. Our discussions in Part II have explained the strategies that the selected Asian governments have adopted to reform their higher education systems in tackling challenges posed by globalization. Comparing and contrasting education reform strategies introduced in these Asian societies, there are a lot of changes in common between the higher education sectors in Hong Kong, Singapore, Taiwan, South Korea, Japan, and mainland China and those elsewhere, which suggests that higher education developments in these societies have been affected by similar trends of globalization. Nonetheless, before we jump to this conclusion, maybe we should also bear in mind an alternative hypothesis that states that local factors are crucial and determining factors for changes. More important, the nation-state/local government of these selected societies still enjoys autonomy and exercises authority to direct higher education reforms.

The continual questioning of the state capacity in the context of globalization has inevitably drawn some people to believe the state is reduced to the role of the "night-watchman" of classical liberalism, hence only taking care of law and order, protecting the sanctity of contract, maintaining the minimum level of welfare to protect those who are really poor and vulnerable, and facilitating the free operation of the market (Brown *et al.* 2001). Moreover, the reformulation of modern states has led some scholars to believe that modern states have to play the roles of "facilitator," "enabler," "regulator," and "builder of market" (Ma 1999; Sbragia 2000) and that new public management is characterized by "governance without government" (Rosenau 1992). In this connection, it seems that the capacity and the role of nation-states have changed in the sense that they become less autonomous and have less exclusive control over the economic, social, and cultural processes and distinctiveness of their territories (Giddens 1998).

Nonetheless, our earlier discussion has indicated that even though similar strategies are adopted by different countries in response to the so-called tide of globalization, different governments may use these similar strategies to serve their own political purposes. As Hallak (2000) rightly suggested, modern states may tactically make use of the globalization discourse to justify their own political agendas or legitimize their own inaction. As for Hong Kong, the call for quality control in higher education must be understood as part of the larger project of the public sector reform started in the late 1980s. The adoption of the managerial approach in university governance is to improve the efficiency and effectiveness of the higher education sector, so that Hong Kong can be maintained as one of the most dynamic and competitive international academic centres. For this reason, we must put the recent higher education reforms within the wider public policy reform/public management reform context in Hong Kong. Hence, reform strategies along the line of managerialism introduced in Hong Kong's higher education could be understood as part of the public sector reengineering project already being developed since 1989 (Mok 2000a).

In the case of Singapore, the use of quality assurance mechanisms in the higher education system can be understood as means to enhance the competitiveness of the city-state in the regional and global market contexts. As I have argued elsewhere (Mok and Lee 2003), the case of Singapore demonstrates how a fragile state can become strong if it gets its developmental priorities and policies right and if education is well resourced, credible, productive, and significant (Gopinathan 1997). The Singapore government has gained legitimacy and the ability to foster rapid economic growth by putting stress on meritocracy, high academic achievement, and the relevance of education to manpower planning (Quah 1998). Unlike Hong Kong, the higher education reforms in Singapore's serve the political agenda to make the city-state a cultural and academic centre in the region, or a "Boston of the East." A state-centric approach for economic and social change requires a proactive and interventionist government to achieve national development and to nurture, influence, and shape the global environment. In this government-made society (Low 1998), the Singapore government has managed to manipulate forces generated from globalization to justify its own local political agendas by pushing higher education reforms to make Singapore a more competitive and economically vibrant society in the global market (Mok and Lee 2003).

As for the case of Taiwan, the call for higher education reforms and quality assurance has to do with the particular sociopolitical environment of the island-state. As Taiwan has become a more politically liberal and democratic society, university academics have become very keen to establish links with the external world, while the state is very keen to make the island-state more international. For this reason, the stress on the importance of international benchmarking and the significance of internationalization can be understood as strategies to allow Taiwan to escape being isolated by the international community. In addition, the rapid expansion of private higher education institutions in Taiwan has caused concern about improving/assuring quality. Recent reform initiatives to promote quality assurance can be seen as the strategy of the government to assert control on the quality of higher education. Similarly, higher education reforms in South Korea and mainland China are directed and orchestrated by the state instead of merely being driven by global forces (Weng 2001; Law 2003). In addition, we should not ignore the role of regional organizations in the process of globalization. More precisely, the Asian Pacific Economic Cooperation affected education internally and externally by both mediating and contributing to globalization. As Dale and Robertson (2002) suggested, despite the fact that there may be a common thread running throughout the globalization processes, the forces of globalization do not sweep all before them and homogenize everything.

Similar reform strategies adopted by the Chinese government in reforming its higher education system may not necessarily mean socialist China commits itself to the ideology underlying the reform measures. Our discussion in Chapter 5 has clearly shown that the policy of decentralization being employed by the Chinese government has not led to a genuine kind of decentralization. Despite the fact that universities in the mainland are now given more flexibility and autonomy in running their own businesses, the state has never withdrawn from regulating higher education. My recent field visits and field interviews conducted on the mainland repeatedly confirm the observations that the Chinese government in general and the Ministry of Education in particular remain the major determining forces in higher education development. The university merging discussion in my recent work (MoK 2004a) once again reflects how a nation-state makes use of global reform strategies to resolve its own local administrative problem.

Our analysis in Chapter 10 also shows how Japan has tried to ride the tides of globalization and the needs to make Japanese education systems more internationalized. Whether the adoption of marketization and corporatization strategies would really transform the traditions of Japanese academia remains an open question. Nonetheless, the Japanese government has successfully introduced and implemented reform strategies along the lines of neoliberalism despite the differences and resistance from the Japanese academia. This indicates that the state is able enough to push its political/reform agendas.

Hence, analyzing current education developments in these societies from a public policy perspective, we may find that the higher education reforms in these East Asian societies have been pursued within the context of managing state building (or government capacity) and economic growth in a state-directed (or government-directed) paradigm of governance rather than to depower the state/government. In addition, the introduction of higher education reforms in these societies can be interpreted as a strategy adopted by the government to cope with problems of political and bureaucratic governance instead of purely problems of severe economic and social difficulties. Even so, our discussions have suggested the presence of diverse national and local agendas which have given different meanings to common management jargons and statements (Cheung 2000). If we accept that diversities in domestic administrative agendas are the norm rather than the exception in global public management and governance, we may better reflect of the globalization impact. Perhaps the usefulness of the globalization claim lies more in its rhetoric; globalization discourse is used to facilitate the accomplishment of domestic purposes such as creating a proper rationale or a legitimate claim for launching institutional reforms, or to sustain a new discourse about the environment confronting institutions (Pratt and Poole 1999, pp. 540–43).

Similar to experiences elsewhere (as in the UK) when strategies of deregulation, contracting-out, agencification, and privatization have been introduced to reform the public sector (Hood 1991; Bache 2003), the reforms may not lead to the "hollowing out of the state" and weakening of state capacity. In contrast, the introduction of new governance, particularly the diversification of nonstate actors and proliferation of policy tools, may enable the state to retain and enhance policy control. As Pierre has rightly argued, "as the state's traditional power bases seem to be losing much of their former strength, there has been a search for alternative strategies through which the state can articulate and pursue the collective interest without necessarily relying on coercive instruments" (2000, p. 2). In short, our scrutiny of the impacts of globalization on education policy/public sector management in these East Asian societies has clearly shown that the revitalization of nonstate sectors (including the market or private actors) in education provision and financing may not necessarily weaken the state's capacity (Knill and Lehmkuhl 2002) but instead may drive modern states to reconstitute and restructure their systems to become activist and proactive in shaping policy agendas and policy directions.

Globalization and the East Asian developmental state

When putting all the observations together, we have found that the selected East Asian countries can manage to exercise their autonomy to direct education reforms. Despite the fact that the governments in these societies have initiated a policy of decentralization in the higher education sector in recent years to allow individual universities to have more autonomy to be responsible for their own development plans, it is wrong to argue that the state/government has retreated entirely from the higher education domain. Instead, the governments of these societies have taken a rather proactive approach to reviewing their higher education systems and have started reforms to nurture more creative and innovative citizens for future developments. Unlike the hyerglobalists" argument that growing globalization trends will eventually weaken the capacity and lessen the autonomy of individual nation-states, this comparative study argues that these selected East Asian governments can enjoy a considerable extent of autonomy and flexibility to direct/shape their own education reform agendas. Contrary to hyperglobalists' arguments, the institutionalized state-society linkages (i.e., the mobilization of nonstate sources and actors to engage in education provision in this case) discussed earlier do not diminish the state's capacity to achieve better public management and social service delivery (Mok 2003c).

According to Weiss (1995), there is a problem with the institutional approach in conceptualizing the role of nation-states in East Asian development. He attacks those who would "kick the state back out." Weiss also argues that:

> in their haste to dispute the "developmental state" idea—to knock down the notion that the East Asian state is in some sense "strong" or distinctive—many recent studies fail to pay sufficient attention to the possible importance of cooperation in a theory of state capacity . . . The danger is that in trying to bring capital back in, the state is being marginalized or diminished, in a negative-sum manner
>
> (1995, pp. 591–92)

Instead of marginalizing nation-states or minimizing the state's capacity in the globalizing economic context, our earlier discussion has also provided evidence of "connectedness" between states and societies. Such a "connectedness" not only generates additional resources for public/social policy provision but also strengthens nation states' capacity to regulate and manage public service delivery. Plenty of comparative studies in education policies have repeatedly reported that decentralization can be a mechanism for *tightening* central control of the periphery instead of allowing far greater decisionmaking power for the lower levels of governments (Neave and van Vught 1994; Hanson 1999; Hawkins 1999). The coexistence of both decentralizing and centralizing trends in education governance is becoming increasingly common. Most important of all, this book has found that the changing modes of governance and the changing role of the state in education have rendered the conventional "public-private distinction" neither adequate nor convincing to describe the restructured state-education relationships especially when we analyze such changes in light of the dynamic and fluid nature of decentralization (Dale 1997; Bray 1999; Hanson 1999; Mok 2000d).

If we conceptualize the processes of decentralization and marketization taking place in the higher education sector of these societies, deregulating some major aspects of education has indeed increased a limited number of state powers and, in turn, strengthened the state's capacity to foster particular interests while appearing to stand outside the frame. As states and governments are the major education service providers, the different roles that they have played are what really changes the education sector of these societies. All these developments suggest: "not only have changes in the nature of the state influenced the reforms of education, but the reforms in education are themselves beginning to change the way we think about the role of the state and what we expect of it" (Whitty 1997, p. 302). As far as the coordination of institutions is concerned in relation to different governance activities in education such as funding, regulation, and provision/delivery, the role of the state, market, and community would normally be identified. Our earlier discussion has suggested that although the nature of the state/government does change in a very broad sense, what is actually transformed is the state itself moving from the primary performer of most of the work of education to determining where the work will be done and by whom. In terms of control, we also observe that the state may take different roles in different governance activities; thus the extent of state intervention is found to be varied.

Concluding remarks

In this book, we have examined how processes of globalization have affected the way that education reforms are launched and how education policies are formulated. Although we can easily find similar policy trends and reform measures adopted by the Asian societies in the present comparative study, we should not come to a sweeping conclusion that globalization is the major or even the only driving force for recent changes taking place in education. When comparing and contrasting education reforms and policy change in these Asian societies, we should look closely into how the systems and policies really change and transform. At the policy level, we may easily find that these governments adopt similar reform strategies. But a closer scrutiny of what really happens at the operational level reveals a contrasting picture that the same reform policy may become merely policy rhetoric instead of policy reality. For this reason, we should pay particular attention to how the changes are really implemented, how reforms have been launched, and to what extent the policy intents or reform objectives are achieved. We must be aware of the gap between policy rhetoric and reality. Equally important, we must look into questions such as what are the consequences after the implementation of reforms and to what extent the outcomes or consequences are the expected results of the reform or intended policy changes.

While there are clear global trends, especially in the economy and in technology, comparative study indicates that these East Asian governments are still powerful actors in shaping national development. Our foregoing discussion points out that not all nations have responded to globalization in the same way because of the specificities of national history, politics, culture, and economy. Therefore, the so-called global tide of market competition, nonstate provision of public services, corporate governance, and system-wide and institutional performance management should not be treated as an undifferentiated universal trend. These different elements undoubtedly reinforce each other, though they are not equivalent or interchangeable everywhere. Instead, they may take different configurations, which remain nation specific as well as global. As Gopinathan argues, "even as educational paradigms and ideas take on a global character, the factors that determine educational policies are essentially national in character" (Gopinathan 1997, p. 8). Instead of being simply the response to a process of globalization, the formulation of national policies is the result of the complicated and dynamic processes of glocalization (Mok and Lee 2003). Therefore, we must not analyze change in education in terms of a one-dimensional movement from "the state" (understood as nonmarket and bureaucratic) to "the market" (understood as nonstate and corporate). Rather, we must contextually analyze the interaction between a range of critical local shaping factors and the impetus for change driven by global trends.

This interaction becomes even more sharply apparent in the reverberations of the Asian financial crisis, which has had a varied economic impact on our four societies, but poses similar challenges. In education, existing tensions generated by globalization and the conflicting pressures produced by the crisis sharpen marketization. This manifests itself on the one hand in a search for increased competitiveness via educational expansion and development. On the other hand, it feeds a desire to control and/or reduce educational expenditure. In all societies, there is thus pressure both for educational development and for cuts in expenditure, alongside attempts to make more effective use of existing resources and pressure on educational institutions to seek alternatives to state funding.

Finally, to what extent does the analysis of education policy in the Tigers support arguments developed elsewhere (Holliday and Wilding 2003) about the fundamentally productivist and political nature of Tiger social policy? It is no accident that education is the largest area of public expenditure in all four societies. Education claims this large share for two main reasons. One relates to its links to fostering economic growth and promoting competitiveness. The other relates to its key role in nation building and in advancing political and social stability. The vigorous reform activity currently taking place in educational sectors in all these societies stems from the perceived economic, political, and social importance of education. At the same time, the state's reluctant collectivism is visible. Combined with a very strong commitment to education is a preference for the government to fund and regulate rather than actually to provide, clearly showing education to be a mixed economy in these East Asian societies.

Notes

1 Globalization and new governance: changing policy instruments and regulatory arrangements in education

1 "Positive coordination" refers to an "attempt to maximize the overall effectiveness and efficiency of government policy by exploring and utilizing the joint strategy of options of several ministerial portfolios," while "negative coordination" is designed to ensure that any new policy initiative designed by a specialized subunit within the ministerial organization will not interfere with the established policies and interests of other ministerial units (see Scharpf 1994).

6 Hong Kong's response to globalization: questing for entrepreneurial universities

1 For details regarding curriculum changes and reform in university curricula, please refer to various websites of UGC-funded universities in Hong Kong. For example, for the University of Hong Kong, please visit www.hku.edu.hk; City University of Hong Kong at www.cityu.edu.hk; Hong Kong University of Science and Technology (www.ust.hk), the Chinese University of Hong Kong (www.cuhk.edu.hk), etc.
2 For details, see the above note.

References

Adams, D. and Gottlieb, E.E. (1993) *Education and Social Change in Korea*, New York: Garland Publishing.

Adamson, B. and Li, S.P. (1999) "Primary and secondary schooling," in M. Bray and R. Koo (eds) *Education and Society in Hong Kong and Macau: Comparative Perspectives on Continuity and Change*, Hong Kong: Comparative Education Research Centre, The University of Hong Kong.

Agelasto, M. and Adamson, B. (1998) *Higher Education in Post-Mao China*, Hong Kong: Hong Kong University Press.

Altbach, P.G. (1998) *Comparative Higher Education: Knowledge, The University and Development*, Hong Kong: Comparative Education Research Centre, The University of Hong Kong.

Altbach, P.G. (2000) "What higher education does right: a millennium accounting," *International Higher Education*, 18: 2–3.

Amano, I. and Poole, G.S. (2004) "The Japan university in crisis," *Higher Education*, 4: 1–24.

Apple, M.W. (2000) "Between neoliberalism and neoconservatism: education and conservatism in a global context," in N.C. Burbules and C.A. Torres (eds) *Globalization and Education: Critical Perspective*, New York: Routledge.

Applebaum, R.P. and Henderson, J. (eds) (1992) *States and Development in the Asian Pacific Rim*, Newbury Park, CA: Sage.

Arimoto, A. (2002) "Globalisation and higher education reforms: the Japanese case," in E. Jurgen and F. Oliver (eds) *Higher Education in a Globalising World: International Trends and Mutual Observations*, Netherlands: Kluwer Academic Publishers.

Asher, M. and Newman, D. (2001) "Hong Kong and Singapore: two approaches to the provision of pensions in Asia," *Journal of Pensions Management: An International Journal*, 7(2): 155–66.

Asia Times, November 27, 2002.

Asonuma, A. (2002) "Finance reform in Japanese higher education," *Higher Education*, 43: 109–26.

Bache, I. (2003) "Governing through governance: education policy control under new labour," *Political Studies*, 51: 300–14.

Ball, S.J. (1990) *Politics and Policy Making in Education*, London: Routledge.

Ball, S.J. (2000) "Performativity and fragmentation in 'postmodern schooling'," in J. Carter (ed.) *Postmodernity and Fragmentation of Welfare*, London: Routledge.

Baltodano, A. (1997) "The study of public administration in times of global interpretation: a historical rationale for a theoretical model 623–26," *Journal of Public Administration Research and Theory*, 7(4): 623–26.

Bellows, T.J. (1995) "Globalization and regionalization in Singapore: a public policy perspective," *Asian Journal of Political Science*, 3(2): 46–65.

Biggs, J. (1999) "Quality in teaching and learning: assurance, enhancement, and feasibility," paper presented at the 16th Annual Conference of the Hong Kong Educational Research Association, the Hong Kong Institute of Education, November 20–21, Hong Kong.

Blaug, M. (1991) *An Introduction to the Economics of Education*, Aldershot, Hampshire: Gregg Revivals.

Bottery, M. (2000) *Education, Policy and Ethics*, London: Continuum.

Brady, A., Abe, K., Takeda, J., and Poole, B. (2003) *Towards a Clearer Understanding of the Socio-economic, Socio-educational, and Socio-political Role of Higher Education in Japan*. Online. Available http://www.soc.hwansei.ac.jp/kiyou/95/95_ch10.ptf (Accessed on August 9, 2004).

Braun, D. and Merrien, F.X. (1999) "Governance of universities and modernization of the state: analytical aspects," in D. Bruan and and F. X. Merrien (eds) *Towards a New Model of Governance for Universities? A Comparative View*, London and Philadelphia, PA: Jessica Kingsley Publishers.

Bray, M. (1997) "Education and colonial transition: the Hong Kong experience in comparative perspective," in M. Bray and W.O. Lee (eds) *Education and Political Transition: Implications of Hong Kong's Change of Sovereignty*, Hong Kong: Comparative Education Research Centre, The University of Hong Kong.

Bray, M. (1999) "Control of education: issues and tensions in centralization and decentralization," in R.F. Arnove and C.T. Torres (eds) *Comparative Education: The Dialectic of the Global and the Local*, Lanham, MD: Rowman & Littlefield.

Bray, M. (2000) "Financing higher education: patterns, trends and options," *Prospects*, XXX: 331–48.

Bray, M. and Lee, W.O. (eds) (2001) *Education and Political Transition: Themes and Experiences in East Asia*, Hong Kong: Comparative Education Research Centre, The University of Hong Kong.

Bridges, D. and McLaughlin, T.H. (eds) (1994) *Education and the Market Place*, London: The Falmer Press.

Broadbent, J. and Gray, A. (2003) "Public–private partnerships: editorial," *Public Money & Management*, 23: 135–36.

Brown, P., Green, A., and Lauder, H. (2001) *High Skills: Globalization, Competitiveness and Skills Formation*, Oxford: Oxford University Press.

Burbules, N.C. and Torres, C.A. (eds) (2000) *Globalization and Education: Critical Perspectives*, New York: Routledge.

Business Times, May 8, 1991.

Carnoy, M. (2000) *Sustaining the New Economy in the Information Age: Reflections on Our Changing World*, University Park, PA: The Pennsylvania State University Press.

Castells, M. (1996) *The Rise of the Network Society*, Oxford: Blackwell.

Census and Statistics Department, Hong Kong (2001a) *Hong Kong Annual Digest of Statistics 2001 Edition*, Hong Kong: Government Printer.

Census and Statistics Department, Hong Kong (2001b) *Population Census: Information Booklet*, Hong Kong: Government Printer.

Census and Statistics Department, Hong Kong (2002) *Hong Kong in Figures 2002 Edition*, Hong Kong: Government Printer.

Cerny, P.G. (1990) *The Changing Architecture of Politics: Structure, Agency, and the Future of the State*, London: Sage.

Cerny, P.G. (1996) "Paradoxes of the competition state: the dynamics of political globalization," *Government and Opposition*, 32: 251–71.

Chae, J. (2003a) *Higher Education Policies (1998–2002)*. Online. Available http://www.moe.go.kr/English/Policy/ (Accessed on January 12, 2004).

Chae, J. (2003b) *Lifelong and Vocational Education Policies (98–02)*. Online. Available http://www.moe.go.kr/English/Policy/ (Accessed on January 12, 2004).

Chan, D. (2002) "Policy implications for adopting a managerial approach in education," in K.H. Mok and D. Chan (eds) *Globalization and Education: The Quest for Quality Education in Hong Kong*, Hong Kong: Hong Kong University Press.

Chan, D. and Mok, K.H. (2001) "Educational reforms and coping strategies under the tidal wave of marketization: a comparative study of Hong Kong and the mainland China," *Comparative Education*, 37(1): 21–41.

Chan, D. and Ngok, K.L. (2000) "Shanghai education into the 21st century: a quest for learning society," *Chulalongkorn Educational Review*, 6(2): 1–14.

Chen, B. and Li, G. (2002) "Minban gaodeng jiaoyu ziketiqu yanjiu baogao" (the research report on people-run higher education), in *Minban Jiaoyu de Gaige yuFazhan* (minban reform and development of people-run education), Beijing: Jiaoyu Kexue Chubanshe [in Chinese].

Chen, S.B. (2001) *The First Ride in the New Century: Reflections of Political Party Rotation in Taiwan*, Taipei: Yuenchen.

Chen, S.F. (1995) Changes in the appointment procedure of university presidents in the Republic of China, *Chinese Education and Society*, 28(4): 50–65.

Cheng, K.M. (1992) "Educational policymaking in Hong Kong: the changing legitimacy," in G.A. Postiglione (ed.) *Education and Society in Hong Kong: Toward One Country and Two Systems*, Hong Kong: Hong Kong University Press.

Cheng, K.M. (1995) "Education—decentralization and the market," in L. Wong and S. MacPherson (eds) *Social Change and Social Policy in Contemporary China*, Aldershot: Avebury.

Cheng, K.M. (1997) "The education system," in G.A. Postiglione and W.O. Lee (eds) *Schooling in Hong Kong: Organization, Teaching and Social Context*, Hong Kong: Hong Kong University Press.

Cheng, K.M. (2002) "The quest for quality education: the quality assurance movement in Hong Kong," in K.H. Mok and D. Chan (eds) *Globalization and Education: The Quest for Quality Education in Hong Kong*, Hong Kong: Hong Kong University Press.

Cheng, W.H. (1995) "Education finance in Taipei, China," paper presented at the Workshop on *Financing Human Resource Development in Asia*, organized by the Asian Development Bank Project, July 11–14, 1995, Manila.

Cheng, Y.C., Mok, M.C.M. and Tsui, K.T. (2002) "Educational reform and research in Hong Kong: a request for comprehensive knowledge," *Educational Research for Policy and Practice*, 1: 7–21.

Cheng, Y.S. (2000) "Educational change and development in Hong Kong: effectiveness, quality and relevance," in Y.S. Cheng and T. Townsend (eds) *Educational Change and Development in the Asia Pacific Region: Challenges for the Future*, Exton: Swets & Zeitlinger Publishers.

Cheng, Y.S. (2002) "Educational reforms in the Asia-Pacific region: trends and implications for research," paper presented at the International Symposium on *Globalization and Educational Governance Change in East Asia*, June 28, 2002, Hong Kong.

Cheng, Y.S. and Townsend, T. (eds) (2000) *Educational Change and Development in the Asia Pacific Region: Challenges for the Future*, Exton: Swets & Zeitlinger Publishers.

Cheung, A. (2000) "Globalization, governance and Asian values: can there be a universal administrative paradigm?," paper presented to the International Conference on Governance, City University of Hong Kong, January 2000, Hong Kong.

Cheung, A. and Scott, I. (eds) (2003) *Governance and Public Sector Reform in Asia*, London and New York: RoutledgeCurzon.

Cheung, B.L. (2001) "Public enterprises and privatization in East Asia: Paths, Policies and Prospects," *Public Finance and Management*, 2: 67–96.

China Education (2000) *Jiao Yu Bu Guan Yu Zho Hao 2001 Nian Pu Tong Gao Kao "3 + X" Ke Mu She Zhi Gai Ge Gong Zuo de Tong Zhi* (Notice about implementing "3 + X" in Standardized Test in 2001 from the Ministry of Education). Online. Available http://www.chinaedu.edu.cn/jyzx/zhengce/00–4/00–4-10–7.htm [in Chinese]. (Accessed on January 13, 2004).

China National Institute of Educational Research (1995) *A Study of NGO-Sponsored and Private Higher Education in China*, Beijing: UNESCO.

China Times, September 1, 1999.

China Times, December 28, 1999.

Chiu, H. (1993) "Constitutional development and reform in the Republic of China on Taiwan," *Issues and Studies*, 29(1): 1–38.

Christiansen, F. (1996) "Devolution on Chinese higher education policy in the 1990s: common establishment and the '211' programme," *Leeds East Asia Papers*, 36: 1–23.

Chu, C.Y. and Tai, H. (1996) *Jiaoyu Songbang*, Taipei: Yuanliu Publisher [in Chinese].

Chu, C.Y. and Yeh, C.H. (1995) "Taiwan's private education," *Chinese Education and Society*, 28(4): 66–69.

Chua, B.L. (2003) *Research Report: Entrepreneurship in Hong Kong: Revitalizing Entrepreneurship*, New York: The Manfield Center for Pacific Affairs.

Chung, B.G. (1999) "A study of the school leaving policy in the republic of Korea: historical review of its genesis, implementation and reforms, 1974–95," EDD Thesis, the University of Hawaii, Hawaii.

Chung, H. (1999) "Contemporary distance education in Taiwan," in K. Harry (ed.) *Higher Education Through Open and Distance Learning: World Review of Distance Education and Open Learning*, London: Routledge.

Chung, W.K. (1992) *The economic dynamism of Hong Kong: partnership of state and capitalists*, unpublished MA Dissertation, Department of Sociology, University of Kentucky.

Clark, B.R. (1998) *Creating Entrepreneurial Universities: Organizational Pathways of Transformation*, Oxford: Pergamon.

Clark, B.R. (2002) *Entrepreneurial Universities*, Comparative Education Policy Occasional Paper Series, No.1, Comparative Education Policy Research Unit, Department of Public and Social Administration, City University of Hong Kong, Hong Kong.

Coleman, J.S. (1990) *Foundations of Social Theory*, Cambridge, MA: Harvard University Press.

Common, R. (1998) *Global impacts on public administration in Hong Kong*, Occasional Paper Series of Department of Public and Social Administration, City University of Hong Kong, Hong Kong.

Communist Party of China Central Committee [CCPCC] (1985) *The Decision of the Central Committee of the Communist Party of China on the Reform of Educational Structure*, Beijing: People's Press.

Communist Party of China Central Committee [CCPCC] (1993) "*Zhonghua Renmin Gongheguo Guowuyuan Gongbao*" (The programme for education reform and development in China), Report of the State Council, People's Republic of China 2: 58–66 [in Chinese].

Council on Education Reform [CER] (1995) *Jiaoyu Gaige Diyiqiziyi Baogaoshu* (Second Report on Consultation for Education Reform), Taipei: Executive Yuan Education Reform Commission.

Council on Education Reform [CER] (1996) *Jiaoyu Gaige Zhongziyi Baogaoshu* (Final Report on Consultation for Education Reform), Taipei: Executive Yuan Education Reform Commission.

Cowen, R. (1996) "Last past the post, comparative education, modernity and perhaps post-modernity," *Comparative Education*, 32(2): 151–70.

Cox, R.W. (1987) *Production, Power, and World Order: Social Forces in the Making of History*, Cambridge: Cambridge University Press.

Crossley, M. (2000) "Bridging cultures and traditions in the reconceptualisation of comparative and international education," *Comparative Education*, 36(3): 319–32.

Curlson, A. (1999) *Market Education: The Unknown History*, New Brunswick: Transaction.

Currie, J. (1998) "Impact of globalization on Australian universities: competition, fragmentation and demoralization," paper presented at the International Association of Sociology World Congress, July 1998, Montreal, Canada.

Currie, J. (2002) "Globalization's impact on the professoriate in Anglo American universities," in A. Welch (ed.) *The Professoriate. Profile of a Profession*, Amsterdam: Kluwer.

Currie, J. and Newson, J. (eds) (1998a) *Globalization and the Universities*, London: Sage.

Currie, J. and Newson, J. (eds) (1998b) *Universities and Globalization: Critical Perspectives*, Thousand Oaks, CA: Sage Publications.

Dale, R. (1997) "The state and the governance of education: an analysis of the restructuring of the state–education relationship," in A.H. Halsey, H. Lauder, P. Brown, and A.S. Well (eds) *Education: Culture, Economy and Society*, Oxford: Oxford University Press.

Dale, R. (1999) "Specifying globalization effects on national policy: a focus on the mechanisms," *Journal of Education Policy*, 14(1): 1–17.

Dale, R. (2000) "Globalisation: a new world for comparative education?" in J. Schriewer (ed.) *Discourse Formation in Comparative Education*, New York and Berlin: Peter Lang.

Dale, R. and Robertson, S. (2002) "The varying effects of regional organizations as subjects of globalization of education," *Comparative Education Review*, 46(1): 10–36.

D'Aveni, R. (1994) *Hypercompetition: Managing the Dynamics of Strategic Maneuvering.* With Gunther, R. New York: Free Press.

De Zilwa, D. (2004) "Using entrepreneurial activities as a means of survival: investigating the processes used by Australian universities to diversify their revenue streams," *Higher Education*, forthcoming.

Deem, R. (2001) "Globalization, new managerialism, academic capitalism in universities: is the local dimension still important?" *Comparative Education*, 37(1): 7–20.

Department of Statistics, Singapore (2002) *Singapore 2002 Statistical Highlights*, Singapore: Singapore Department of Statistics.

Department of Statistics (2003) *Statistics of Taiwan*, Taipei: Department of Statistics, Government of Taiwan.

Department of Statistics (2004) *Statistics of Taiwan*, Taipei: Department of Statistics, Government of Taiwan.

Development and Planning Bureau, Ministry of Education [DPBMOE] and Shanghai Academy of Educational Sciences [SAES] (2003) *Green Paper on Non-governmental Education in China*, Shanghai: Shanghai Jiaoyu Chubanshe.

Dill, D.D. (2001) "The regulation of public research universities: changes in academic competition and implications for university autonomy and accountability," *Higher Education Policy*, 14(1): 21–35.

Doong, S.L. (2002) "Decentralization and diversification: review of Taiwan's educational reform policies in secondary education," paper presented at the *Pacific Consortium 26th Annual Conference*, May 2002, Seoul, South Korea.

Duke, C. (1992) *The Learning University: Towards a New Paradigm*, Buckingham: The Society for Research into Higher Education and Open University Press.

Dunsire, A. (1993) "Modes of governance," in J. Kooiman (ed.) *Modern Governance: New Government–Society Interactions*, London: Sage.

Education and Manpower Branch and Education Department (1991) *School Management Initiative*, Hong Kong: The Government Printer.

Education and Manpower Bureau (1997) *Policy Program: The 1997 Policy Address*, Hong Kong: Printing Department, HKSAR Government.

Education and Manpower Bureau (2004a). Online. Available http://www.emb.gov.hk (Accessed on December 23, 2004).

Education and Manpower Bureau (2004b) *Education Statistics*, Hong Kong: Hong Kong Government Printer.

Education Commission (1997) *Education Commission Report No. 7*, Hong Kong: Printing Department, HKSAR Government.

Education Commission (2000a) *Learning for Life, Learning through Life: Reform Proposals for the Education System in Hong Kong*, Hong Kong: Printing Department, HKSAR Government.

Education Commission (2000b) *Review of Education System: Reform Proposals*, Hong Kong: Hong Kong Government Printer.

Education Department, Hong Kong (2001) *Education Indicators for the Hong Kong School Education System: 2002 Abridged Report*, Hong Kong: Government Printer.

Education Department, Hong Kong (2002) *What is "Direct Subsidy" School?* Hong Kong: Government Printer [in Chinese].

Education Testing Service (2000) *TOEIC Report on Test-Takers Worldwide 1997–98*. Online. Available http://www.ets/org/ell/research/toeic.html (Accessed on September 23, 2004).

Educational Development Institute [KEDI] (2000) *Handbook of Educational Statistics*, Seoul: Korean Educational Development Institute.

Ekong, D. and Cloete, N. (1997) "Curriculum responses to a changing national and global environment in an African continent," in N. Cloete, J. Muller, M.W. Makgoba, and D. Ekong (eds) *Knowledge, Identity and Curriculum Transformation in Africa*, London: Maskew Miller Longman.

Etzkowitz, H. (2003) "Research groups as 'quasi-firms': the invention of the entrepreneurial university," *Research Policy*, 32: 109–21.

Etzkowitz, H. and Leydesdorff, L. (eds) (1997) *Universities and the Global Knowledge Economy*, London: Pinter.

Evans, P. (1999) "Transferable lessons? Re-examining the institutional prerequisites of East Asian economic policies," in Y. Akyuz (ed.) *East Asian Development: New Perspectives*, London: Frank Cass.

Fan, L. (1995) "The administrative adjustment of higher education in mainland China," *Issues and Studies*, 31(2): 36–54.

Faulk, K. (2000) *Political Sociology: A Critical Introduction*, New York: New York University Press.

Ferlie, E., Pettigrew, A., Ashburner, L., and Fitzgerald, L. (1996) *The New Public Management in Action*, Oxford: Oxford University Press.

FitzPatrick, P. (2003) "Reinventing Singapore: changing a country's mindset by changing its education system," *International Higher Education*, 31: 22–23.

Flynn, N. (1997) *Public Sector Management*, Hempstead: Harvester Wheatsheaf.

Foreign Press Centre (1995) *About Japan Series 8: Education in Japan*, 2nd edition, Japan: Foreign Press Center/Japan.

Fukuyama, F. (1992) *The End of History and the Last Man*, New York: Free Press.

Gamble, A. (2000) "Economic governance," in J. Pierre (ed.) *Debating Governance*, Oxford: Oxford University Press.

Gao Fiao Fian Xun, June 10, 1993.

Giddens, A. (1998) *The Third Way: The Renewal of Social Democracy*, Cambridge: Polity Press.

Giddens, A. (1999) *Runaway World*, London: Profile Books Ltd.

Giddens, A. (2000) *The Third Way and its Critics*, Cambridge: Polity Press.

Goh, C.T. (1997) "Shaping our Future: 'Thinking schools' and a 'learning nation'," speech at the opening of the 7th *International Conference on Thinking*, June 2, 1997, Singapore.

Goh, C.T. (1999) "Making globalisation work with social accountability," keynote address by Singapore Prime Minister Goh Chok Tong at the *Commonwealth Business Forum*, Ministry of Information and the Arts, November 11, 1999, Singapore.

Goh, C.T. (2000) "Education—meeting the challenge of globalization," opening address by Prime Minister Goh Chok Tong at the *APEC Education Ministers Meeting*, Ministry of Education, April 6, 2000, Singapore.

Goh, C.T. (2001) "Shaping lives, moulding nation," speech by Prime Minister Goh Chok Tong at the *Teachers Day Rally*, August 31, 2001, Singapore.

Gold, T. (1986) *State and Society in the Taiwan Miracle*, Armonk, NY: M.E. Sharpe.

Good, T.L. and Barden, J.S. (2000) *The Great School Debate: Choice, Vouchers and Charters*, Lawrence Erlbaum Associates.

Gopinathan, S. (1989) "University education in Singapore: the making of a national university," in P.G. Altbach and V. Selvaratnam (eds) *From Dependence to Autonomy*, Dordrecht: Kluwer Academic Publishers.

Gopinathan, S. (1996) "Globalisation, the state and education policy in Singapore," in W.O. Lee and M. Bray (eds) *Education and Political Transition: Perspectives and Dimensions in East Asia*, Hong Kong: Comparative Education Research Centre, University of Hong Kong.

Gopinathan, S. (1997) "Singapore educational development in a strong developmentalist state: the Singapore experience," in W.K. Cummings and N.F. McGinn (eds) *International Handbook of Education and Development: Preparing Schools, Students and Nations for the Twenty-first Century*, London: Pergamon.

Gopinathan, S. (1999) "Thinking schools and learning nation in Singapore," paper presented to the MERA-ERA Joint Conference 1999 *Educational Challenges in the New Millennium*, December 1–3, Malacca, Malaysia.

Gopinathan, S. (2001a) "Globalization, the state and education policy in Singapore," in J. Tan, S. Gopinathan, and W.K. Ho (eds) *Challenges Facing the Singapore Education System Today*, Singapore: Prentice Hall.

Gopinathan, S. (2001b) "Globalization, the state and education policy in Singapore," in M. Bray and W.O. Lee (eds) *Education and Political Transition: Themes and Experiences in East Asia*, Hong Kong: Comparative Education Research Centre, The University of Hong Kong.

Gopinathan, S. (2005) "Globalization, the Singapore developmental state and education policy: a thesis revisited," Working paper, National Institute of Education, Singapore.

Gopinathan, S. and Ho, W.K. (2000) "Educational Change and development in Singapore," in T. Townsend and Y.C. Cheng (eds) *Educational change and Development in the Asia-Pacific Region*, Lisse: Swets and & Zeitlinger Publishers.

Gopinathan, S. and Morriss, B. (1997) "Trends in university reform in the context of massification," *RIHE International Seminar Reports*, 10: 127–60.

Gouri, G., Sankar, T.L., Reddy, Y.V., and Shams, K. (1991) "Imperatives and perspectives," in G. Gouri (ed.) *Privatisation and Public Enterprise*, New Delhi: Oxford and IBH Publishing.

Government Information Office, Republic of China (2002) *The Republic of China Yearbook 2002*, Taipei: Government Information office.

Government Information Service, Taiwan (2003) *Taiwan Yearbook 2003*, Taipei: Author.

Government Information Service, Taiwan (2004) *Taiwan Yearbook 2004*, Taipei: Author.

Green, A. (1997) *Education, Globalization and the Nation State*, Basingstoke: Macmillan.

Green, A. (1999) "Education and globalization in Europe and East Asia: convergent and divergent trends," *Journal of Education Policy*, 14(1): 55–71.

Greene, B.I. (1995) "Meeting higher education needs in the 21st century," *Asia-Pacific Exchange Journal*, 2(1): 2.

Haggard, S. and Cheng, T.J. (1987) "State and foreign capital in the East Asian NICs," in F.C. Deyo (ed.) *The Political Economy of New Asian Industrialization*, Ithaca, NY: Cornell University.

Hakim, S., Seidenstat, P., and Bowman, G. (1994) *Privatizing Education and Educational Choice: Concepts, Plans and Experiences*, Westport: Praeger.

Hallak, J. (2000) "Globalization and its impact on education," in T. Mebrahtu, M. Crossley, and D. Johnson (eds) *Globalization, Educational Transformation and Societies in Transition*, Oxford: Symposium Books.

Hanson, E.M. (1998) "Strategies of educational decentralization: key questions and core issues," *Journal of Educational Administration*, 36(2): 111–28.

Hanson, E.M. (1999) "National centralization and regional decentralization in Spain: a study of educational reform," paper presented to the Workshop on *Centralization versus Decentralization: Educational Reform in East and West*, Comparative Education Research Centre, University of Hong Kong, October 20–21, Hong Kong.

Harmer, D. (1994) *School Choice: Why You Need It—How You Get It*, Washington, DC: CATO Institute.

Harris, N. (1986) *The End of the Third World*, London: Penguin.

Hau, Y. (2001) "Entrepreneurship in Hong Kong." Online. Available http://www.mit.Edu/afs (Accessed on September 18, 2003).

Hawkins, J.N. (1999) "Centralization, decentralization, recentralization: educational reform in China," paper presented at the *Workshop on Centralization versus Decentralization: Educational Reform in East and West*, Comparative Education Research Centre, University of Hong Kong, October 20–21, Hong Kong.

Hawkins, J.N. (2000) "Centralization, decentralization, recentralization: educational reform in China," *Journal of Educational Administration*, 38(5): 442–54.

Hawthorne, E. (1996) "Increasing understanding of decision making in higher education: the case of Taiwan," *Quality in Higher Education*, 2(1): 65–77.

Hayhoe, R. (1989) *China's Universities and the Open Door*, New York: M.E. Sharpe.

Hayhoe, R. (1996) *China's Universities 1895–1995: A Century of Cultural Conflict*, New York and London: Garland Press.

HEFCE-OCED/IMHE (2004) *Financial Management and Governance in HEIS: Japan*, Paris: OECD.

Held, D. (ed.) (2000) *A Globalizing World? Culture, Economics, Politics*, London: Routledge.

Held, D., McGrew, A., Glodblatt, D., and Parraton, J. (1999) *Global Transformation: Politics, Economics and Culture*, Stanford, CA: Stanford University Press.

Hendry, J. (2003) *Understanding Japanese Society*, 3rd edition, London: RoutledgeCurzon.

Henkel, M. (1998) "Evaluation in higher education: conceptual and epistemological foundations," *European Journal of Education*, 33(3): 283–97.

Henry, M.L. (1987) "Education as a public and private good," *Journal of Policy Analysis and Management*, 6(4): 628–41.

Henry, M., Lingard, B., Rizvi, F., and Taylor, S. (1999) "Working with/against globalization in education," *Journal of Education Policy*, 14(1): 85–97.

Hinnfors, J. and Pierre, J. (1998) "The Politics of currency crises in Sweden: domestic policy choice in a globalized economy," *West European Politics*, 21: 103–19.

Hirota, T. (2003) "Theorising cohesion and conflict between industry-labour system and education system: from Japan's perspectives," paper presented at the International Workshop on *Comparative Sociology on Cohesion and Conflict between Industry–Labour Policies and Education Policies in the Process of Modernization*, University of Tokyo, December 12, 2003, Tokyo.

Hirst, P. and Thompson, G. (1999) *Globalization in Question*, Cambridge: Polity Press.

HKSAR Government (2001) *Hong Kong 2000*, Hong Kong: Government Printer.

HKSAR Government (2002) *Hong Kong 2001*, Hong Kong: Government Printer.

Hoggett, P. (1991) "A new management in the public sector?" *Policy and Politics*, 19(4): 243–56.

Holliday, I. (2000) "Productivist welfare capitalism: social policy in East Asia," *Political Studies*, 48: 706–23.

Holliday, I. and Wilding, P. (eds) (2003) *Welfare Capitalism in East Asia: Social Policy in the Tiger Economies*, Basingstoke: Palgrave Macmillan.

Hong Kong Government (1965) *Education Policy*, Hong Kong: The Government Printer.

Hong Kong Government (1974) *Secondary Education in Hong Kong over the Next Decade*, Hong Kong: The Government Printer.

Hong Kong Government (1978) *The Development of Senior Secondary and Tertiary Education*, Hong Kong: The Government Printer.

Hood, C. (1991) "A public management for all seasons," *Public Administration*, 69(1): 3–19.

Hood, C. (1999) *Regulation inside Government*, Oxford: Oxford University Press.

Howlett, M. and Ramesh, M. (1995) *Studying Public Policy: Policy Cycles and Policy Subsytems*, Toronto: Oxford University Press.

Hsieh, Y.L. and Tseng, S.F. (2002) "The welfare in the information age, hollowing out or restructuring in the changing labour market in Singapore?" *International Journal of Human Resources Management*, 13(3): 501–21.

Hu, W. (1997) "Woguo Minban Jiaoyu de Sizhong Moshui Ji Qi Tedian" (Four models and their characteristics of minban education in China), *Jiaoyu Zhiye* (Educational Perspective), 6: 44–45 [in Chinese].

Huang, G.C. (1992) *Zhongguo Yishi Yu Taiwan Yishi* (*Chinese Consciousness and Taiwan Consciousness*), Taipei: Wunan Publishing Company.

Husen, T. and Postlethwaite, T.N. (1985) *The International Education: Research and Studies*, Oxford: Pergamon Press.

Information Services Department (2003) *Hong Kong 2002*, Hong Kong: Government Logistics Department, HKSAR Government.

Innovation and Technology Committee (2002) *Innovation and Technology Fund Annual Report 2002*, Hong Kong: Innovation and Technology Committee, HKSAR Government.

Innovation and Technology Committee (2004) *Innovation and Technology Fund Annual Report 2004*, Hong Kong: HSKAR.

Institute of Policy Studies (2003) *Re-inventing the Asian Model: The Case of Singapore*, Singapore: Eastern Universities Press.

Jarvis, P. (2000) "The changing university: meeting a need and needing to change," *Higher Education Quarterly*, 54(1): 43–67.

Jayasurya, K. (2001) "Globalization and the changing architecture of the state: the regulatory state and the politics of negative coordination," *Journal of European Public Policy*, 8: 102–23.

Jomo, K.S., Khoo, B.T., and Chang, Y.T. (1995) *Vision, Policy and Governance in Malaysia*, PSD Occasional Paper No 10, Washington, DC: World Bank.

Jones, P. (1998) "Globalisation and internationalism: democratic prospects for world education," *Comparative Education*, 34(2): 143–55.

Jung, I. and Rha, I. (2001) "A virtual university trial project: its impact on higher education in South Korea," *Innovations in Education & Teaching International*, 38(1): 31–41.

Kan, M.Y. (2000) "Political development and democratization in Taiwan," in K.H. Mok and Y.W. Ku (eds) *A Comparative Study of Social Development in Hong Kong, Taiwan and Mainland China*, Hong Kong: Hong Kong Humanities Press.

Kim, J. (2000) "Curriculum and management," in J.C. Weidman and N. Park (eds) *Higher Education in Korea: Tradition and Adaptation*, New York: Falmer Press.

Kim, Y.H. (2000) "Recent changes and development in Korean school education," in T. Townsend and Y.C. Cheng (eds) *Educational Change and Development in the Asia-Pacific Region: Challenges for the Future*, Lisse: Swets & Zeitlinger Publishers.

Klijn, E.H. and Teisman, G.R. (2003) "Institutional and strategic barriers to public-private partnership: an analysis of Dutch cases," *Public Money & Management*, 23: 137–46.

Knill, C. and Lehmkuhl, D. (2002) "Private actors and the state: internationalization and changing patterns of governance," *Governance*, 15: 41–63.

Knowles, A.S. (1978) *The International Encyclopedia of Higher Education*, San Francisco, CA: Jossey-Bass Publishers.

Kogan, M. and Hanney, S. (2000) *Reforming Higher Education*, London: Jessica Kingsley Publishers.

Koo, H. (1993) *State and Society in Contemporary Korea*, Ithaca, NY: Cornell University.

Kooiman, J. (1993) "Social-political governance: introduction," in J. Kooiman (ed.) *Modern Governance: New Government–Society Interactions*, London: Sage.

Korean Educational Development Institute [KEDI] (2000) *Handbook of Educational Statistics*, Seoul: Korean Educational Development Institute.

Ku, Y.W. (2000) "Economic growth and social development: the challenges to Taiwan," in K.H. Mok and Y.W. Ku (eds) *A Comparative Study of Social Development in Hong Kong, Taiwan and Mainland China*, Hong Kong: Hong Kong Humanities Press.

Kwak, B.S. (2000) "Higher education reform in Korea," paper presented at the International Conference on *Massification of Higher Education and Education Reform*, 2000, Taipei.

Kwak, B.S. (2001) *Leading the Future: Policy Directions and Tasks of Education in Korea*, Seoul: Korean Educational Development Institute.

Kwak, B.S. (2002) "Korea's experiences in education for national and regional development," paper presented at the International Symposium on *Globalization and*

Educational Governance Change in East Asia, City University of Hong Kong, June 28, 2002, Hong Kong.

Kwon, H.J. (1997) "Beyond European welfare regimes: comparative perspectives on East Asian welfare systems," *Journal of Social Policy*, 26(4): 467–84.

Kwong, J. (2000) "Introduction," *International Journal of Educational Development*, 20: 1–10.

Lai, G. (2002) *Primary Admission System and Parental Choice in Hong Kong*, unpublished MA dissertation, Department of Public and Social Administration, City University of Hong Kong.

Lai, P.S. (2003) "Report on entrepreneurship environment in Singapore," Paper downloaded from www.mit.edu (Accessed on September 10, 2004).

Lane, J. and Ersson, S. (2002) *Government and the Economy: A Global Perspective*, London: Continuum.

Law, W.W. (1996a) "Fortress state, cultural continuities and economic change: higher education in mainland China and Taiwan," *Comparative Education*, 32(1): 377–93.

Law, W.W. (1996b) "The Taiwanisation, democratisation and internationalisation of higher education in Taiwan," *Asia Pacific Journal of Education*, 16(1): 5–20.

Law, W.W. (1996c) "The Taiwanisation, democratisation and internationalisation of higher education in Taiwan," *Asia Pacific Journal of Education*, 16(1): 58.

Law, W.W. (1998a) "Higher education in Taiwan: the rule of law and democracy," *International Higher Education*, 11: 4–6.

Law, W.W. (1998b) "Higher education in Taiwan: the rule of law and democracy," *International Higher Education*, Internet Edition.

Law, W.W. (2003) "Globalization, localization and education reform in a new democracy: the Taiwan experience," in K.H. Mok and A. Welch (eds) *Globalization and Educational Restructuring in the Asian Pacific Region*, Basingstoke: Palgrave Macmillan.

Lee, E. and Tan, T.Y. (1995) *Beyond Degrees: The Making of the National University of Singapore*, Singapore: Singapore University Press.

Lee, H.H. (2000) "Higher education in Hong Kong and Singapore: an optimistic or pessimistic future?," paper presented at the Australian Association for Research and Education (AARE), the University of Sydney, December 4–7, Sydney.

Lee, H.H. (2001) "The impacts of marketization on higher education reform in Singapore," paper presented at the International Conference on *Marketization and Higher Education in East Asia*, April 7–8, 2001, Shanghai.

Lee, H.H. (2003a) "A tale of two cities: comparing higher education policies and reforms in Hong Kong and Singapore," *Australian Journal of Education*, 46(3): 255–86.

Lee, H.H. (2003b) "Globalization and national responses: Singapore," paper presented at the International Workshop on *Emergence of Global Market of Higher Education and Roles of State Governments*, National Institute for Educational Policy Research, December 15, Tokyo.

Lee, H.H. (2003c) *A Comparative Study of Globalization Impacts on Higher Education in Hong Kong and Singapore*, unpublished MPhil thesis, Department of Public and Social Administration, City University of Hong Kong, Hong Kong.

Lee, H.H. and Gopinathan, S. (2001) "Centralized decentralization of higher education in Singapore," *Education and Society*, 19(3): 79–96.

Lee, H.H. and Gopinathan, S. (2002) "Comparison of education reforms in Hong Kong and Singapore," paper presented at the International Symposium on *Globalization and Educational Governance Change in East Asia*, June 28, 2002, Hong Kong.

Lee, H.Y., Baik E.S., and Seo H.A. (2000) *The Credit Bank System: An Innovative Approach to Adult Lifelong Learning in Korea*, Seoul: Korean Educational Development Institute.

Lee, J.K. (2000) "Main reform on higher education systems in Korea," *Revista electronica de Investigacion Educativa*, 2(2): 61–76.

Leung, J. (2001) "The politics of decentralization: a case study of school management reform in Hong Kong," *Education and Society*, 19(3): 17–36.

Leung, Y.H. (2003) "The politics of decentralization: a case study of the school management reform in Hong Kong," in K.H. Mok (ed.) *Centralization and Decentralization: Educational Reforms and Changing Governance in Chinese Societies*, Hong Kong: Comparative Education Research Centre, University of Hong Kong.

Levin, H.M. (1987) "Education as a public and private good," *Journal of Policy Analysis and Management*, 6(4): 628–41.

Leydesdorff, L. and Etzkowitz, H. (2001) "The transformation of university–industry–government relations," *Electronic Journal of Sociology*, 5(4): 1–17.

Lim, S.G. (1998) "PS21: gearing up the public service for the 21st Century," in A. Mahizhnan and T.Y. Lee (eds) *Singapore Re-Engineering Success*, Singapore: Institute of Policy Studies and Oxford University Press.

Lin, J. (2004) "China: private trends," *International Higher Education*, 36: 17–18.

Lin, J. and Yu, Z. (2004) "Educational expansion and shortage of secondary schools," *Journal of Contemporary China*, forthcoming.

Lin, J.M. (1998) "Wannian Xiaochang Jiaogai Yidafengci" (Principals-for-life: A Big Joke to Education Reform), *Zhongguo Shibao* (China Times).

Linder, S. and Peters, G. (1989) "Instruments of government: perceptions and contexts," *Journal of Public Policy*, 9: 35–58.

Lissenburgh, S. and Harding, R. (2000) *Knowledge Links: Innovation in University/Business Partnerships*, London: IPPR.

Lo, H.C. and Tai, H.H. (2003) "Centralization and decentralization in higher education: a comparative study of Hong Kong and Taiwan," in K.H. Mok (ed.) *Centralization and Decentralization: Educational Reforms and Changing Governance in Chinese Societies*, Hong Kong: Comparative Education Research Centre, University of Hong Kong and Kluwer Academic Publishers.

Lo, Y.W. and Weng, F.Y. (2005) "Taiwan's responses to globalization: decentralization and internationalization of higher education," in K.H. Mok and R. James (eds) *Globalization and Higher Education in East Asia*, Singapore: Marshall Cavendish International.

Low, L. (1998) *The Political Economy of a City-State: Government-made Singapore*, Singapore: Oxford University Press.

Low, L. (2001) "Political economy of Singapore's policy on foreign talents and high skills society," paper downloaded from www.fba.nus.edu.sg (Accessed on July 10, 2004).

Lu, M.L. (2004) "The blueprint and competitiveness of Taiwan's higher education," paper presented at the *Cross Strait Seminar on Review and Prospects of the Policy of University Excellence*, Tamkang University, March 25–26, 2004, Taipei.

Luo, L. and Wendel, F.C. (1999) "Junior high school education in China," *The Clearing House*, 72(5): 279–84.

Ma, S.Y. (1999) "The state, foreign capital and privatization in China," *Journal of Communist Studies and Transition Politics*, 26(7–9): 1078–90.

Mahmood, I.P. and Singh, J. (2003) "Technological dynamism in Asia," *Research Policy*, 32(6): 1031–54.

Manfield, E. (1991) "Academic research and industrial innovation," *Research Policy*, 21(1): 1–12.

Marginson, S. (1999) "After globalization: emerging politics of education," *Journal of Education Policy*, 14(1): 19–31.

Marginson, S. (2000) "The enterprise university," paper presented at the Annual Conference of the Australian Association for Research in Education, November 29–December 2, 2000, Melbourne.

Marginson, S. and Considine, M. (2000) *The Enterprise University: Power, Governance and Reinvention in Australia*, Cambridge: Cambridge University Press.

Marginson, S. and Rhodes, G. (2002) "Beyond national states, markets and systems of higher education: a glonacal agency heuristic," *Higher Education*, 43(3): 281–309.

Marrow, R.A. and Torres, C.A. (2000) "The state, globalization, and educational policy," in N. Burbules and C.A. Torres (eds) *Globalization and Education: Critical Perspectives*, London: Routledge.

Massey, A. (ed.). (1997) *Globalization and Marketization of Government Services* Basingstoke: Macmillan.

MEXT (1998) *A Vision of Universities in the 21st Century and Reform Measures To be Distinctive Universities in a Competitive Environment (University Council Report (Outline))*. Online. Available http://www.mext.go.jp/english/news/1998/10/981010.htm (Accessed on September 20, 2003).

MEXT (2002) *A New Image of National University Corporations*. Online. Available http://www.mext.go.jp/english/news/2003/07/03120301/004.htm

MEXT (2003a) *Legislation of the National University Corporation Law*. Online. Available http://www.mext.go.jp/english/news/2003/07/03120301.html (Accessed on January 16, 2004).

MEXT (2003b) *Partnership between Universities and Industries (2003 edition)*. Online. Available http://www.mext.go.jp/English/org/science/07d/03061301.html (Accessed on January 16, 2004).

MEXT (2004a) *Educational Reform-Education Reform Plan for the 21st Century*. Online. Available http://www.mext.go.jp/english/org/reform/07.html (Accessed on July 3, 2004).

MEXT (2004b) *Enrollment and Advancement Rate, 1948 to 2003*. Online. Available http://www.mext.go.jp/english/statist/gif/013.gif (Accessed on October 10, 2004).

MEXT (2004c) University and Junior Colleges. Online. Available www.mext.go.jp/english/statist/gif/078.gif (Accessed on October 10, 2004).

MEXT (2004d) *Formal Education*. Online. Available http://www.mext.go.jp/english/org/formal/05i.htm (Accessed on October 10, 2004).

MEXT (2004e) *Total Expenditure and Public Expenditure on Education, Science, Sports and Culture, relative to Total Public Expenditure and Gross Domestic Product*. Online. Available http://www.mext.go.jp/english/statist/gif/172.gif (Accessed on October 12, 2004).

Meyer, H.D. (2001) "Civil society and education—the return of an idea," in H.D. Meyer and W.L. Boyd (eds) *Education between States, Markets and Civil Society: Comparative Perspectives*, New Jersey: Lawerence Erlbaum Associates, Publishers.

Meyer, H.D. and Boyd, W.L. (eds) (2001) *Education between States, Markets and Civil Society: Comparative Perspectives*, New Jersey: Lawerence Erlbaum Associates, Publishers.

Min, W. (1994) "People's Republic of China: autonomy and accountability: an analysis of the changing relationships between the government and universities," in G. Neave and F. van Vught (eds) *Government and Higher Education Relationships Across Three Continents: The Winds of Change*, Oxford: Pergamon.

Ming Pao (2003), various issues in May and June.

Ministry of Education (1999) *Preparing Graduates for a Knowledge Economy: A New University Admission System for Singapore*, Singapore: Ministry of Education.

Ministry of Education (2000a) "Greater autonomy for NUS and NTU, along with greater accountability," press release on January 27, Singapore: Ministry of Education.

Ministry of Education (2000b) "Government accepts recommendations on university governance and funding," press release on July 3, Singapore: Ministry of Education.

Ministry of Education (2000c) "FY2000 committee of supply debate Minister's fourth reply on university issues," press release on March 13, Singapore: Ministry of Education.

Ministry of Education (2003) *Autonomy and Accountability*, Review Report on Higher Education, Singapore: Ministry of Education.

Ministry of Education, Korea (1999) *Education in Korea 1998–1999*, Seoul: Ministry of Education.

Ministry of Education, Korea (2000a) *Brain Korea 21 Project*, Seoul: Ministry of Education, Republic of Korea.

Ministry of Education, Korea (2000b) *Education in Korea 1999–2000*, Seoul: Ministry of Education.

Ministry of Education, Korea (2001) *Education in Korea 2000–2001*, Seoul: Ministry of Education.

Ministry of Education, Korea (2004) Online. Available http://www.moe.go.kr/en/down/ Studyin Korea.pdf (Accessed on Janaury 20, 2005).

Ministry of Education PRC (2001) *2000 Nian Quan Gro Jaiio Yu Shi Ye Fa Xhan Tong Ji Gong Bao* (Statistic report on country's education development 2000). Online. Available http://www.moe.gov.cn/ [in Chinese] (Accessed on October 2, 2004).

Ministry of Education PRC (2002a) *2001 Nian Quan Gro Jaiio Yu Shi Ye Fa Xhan Tong Ji Gong Bao* (Statistic report on country's education development 2001). Online. Available http://www.moe.gov.cn/ [in Chinese] (Accessed on October 2, 2004).

Ministry of Education PRC (2002b) *Zhong Guo de Ji Chu Jian Yo* (China's foundation education). Online. Available http://www.moe.gov.cn/ [in Chinese] (Accessed on October 2, 2004).

Ministry of Education PRC (2004) *2003–2007 Nian Jiao Yu Zhen Xing Xing Dong Ji Hua* (Revitalizing education action planning 2003–2007). Online. Available http:// www.moe.gov.cn/ [in Chinese] (Accessed on Janaury 13, 2005).

Ministry of Education, Singapore [MOES] (1998) *The Desired Outcomes of Education*, Singapore: Ministry of Education.

Ministry of Education, Singapore [MOES] (2001) *Education Statistics Digest 2001*, Singapore: Ministry of Education.

Ministry of Education, Singapore [MOES] (2002a) *School Excellence Model*, Singapore: Ministry of Education.

Ministry of Education, Singapore [MOES] (2002b) *Apply to Teach*. Online. Available http://www1.moe.edu.sg/teach (Accessed on May 16, 2004).

Ministry of Education, Singapore [MOES] (2002c) *Programme for Rebuilding and Improving Existing Schools*. Online. Available http://www1/moe.edu.sg/prime (Accessed on May 16, 2004).

Ministry of Education, Singapore [MOES] (2003) *Education Statistics Digest 2003*, Singapore: Ministry of Education.

Ministry of Education, Singapore (2004) Online. Available http://www1.moe.edu.sg/ primary.htm (Accessed on February 18, 2005).

Ministry of Education, South Korea [MOEROK] (2000) *Education in Korea 1999–2000*, Seoul: Ministry of Education.

Ministry of Education, South Korea [MOEROK] (2001) *Education in Korea 2000–2001*, Seoul: Ministry of Education.

Ministry of Education, South Korea [MOEROK] (2003) *Education in Korea 2002–2003*, Seoul: Ministry of Education.

Ministry of Education, Taiwan (1993) *Daxuefa Xiuzhengan* (Revised Drafts of the University Act), Taipei: Ministry of Education.

Ministry of Education, Taiwan (1994) *Documents of Legislative Yuan: The University Act*, Taipei: Ministry of Education.

Ministry of Education, Taiwan (1995) *Zhonghuaminguo Jiaoyu Baogaoshu: Maixiang Ershiyi De Jiaoyu Yuanjing* (A Report on Education of the Republic of China: An Educational Prospect Towards the 21st Century), Taipei: Ministry of Education.

Ministry of Education, Taiwan (1997a) *Jiaoyu Gaige Zhongtijihua Gangyao* (A Comprehensive Plan for Education Reform), Taipei: Ministry of Education.

Ministry of Education, Taiwan (1997b) *Bashiliu Xueniandu Daixue Zonghe Pingjian Shiban Jihua Pingjian Shouce (The Handbook of the Pilot Comprehensive Evaluation on Higher Education Institutions)*, Taipei: Ministry of Education.

Ministry of Education, Taiwan (1998a) *Education in the Republic of China, 1998*, Taipei: Ministry of Education.

Ministry of Education, Taiwan (1998b) *Maixiang Xuexi Shehui* (Towards a Learning Society), Taipei: Ministry of Education.

Ministry of Education, Taiwan (1999a) *Education Statistics of the Republic of China, 1998*, Taipei: Ministry of Education.

Ministry of Education, Taiwan (1999b) *Bashiba Xueniandu Gaoji Zhiye Xuexiao Ziwo Pingjian Shouce* (The Handbook of Self-evaluation for Senior Vocational Schools), Taipei: Ministry of Education.

Ministry of Education, Taiwan (2001) *White Paper on Higher Education*, Taipei: Ministry of Education.

Ministry of Education, Taiwan (2002) *Programme for Promoting University International Competitive Capacity 2002*, Taipei: Ministry of Education.

Ministry of Education, Taiwan (2003) *Educational Statistical Indicators: Republic of China*, Taipei: Ministry of Education.

Ministry of Education, Taiwan (2004a) Online. Available http://www.moe.edu.tw (Accessed on January 20, 2005).

Ministry of Education, Taiwan (2004b) Online. Available http://www.high.edu.tw (Accessed on December 20, 2004).

Ministry of Education, Taiwan [MOEROC] (2000) *Education Statistical Indicators, Republic of China 2000*, Taipei: Ministry of Education.

Ministry of Education, Taiwan [MOEROC] (2001a) *White Paper on Higher Education*, Taipei: Ministry of Education.

Ministry of Education, Taiwan [MOEROC] (2001b) *Education Statistics of the Republic of China 2001*, Taipei: Ministry of Education.

Ministry of Education, Taiwan [MOEROC] (2001c) *Education Statistical Indicators, Republic of China 2001*, Taipei: Ministry of Education.

Ministry of Education, Taiwan [MOEROC] (2002) *Education Statistical Indicators, Republic of China 2002*, Taipei: Ministry of Education.

Ministry of Education and Human Resources Development, Korea [MOE] (2001) *Educational Reform Initiatives—Brain Korea*, Seoul: Ministry of Education [Internet source].

Ministry of Education and Human Resources Development (2002) *Education in Korea 2001–2002*, Seoul: Author.

Ministry of Education and Human Resources Development, Korea [MOE] (2003) *Education in Korea 2002–2003*, Seoul: Ministry of Education.

Ministry of Health, Labor and Welfare (1997) *On the Basic Viewpoint Regarding the Trend Toward Fewer Children—a Society of Decreasing Population: Responsibilities and Choices for the Future.* Online. Available http://www1.mhlw.go.jp/english/council/c0126–2.html (Accessed on June 12, 2004).

Ministry of Information, Communications and the Arts (2001) *Singapore 2001*, Singapore: Ministry of Information, Communications and the Arts.

Ministry of Information, Communications and the Arts (2002) *Singapore 2002*, Singapore: Ministry of Information, Communications and the Arts.

Ministry of Information, Communications and the Arts (2003) *Singapore 2003*, Singapore: Ministry of Information, Communications and the Arts.

Minogue, M. (1998) "Changing the state: concepts and practice in the reform of the public sector," in M. Minogue, C. Polidana, and D. Hulme (eds) *Beyond the New Public Management*, Cheltenham: Edward Elgar.

Mittleman, J. (2000) *The Globalization Syndrome: Transformation and Resistance*, New Jersey: Princeton University Press.

Mok, K.H. (1996) "Marketization and decentralization: development of education and paradigm shift in social policy," *Hong Kong Public Administration*, 5(1): 35–56.

Mok, K.H. (1999) "Education and the market place in Hong Kong and Mainland China," *Higher Education*, 37: 133–58.

Mok, K.H. (2000a) "Impact of globalization: a study of quality assurance systems of higher education in Hong Kong and Singapore," *Comparative Education Review*, 44(2): 148–74.

Mok, K.H. (2000b) "Reflecting globalization effects on local policy: higher education reform in Taiwan," *Journal of Education Policy*, 15(6): 637–60.

Mok, K.H. (2000c) "Similar trends, diverse agendas: higher education reforms in Hong Kong, Taiwan and Singapore," paper presented at the Faculty of Education, University of Manchester, February 24, 2000. Manchester, NH.

Mok, K.H. (2000d) "Marketizing higher education in post-Mao China," *International Journal of Educational Development*, 20: 109–26.

Mok, K.H. (2000e) "Reflecting globalization effects on local policy: higher education reform in Taiwan," *Journal of Education Policy*, 15(6): 637–60.

Mok, K.H. (2001a) "Academic capitalisation in the new millennium: the marketization and corporatization of higher education in Hong Kong," *Policy & Politics*, 29(3): 299–316.

Mok, K.H. (2001b) "Education and Policy Reform," in L. Wong and F. Norman (eds) *The Market in Chinese Social Policy*, Basingstoke: Palgrave.

Mok, K.H. (2001c) "Globalization, marketization and higher education: trends and developments in East Asia," paper presented at the *International Conference on Marketization and Higher Education in East Asia*, April 7–8, 2001, Shanghai.

Mok, K.H. (2002a) "Policy of decentralization and changing governance of higher education in post-Mao China," *Policy Administration and Development*, 22: 261–73.

Mok, K.H. (2002b) "Globalization and university merging: international perspectives," paper presented at the International Conference on University Merging, Tamkang University, December 6–7, Taipei [in Chinese].

Mok, K.H. (2002c) "Overview and common research agendas in comparative education," paper presented at the International Symposium on *Globalization & Educational Governance Change in East Asia*, June 2002, Hong Kong.

Mok, K.H. (2002d) "From nationalization to marketization: changing governance in Taiwan's higher education system," *Governance*, 15(2): 137–60.

Mok, K.H. (2003a) "Decentralization and marketization of education in Singapore: a case study of the school excellence model," *International Journal of Educational Administration*, 41(4): 348–66.

Mok, K.H. (2003b) "Globalization and structural adjustment: analysing comparative education from public policy perspectives, key-note speech," paper presented at the Annual Conference 2003, Comparative Education Society of Hong Kong, Chinese University of Hong Kong, January 2003, Hong Kong.

Mok, K.H. (2003c) "Similar trends, diverse agendas: higher education reforms in East Asia," *Globalization, Societies & Education*, 1(2): 201–21.

Mok, K.H. (2003d) "Globalization and structural adjustments: changing policy instruments and regulatory arrangements in education," unpublished paper under review by *Journal of Education Policy*.

Mok, K.H. (2003e) "Riding over autonomy and accountability: changing university governance in Hong Kong and Singapore," paper presented at the *International Seminar on Organizational Reforms and University Governance: Autonomy and Accountability*, Hiroshima University, December 17–18, 2003, Hiroshima, Japan.

Mok, K.H. (2004a) "Globalization and educational restructuring: university merging and changing governance in China," *Higher Education*, 47: 1–32.

Mok, K.H. (2004b) "Riding over autonomy and accountability: reform of university governance in Hong Kong and Singapore," *COE Publication Series*, 2: 51–80.

Mok, K.H. (2005a) "Riding over socialism and global capitalism: changing education governance and social policy paradigms in post-Mao China," *Comparative Education*, 41(2): 217–42.

Mok, K.H. (2005b) "The quest for world class university: quality assurance and international benchmarking in Hong Kong," *Journal of Quality Assurance in Education*, December 2005, forthcoming.

Mok, K.H. (2005c) "Globalization and governance: educational policy instruments and regulatory," *International Review of Education*, 51(4): 337–79.

Mok, K.H. and Chan, D. (eds) (2002) *Globalization and Education: The Quest for Quality Education in Hong Kong*, Hong Kong: Hong Kong University Press.

Mok, K.H. and Currie, J. (2002) "Reflections on the impact of globalization on educational restructuring in Hong Kong," in K.H. Mok and D. Chan (eds) *Globalization and Education: The Quest for Quality Education in Hong Kong*, Hong Kong: Hong Kong University Press.

Mok, K.H. and Lee, H.H. (2000) "Globalization or recolonization: higher education reforms in Hong Kong," *Higher Education Policy*, 13(4): 361–77.

Mok, K.H. and Lee, H.H. (2001) "Globalization or glocalization? Higher education reforms in Singapore," paper presented at the International Conference of *Cultures of Learning: Risk, Uncertainty and Education*, University of Bristol, April 19–22, 2001, Bristol.

Mok, K.H. and Lee, H.H. (2002) "A reflection on quality assurance in Hong Kong's higher education," in K.H. Mok and D. Chan (eds) *Globalization and Education: The Quest for Quality Education in Hong Kong*, Hong Kong: Hong Kong University Press.

Mok, K.H. and Lee, H.H. (2003) "Globalization or glocalization? Higher education reforms in Singapore," *Asia Pacific Journal of Education*, 23(1): 15–42.

Mok, K.H. and Lee, M. (2000) "Globalization or recolonization: higher education reforms in Hong Kong," *Journal of Education Policy*, 14(4): 361–77.

Mok, K.H. and Lo, H.C. (2001) "Marketization and the changing governance in higher education: a comparative studies of Hong Kong and Taiwan," paper presented at the International Conference on *Marketization and Higher Education in East Asia*, April 7–8, 2001, Shanghai.

Mok, K.H. and Lo, H.C. (2002) "Marketization and the changing governance in higher education: a comparative study," *Higher Education Management and Policy*, 14(1): 51–82.

Mok, K.H. and Tan, J. (2004) *Globalization and Marketization in Education: A Comparative Analysis of Hong Kong and Singapore*, Cheltenham: Edward Elgar.

Mok, K.H. and Welch, A. (2002) "Economic rationalism, managerialism and structural reform in education," in K.H. Mok and D. Chan (eds) *Globalization and Education: The Quest for Quality Education in Hong Kong*, Hong Kong: Hong Kong University Press.

Mok, K.H. and Welch, A. (eds) (2003) *Globalization and Educational Restructuring in the Asia Pacific Region*, Basingstoke: Palgrave Macmillan.

Mok, K.H. and Wilding, P. (2003) "The quest for quality education and a learning society in Hong Kong" in K.H. Mok and A. Welch (eds) *Globalization and Educational Restructuring in the Asia Pacific Region*, Basingstoke: Palgrave Macmillan.

Mok, K.H., Tan, J., and Lee, H.H. (2000) "Positioning Singapore for the 21st century: 'thinking schools, learning nation' vision," *Chulalongkorn Educational Review*, 6(2): 33–51.

Moon, Y.L. (1997) "Education reform in Korea and further tasks," paper presented at the International Conference on *Education reform, Megatrends of Education Reform: OECD Member Countries*, Seoul, Korea.

Moon, Y.L. (1998) "The education reform in Korea and future tasks," *Korea Observer*, 19(2): 235–58.

Morris, P. (1996) "Asia's four little tigers: a comparison of the role of education in their development," *Comparative Education*, 32(1): 95–109.

Morris, P. and Scott, I. (2003) "Educational reform and policy implementation in Hong Kong," *Journal of Education Policy*, 18(1): 71–84.

Morris, P. and Sweeting, A. (eds) (1995) *Education and Development in East Asia*, New York: Garland Publishing, Inc.

Nanyang Technological University [NTU] (1998) *NTU Fund*, Singapore: NTU.

Nanyang Technological University [NTU] (1999) *Nanyang Technological University Annual Report 1998/99*, Singapore: NTU.

Nanyang Technological University [NTU] (2000) *Nanyang Technological University Annual Report 1999/2000*, Singapore: NTU.

National Institute of Educational Resources and Research (1999) *Education Yearbook of the Republic of China 1998*, Taipei: National Institute of Educational Resources and Research.

National Institute of Educational Resources and Research (2000) *Education Yearbook of the Republic of China 1999*, Taipei: National Institute of Educational Resources and Research.

National Institute of Population and Social Security Research (2002) *Population Projection for Japan: 2001–2050*. Online. Available http://www.ipss.go.jp/English/ppfj02/suikei_g_e.html (Accessed on June 12, 2004).

National University of Singapore [NUS] (1998) *Strategic Directions for the Twenty-First Century*, Singapore: NUS.

National University of Singapore [NUS] (2000) *National University of Singapore Yearbook 2000*, Singapore: NUS.

Neave, G. (2001) "The changing frontiers of autonomy and accountability," *Higher Education Policy*, 14(1): 1–5.

Neave, G. and Vught, F. van (1994) "Government and higher education in developing nations: a conceptual framework," in G. Neave and F. van Vught (eds) *Government and Higher Education Relationships Across Three Continents: The Winds of Change*, London: Pergamon.

Ng, P.T. (2003) "The Singapore school and the school excellence model," *Educational Research for Policy and Practice*, 2: 27–39.

Oba, J. (2003) "Incorporation of national universities in Japan—a reform toward the enhancement of autonomy in search of excellence," paper presented at the RIHE International Seminar on *Organizational reforms and University Governance: Autonomy and Accountability*, Hiroshima University, Hiroshima, Japan, December 17–18, 2003, Hiroshima, Japan.

Oba, J. (2004) "Incorporation of national universities in Japan—a reform toward the enhancement of autonomy in search of excellence," *COE Publication Series*, 11: 15–50.

Ogawa, Y. (1999) *Japanese Higher Education Reform: The University Council Report*. Online. Available http://www.bc.edu/bc_org/avp/soe/cihe/newsletter/News14/text11.html (Accessed on September 23, 2004).

Ogawa, Y. (2002) "Challenging the traditional organization of Japanese universities," *Higher Education*, 43: 85–108.

Ohmae, K. (1990) *The Borderless World: Power and Strategy in the Interlinked Economy*, New York: Harper Perennial.

Ohmae, K. (1995) *The End of the Nation-state*, New York: Harper Perennial.

Ohmae, K. (1999) *The Borderless World: Power and Strategy in the Interlinked Economy* (Revised Edition), New York: Harper Perennial.

Okano, K. and Tsuchiya, M. (eds) (1999) *Education in Contemporary Japan*, United Kingdom: Cambridge University Press.

Organisation for Economic Cooperation and Development [OECD] (1998) *Reviews of National Policies for Education: Korea*, Paris: Organisation for Economic Cooperation and Development.

Organisation for Economic Cooperation and Development [OECD] (2000) *Korea and the Knowledge-based Economy: Making the Transition,* Paris: Organisation for Economic Cooperation and Development.

Osborne, D. and Gaebler, T. (1992) *Reinventing Government: How the Entrepreneurial Spirit in Transforming the Public Sector*, New York: Plume Books.

Palan, R. and Abbott, J. (1996) *State Strategies in the Global Economy*, With Deans, P., London: Pinter.

Park, N. (2000a) "The 31 May 1995 higher education reform," in J.C. Weidman and N. Park (eds) *Higher Education in Korea: Tradition and Adaptation*, New York: The Falmer Press.

Park, N. (2000b) "Continuing debates: government financial aid to the private higher education sector and faculty tenure," in J.C. Weidman and N. Park (eds) *Higher Education in Korea Tradition and Adaptation*, New York: Falmer Press.

Park, N. (2000c) "Higher education in a rapidly developing country: the case of the Republic of Korea," in M.S. McMullen, J.E. Mauch, and B. Donnorummo (eds) *The Emerging Markets and Higher Education*, New York: RoutledgeFalmer.

Partick, H. (ed.) (1991) *Pacific Basin Industries in Distress*, New York: Columbia University Press.

Pempel, T.J. (1998) *Regime Shift: Comparative Dynamics of the Japanese Political Economy*, Ithaca, NY and London: Cornell University Press.

People's Republic of China (1982) *The Constitution of China*, Beijing: Chinese Legal Press.

Peters, G. (1995) *The Future of Governing*, Lawrence: University of Press of Kansas.

Peters, G. (2000) "Governance and comparative politics," in J. Pierre (ed.) *Debating Governance*, Oxford: Oxford University Press.

Peters, G. (2002) "The politics of tool choice," in L.M. Salomon (ed.) *The Tools of Government: A Guide to the New Governance*, Oxford: Oxford University Press.

Pierre, J. (ed.) (2000) *Debating Governance*, Oxford: Oxford University Press.

Pierre, J. and Peters, G. (2000) *Governance, Politics and State*, Basingstoke: Macmillan.

Poole, G. (2003a) "Retention strategies at a Japanese private university: cultural debates on curriculum reform and faculty identity," paper presented at the Daiwa Anglo-Japanese Foundation, February 2003, London.

Poole, G. (2003b) "Higher education reform in Japan: Amano Ikuo on 'the university in crisis'," *International Education Journal*, 40(3): 149–76.

Post, D. (1996) "The massification of education in Hong Kong: effects on the quality of opportunity, 1981–1991," *Sociological Perspectives*, 39(1): 155–74.

Power, M. (1997) *The Audit Society*, Oxford: Oxford University Press.

Pratt, G. and Poole, D. (1999) "Globalization and Australian universities: policies and impacts," *International Journal of Public Sector Management*, 12(6): 533–44.

Pring, R. (1987) "Privatization in education," *Education Policy*, 2(4): 89–99.

PS21 Office (2001) *Public Service for the Twenty-first Century*, Singapore: PS21 Office.

Quah, J.S.T. (2001) "Singapore: meritocratic city-state," in J. Funston (ed.) *Government and Politics in Southeast Asia*, Singapore: Institute of Southeast Asian Studies.

Quah, S.T. (1998) "Singapore's model of development: is it transferable?" in H.S. Rowen (ed.) *Behind East Asian Growth: The Political and Social Foundations of Prosperity*, London: Routledge.

Quah, S.T. (1999) "Learning from Singapore's Development," *The International Journal of Technical Cooperation*, 4(1): 54–68.

Rabushka, A. (1979) *Hong Kong: A Study of Economic Freedom*, Chicago: University of Chicago Press.

Ramamurti, R. (1999) "Why haven't developing countries privatized deeper and faster?" *World Development*, 27: 137–55.

Reesor, M. (2003) "Japanese attitudes to English: towards an explanation of poor performance," *NUCB JLCC*, 5(2): 57–65.

Reeves, E. (2003) "Public–private partnership in Ireland: policy and practice," *Public Money & Management*, 23: 163–70.

Rhodes, R.A.W. (1997) *Understanding Governance: Policy Networks, Governance, Reflexivity and Accountability*, Buckingham: Open University Press.

Rhodes, R.A.W. (2000) "Governance and public administration," in J. Pierre (ed.) *Debating Governance*, Oxford: Oxford University Press.

Richard, J. and Mok, K.H. (eds) (2003) "Special issue on going global: the internationalization of higher education in the Asian region," *Higher Education Research and Development*, 22(2): 115–228.

RIHE (2003) *Incorporation of National Universities in Japan—A Reform Toward the Enhancement of Autonomy in Search of Excellence*, Japan: RIHE.

Ringeling, A.B. (2002) "European experience with tools of government," in L.M. Salomon (ed.) *The Tools of Government: A Guide to the New Governance*, Oxford: Oxford University Press.

Robertson, R. (1995) "Globalization: time–space and homogeneity–heterogeneity," in M. Featherstone, S. Lash, and R. Robertson (eds) *Global Modernities*, London: Sage.

Robertson, R. and Dale, R. (2000) "Competitive contractualism: a new social settlement in New Zealand education," in D. Coulby, R. Cowen, and C. Jones (eds) *World Yearbook of Education 2000: Education in Times of Transition*, Auckland: Kogan.

Robertson, S. (1999) "Strip away the bark, expose the heartwood, get to the heart of the matter: re/regulation teachers' labour in New Zealand," *New Zealand Journal of Educational Studies*, 34: 121–32.

Robertson, S. and Dale, R. (2000) "Competitive contractualism: a new social settlement in New Zealand education," in D. Coulby, R. Cowen, and C. Jones (eds) *World Yearbook of Education 2000: Education in Times of Transition*, London: Kogan Page.

Rodrik, D. (1997) "Sense and nonsense in the globalization debate," *Foreign Policy*, 107: 14–37.

Rosenau, J.N. (1992) "Citizenship in a changing global order," in J.N. Rosenau and E.-O. Czempiel (eds) *Governance without Government: Order and Change in World Politics*, Cambridge: Cambridge University Press.

Rosenau, J.N. (1997) *Along the Domestic-Foreign Frontier*, Cambridge: Cambridge University Press.

Rozman, G. (1992) "The Confucian faces of capitalism," in M. Borthwick (ed.) *Pacific Century*, Boulder, CO: Westview.

Sahlin-Andersson, K. (2001) "National, international and transnational constructions of new public management," in T. Christensen and P. Laegreid (eds) *New Public Management: The Transformation of Ideas and Practice*, Aldershot: Ashgate.

Salomon, L.M. (ed.) (2002) *The Tools of Government: A Guide to the New Governance*, Oxford: Oxford University Press.

Sassen, S. (1998) *Globalization and its Discourse*, New York: The New Press.

Sbragia, A. (2000) "Governance, the state, and the market: what is going on?" *Governance*, 13: 243–50.

Scharpf, F.W. (1994) "Games real actors could play: positive and negative coordination in embedded negotiations," *Journal of Theoretical Politics*, 61: 27–53.

Schiffer, J.R. (1983) *Anatomy of a Laissez-faire Government: The Hong Kong Growth Model Reconsidered*, Hong Kong: Centre of Urban Studies, University of Hong Kong.

Schneider, M., Teske, P., and Marschall, M. (2000) *Choosing Schools: Consumer Choice and the Quality of American Schools*, New Jersey: Princeton University Press.

Selvaratnam, V. (1994) *Innovations in Higher Education: Singapore at the Competitive Edge*, Washington, DC: The World Bank.

Shan, P. and Chang, J. (2000) "Social change and educational development in Taiwan," in T. Townsend and Y.C. Cheng (eds) *Educational Change and Development in the Asia-Pacific Region: Challenges for the Future*, Lisse: Swets & Zeitlinger Publishers.

Shan, W.J. and Chang, C.C. (2000) "Social change and educational development in Taiwan, 1945–1999," in T. Townsend and Y.C. Cheng (eds) *Educational Change and Development in the Asia-Pacific Region: Challenges for the Future*, Lisse: Swets & Zeitlinger Publishers.

Sharpe, L. and Gopinathan, S. (2002) "After effectiveness: new directions in the Singapore school system," paper presented at the International Forum on *Education reforms in Singapore, South Korea, Taiwan and Hong Kong*, City University of Hong Kong, June 29, 2002, Hong Kong.

Singapore Department of Statistics (1998) *Yearbook of Statistics Singapore 1997*, Singapore: Singapore Department of Statistics.

Singapore Department of Statistics (1999) *Singapore 1998 Statistical Highlights*, Singapore: Singapore Department of Statistics.

Singapore Department of Statistics (2000) *Singapore 1999 Statistical Highlights*, Singapore: Singapore Department of Statistics.

Singapore Department of Statistics (2001) *Singapore 2001 Statistical Highlights*, Singapore: Singapore Department of Statistics.

Singapore Department of Statistics (2002) *Singapore 2002 Statistical Highlights*, Singapore: Singapore Department of Statistics.

Singapore Government (1999) *Singapore 21: Together, We Make the Difference*, Singapore: Singapore 21 Committee.

Sklair, L. (1995) *Sociology of the Global System*, Baltimore, MD: Johns Hopkins University Press.

Sklair, L. (1999) "Globalization," in S. Taylor (ed.) *Sociology: Issues and Debates*, Basingstoke: Macmillan.

Slaughter, S. (1998) "National higher education policies in a global economy," in J. Currie and J. Newson (eds) *Universities and Globalization*, Thousand Oaks, CA: Sage Publications.

Slaughter, S. and Leslie, L.L. (1997) *Academic Capitalism: Politics, Policies and the Entrepreneurial University*, Baltimore, MD: Johns Hopkins University Press.

Smith, D.A., Solinger, D.J., and Topik, S.C. (eds) (1999) *States and Sovereignty in the Global Economy*, London: Routledge.

So, A. (2003) "Is SARS anti-globalization?" paper presented at the Workshop on *Globalization and Challenges to Modern States*, Lingnan University, June 7, 2003, Hong Kong.

So, A. and Chiu, S. (1995) *East Asia and the World Economy*, Thousand Oaks, CA: Sage Publications.

Soong, C.Y. (1997) "Explaining Taiwan's transition," in L. Diamond, M.F. Plattner, Y.H. Chu, and M.H. Tien (eds) *Consolidating the Third Wave Democracies: Regional Challenges*, Baltimore, MD: Johns Hopkins University Press.

Space, HKU (2003) *Annual Report*, Hong Kong: SPACE, University of Hong Kong.

Spring, J.H. (1998) *Education and the Rise of Global Economy*, Mahwah, NJ: Lawrence Erlbaum.

Stiglitz, J.E. (2002) *Globalization and Its Discontents*. London: Allen Lane.

Strange, S. (1996) *The Retreat of the State: The Diffusion of Power in the World Economy*, Cambridge: Cambridge University Press.

Stromquist, N. (2002) "Preface," *Comparative Education Review*, 46(1): iii–viii.

Su, Z. (1999) "Asian education," in R.F. Arnove and C.A. Torres (eds) *Higher Education: The Dialectic of the Global and the Local*, New York: Rowman & Littlefield.

Sutz, J. (1997) "The new role of the university in the productive sector," in H. Etzkowitz and L. Leydesdorff (eds) *Universities and the Global Knowledge Economy*, London: Pinter.

Tai, H.H. (2000a) "Towards the new century: the transformation of higher education," *Bulletin of Educational Research*, 44: 35–60.

Tai, H.H. (2000b) *The Massification and Marketization of Higher Education*, Taipei: Yang-Chih Book Co., Ltd. [in Chinese].

Tai, H.H. (2001) "Globalization and the change of state/market relationships: a contextual analysis of the marketization of higher education," *Bulletin of Educational Research*, 47: 301–28.

Tai, H.H. (2002) "A comparative study of higher education merging: international experiences," paper presented at the International Conference on University Merging, Tamkang University, December 6–7, 2002, Taipei [in Chinese].

Tan, J. (1997) "Independent schools in Singapore: implications for social and educational inequalities," in J. Tan, S. Gopinathan, and W.K. Ho (eds) *Education in Singapore: A Book of Readings*, Singapore: Prentice Hall.

Tan, J. (1998) "The marketization of education in Singapore: policies and implications," *International Review of Education*, 44: 47–63.

Tan, J. (1999) "Education in Singapore in the early 21st century: challenges and dilemmas," paper presented at the Institute of Southeast Asian Studies Conference on *Singapore in the New Millennium: Challenges Facing the City-State*, August, 25.

Tan, J. (2002) "Education in the early 21st century: challenges and dilemmas," in D. da Cunha (ed.) *Singapore in the New Millennium: Challenges Facing the City-State*, Singapore: Institute of Southeast Asian Studies.

Tan, J. (2003) "Reflections on Singapore's education policies in an age of globalization," in K.H. Mok and A. Welch (eds) *Globalization and Educational Restructuring in the Asia Pacific Region*, Basingstoke: Palgrave Macmillan.

Tan, T.K.Y. (2000) "Universities in the knowledge era—challenges and responses," lecture by Dr. Tony Tan Keny Yam, Deputy Prime Minister and Minister for Defence, at the Chualongkorn University, Thailand, on January 14, 2000, Singapore: Ministry of Education [Internet source].

Tan, W.L. and Tan, T.M. (2002) "The usefulness of networks to SMEs: the case of Singapore," paper downloaded from www.usasbe.org/knowledge/proceedings/2002.

Teo, C.H. (2000) speech by RADM Teo Chee Hean, Minister for Education and Second Minister for Defence at the Second Reading of the Singapore Management University Bill in Parliament on February 21, 2000, Singapore: Ministry of Education [Internet source].

Teo, C.H. (2001) Speech by RADM(NS) Teo Chee Hean, Minister for Education and Second Minister for Defence at SMU's Convocation Ceremony on August 12, Singapore: Ministry of Education.

The Straits Times, various issues in 1991, 1997, 1999, 2000.

The Straits Times Weekly Edition, April 28, 2001.

Tilak, J. (2000) *Education and Development: Lessons from Asian Experience*, New Delhi: National Institute of Educational Planning and Administration.

Tomlinson, J. (1986) "Public education, public good," *Oxford Review of Education*, 12(3): 211–22.

Townsend, T. (1998) "The primary school of the future: third world or third millennium?" in T. Townsend (ed.) *The Primary School in Changing Times: The Australian Experience*, London: Routledge.

Townsend, T. and Cheng, Y.C. (2000) "Charting the progress: influences that have shaped education in the Asia-Pacific region," in Y.C. Cheng and T. Townsend (eds) *Educational Change and Development in the Asia Pacific Region: Challenges for the Future*, Exton: Swets & Zeitlinger Publishers.

Trow, M. (1975) "Problems in the transition from elite to mass higher education," paper prepared for a Conference on Mass Higher Education held by the Organization for Economic Cooperation and Development, October 5–9, 1975, Paris.

Tsai, C.W. (1996a) "The deregulation of higher education in Taiwan," *International Higher Education*, 4: 11–13.

Tsai, C.W. (1996b) "The deregulation of higher education in Taiwan," *International Higher Education*, Spring: 1–3.

Tsang, M.C. (2003) "School choices in the People's Republic of China," in D.N. Plank and G. Sykes (eds) *Choosing Choice: School Choice in International Perspectives*, New York: Teachers College Press.

Tsang, W.K. (1998) *An Analysis of Education Policy in Hong Kong: A Sociological Perspective*, Hong Kong: Joint Publishers [in Chinese].

Tsang, W.K. (2002) "Hong Kong education reform in the context of globalization," paper presented at the International Symposium on *Globalization and Educational Governance Change in East Asia*, City University of Hong Kong, June 28, 2002, Hong Kong.

Tsay, R.M. (2000) "Social change and social stratification in Taiwan," in K.H. Mok and Y.W. Ku (eds) *A Comparative Study of Social Development in Hong Kong, Taiwan and Mainland China*, Hong Kong: Hong Kong Humanities Press.

Tse, K.L. (1998) *The Denationalization and Depoliticization of Education in Hong Kong, 1945–1992*, PhD Thesis, University of Wisconsin, Madison.

Tse, K.L. (2002) "A critical review of the quality education movement in Hong Kong," in K.H. Mok and D. Chan (eds) *Globalization and Education: The Quest for Quality Education in Hong Kong*, Hong Kong: Hong Kong University Press.

Tsuruta, Y. (2003a) "On-going changes to higher education in Japan and some key issues," paper presented at the Daiwa Anglo-Japanese Foundation, February 2003, London.

Tsuruta, Y. (2003b) "Globalization and the recent reforms in Japanese higher education," in G. Roger and D. Phillips (eds) *Can the Japanese Reform their Education System?* London: Symposium Books.

Tung, C.H. (2001) *Policy Address 2001*, Hong Kong: Printing Department, HKSAR Government.

Tung, C.H. (2004) *Policy Address 2004*, Hong Kong: Government Printer.

United News, December 28, 1999.

University Grants Committee [UGC] (1996) *Higher Education in Hong Kong*, Hong Kong: University Grants Committee.

University Grants Committee [UGC] (2000) *University Grants Committee Facts and Figures 1999*, Hong Kong: Government Printer.

University Grants Committee [UGC] (2001) *University Grants Committee Facts and Figures 2000*, Hong Kong: Government Printer.

University Grants Committee [UGC] (2002a) *Higher Education in Hong Kong: Report of the University Grants Committee*, Hong Kong: Printing Department, HKSAR Government.

University Grants Committee [UGC] (2002b) *Higher Education in Hong Kong: Report of the University Grants Committee*, Hong Kong: University Grants Committee.

Vogel, S.K. (1996) *Freer Markets, More Rules*, Ithaca, NY: Cornell University Press.

Wang, T. (2003) *Minban Jiaoyu Yinlun* (Introduction to people-run education), Beijing: Zhongguo Shehui Kexue Chubanshe [in Chinese].

Wang, Y. (1988) "The Structure and Governance of Chinese higher Education," in *The Role of Government in Asian Higher Education*, Research Institute of Higher Education, Hiroshima University.

Waters, M. (1995) *Globalization*, London: Routledge.

Waters, M. (2001) *Globalization*, London: Routledge.

Watson, K. (1996) "Banking on key reforms for educational development: a critique of the World Bank review," *Mediterranean Journal of Educational Studies*, 1: 43–61.

Wei, Y.T. and Zhang, G.C. (1995) "A historical perspective on non-governmental higher Education in China," paper presented to at the *International Conference on Private Education in Asia and the Pacific Region*, University of Xiamen, Xiamen, China, November 1995, Xiamen, China.

Weiss, L. (1995) "Governed interdependence: rethinking the government-business relationship in East Asia," *The Pacific Review*, 8(4): 589–616.

Weiss, L. (1998) *The Myth of Powerless State*, Cambridge: Cambridge University Press.

Welch, A. (1996) *Australian Education: Reform or Crisis?* Sydney: Allen & Unwin.

Welch, A. (1998) "Education and the cult of efficiency: comparative reflections on the reality and the rhetoric," *Comparative Education*, 34(2): 157–75.

Welch, A. (2000) "Quality and equality in third world education," in A. Welch (ed.) *Third World Education: Quality and Equality*, New York: Garland.

Welch, A. (2001) "Globalisation, post-modernity and the state: comparative education facing the third millennium," *Comparative Education*, 37: 475–92.

Welch, A. (2004) *Educational Services in Southeast Asia*, BICA 2003–04 Report Booklet, 7, 2004.

Weng, F.Y. (1999a) "Educational reform and development in Taiwan," in K.H. Mok and Y.W. Ku (eds) *A Comparative Study of Social Development in Hong Kong, Taiwan and Mainland China*, Hong Kong: Hong Kong Humanities Press.

Weng, F.Y. (1999b) "The implementation of equality of educational opportunities in Taiwan in the early 1990s: a post-Fordist perspective," *Comparative Education*, 47: 28–54.

Weng, F.Y. (2000a) "Educational reform and development in Taiwan," in K.H. Mok and Y.W. Ku (eds) *A Comparative Study of Social Development in Hong Kong, Taiwan and Mainland China*, Hong Kong: Hong Kong Humanities Press.

Weng, F.Y. (2000b) "Social change and educational development in Taiwan," in K.H. Mok and Y.W. Ku (eds) *A Comparative Study of Social Development in Hong Kong, Taiwan and Mainland China*, Hong Kong: Hong Kong Humanities Press [in Chinese].

Weng, F.Y. (2001) "Towards a global trend: decentralization or centralization in educational governance in Taiwan," paper presented at the Symposium on *Comparative Education Policy Developments in Chinese Societies*, City University of Hong Kong, April 9, 2001, Hong Kong.

Weng, F.Y. (2002) "The reform of education policy in Taiwan: a sociological analysis," paper presented at the International Symposium on *Globalization & Educational Governance Change in East Asia*, City University of Hong Kong, June 2002, Hong Kong.

Weng, F.Y. (2003) "Centralization and decentralization in educational governance," in K.H. Mok (ed.) *Centralization and Decentralization: Educational Reforms and Changing Governance in Chinese Societies*, Kluwer Academic Publishers and Hong Kong: Comparative Education Research Centre, University of Hong Kong and Kluwer Academic Publishers.

White, G. and Goodman, R. (1998) "Welfare orientalism and the search for an East Asian welfare model," in R. Goodman, G. White, and H.J. Kwon (eds) *The East Asian Welfare Model: Welfare Orientalism and the State*, London: Routledge.

White, G. and Hauck, F. (2000) *Campus, Inc*, New York: Prometheus Books, Amherst.

Whitty, G. (1997) "Marketization, the state and the re-formation of the teaching profession," in A.H. Halsey, H. Lauder, P. Brown, and A.S. Wells (eds) *Education: Culture, Economy and Society*, Oxford: Oxford University Press.

William, G. and Fry, H. (1994) *Longer Term Prospects for British Higher Education: A Report to the Committee of Vice-Chancellors and Principals*, London: University of London.

Woods, N. (2000) *The Political Economy of Globalization*, Basingstoke: Macmillan.

World Bank (1991) *Skills for Productivity: Policies for Vocational and Technical Education in Developing Countries*, Washington, DC: The World Bank.

World Bank (1993) *The East Asian Miracle: Economic Growth and Public Policy*, New York: Oxford University Press.

World Bank (1994a) *Higher Education: The Lessons of Experience*, Washington, DC: The World Bank.

World Bank (1994b) *Priorities and Strategies for Education*, Washington, DC: World Bank.

World Bank (1995a) *Higher Education: The Lessons of Experience*, Washington, DC: The World Bank.

World Bank (1995b) *Priorities and Strategies for Education*, Washington, DC: The World Bank.

World Bank (1995c) *Higher Education: The Lessons of Experience*, Washington, DC: The World Bank.

World Bank (2000) *Higher Education in Developing Countries: Peril and Promise*, Washington, DC: The World Bank.

Wu, D. (2003) "Marketization: choice and response of the private higher education in China," in X.X. Dai, K.H. Mok, and A.B. Xie (eds) *The Marketization of Higher Education: A Comparative Study of Taiwan, Hong Kong and China*, Taibei: Gaodeng Jiaoyu Wenhua Shiye Youxiangongsi [in Chinese].

Xu, Y.F. (2002) "Lun Wanli Moshui" (Discussing wanli model), *Journal of Zhejiang Wanli University*, 15(2): 1–3 [in Chinese].

Yamamoto, K. (2004) "Corporatization of national universities in Japan: revolution for governance or rhetoric for downsizing?" *Financial Accountability & Management*, 20(2): 153–81.

Yamato, Y. and Bray, M. (2002) "Education and socio-political change: the continued growth and evolution of the international school sector in Hong Kong," *Asia Pacific Education Review*, 3(1): 24–36.

Yang, D.P. (2002) "Development of education and related issues in China in the new century," in L. Jiang, X. Xu, and P.L. Li (eds) *2002: Analysis and Forecast of China's Social Situation*, Beijing: Social Sciences Documentation Publishing House.

Yang, K.T. (2000) "The construction of a lifelong learning environment," in Institute of Education, Zhongcheng University of Taiwan (ed.) *Education in the New Millennium: Theory and Practice*, Taipei: Leiman Cultural Publishing Company.

Yang, R. (2000) "Tensions between the global and the local: a comparative illustration of the reorganization of China's higher education in the 1950s and 1990s," *Higher Education*, 39: 319–37.

Yang, R. (2003) "Globalization and higher education development: a critical analysis," *Higher Education*, 49(3–4): 269–91.

Yang, R. (2004) "Openness and reform as dynamics for development: a case study of internationalisation of South China University of Technology," *Higher Education*, 47(4): 473–500.

Yao, R.B. (1984) *Zhongguo Jiaoyu 1949–1982* (China's education 1949–1982), Hong Kong: Wah Fong Bookshop Press.

Yeates, N. (2001) *Globalization and Social Policy*, London: Sage Publications.

Yin, Q. and White, G. (1994) "The marketization of Chinese higher education: a critical assessment," *Comparative Education*, 30(3): 217–37.

Yip, J., Eng S.P., and Yap, J. (1997) "25 years of educational reform," in J. Tan, S. Gopinathan, and W.K. Ho (eds) *Education in Singapore: A Book of Readings*, Singapore: Prentice Hall.

Yonezawa, A. (2002a) "The new quality assurance system for Japanese higher education: its social background, tasks and future," *The Journal of University Evaluation of National Institution for Academic Degrees*, No. 2, December.

Yonezawa, A. (2002b) "The quality assurance system and market forces in Japanese higher education," *Higher Education*, 43: 127–39.

Yonezawa, A. (2003a) "Making 'world-class universities': Japan's experiment," *Higher Education Management and Policy*, 15(2): 9–23.

Yonezawa, A. (2003b) "The impact of globalisation on higher education governance in Japan," *Higher Education Research and Development*, 22(2): 145–54.

Yonezawa, A., Nakatsui, I., and Kobayashi, T. (2002) "University rankings in Japan," *Higher Education in Europe*, XXVII (4): 373–82.

Yoon, K. (2000) "Reforming higher education in Korea: the general trends and teacher education institutions," paper presented at the 19th Comparative Education Society in Europe Conference, Bologna, Italy, September 3–7, Bologna, Italy.

Yoon, K. (2001) "Higher education in Korea: changes and reactions," paper presented at the International Conference on *Marketization and Higher Education in East Asia*, Shanghai, April 7–8, Shanghai.

Young, Y.H. (2000) "Recent changes and developments in Korean school education," in T. Townsend and Y.C. Cheng (eds) *Educational Change and Development in the Asia-Pacific Region: Challenges for the Future*, Lisse: Swets & Zeitlinger Publishers.

Yuan, Z. and Zhou, S. (2003) *Zhongguo Minban Jiaoyu Zhengce Fenxi* (Policy analysis of people-run education in China), Beijing: Zhongguo Shehui Kexue Chubanshe [in Chinese].

Yung, K.C. (1999) "Implementing sustainable education reform in diverse contexts," paper presented to the South East Asia & Pacific Region Educational Administrators & Managers Symposium, National Taiwan Normal University, December 13–17, 1999, Taipei.

Zemsky, R. (1997) "Situation and perspective in the massification stage of higher education," paper presented at the *Six-Nation Higher Education Project Seminar Academic Reforms in the World*, February 6–7, 1997, Hiroshima.

Zhu, Y. (1994) "Perspectives on minban schools in China" paper presented at the Shanghai International House for Education, Shanghai, August 15–20, 2004, Shanghai.

Index

Note: Page numbers in italics refer to tables and figures.

For Product Safety Concerns and Information please contact our EU
representative GPSR@taylorandfrancis.com
Taylor & Francis Verlag GmbH, Kaufingerstraße 24, 80331 München, Germany